The Revolution Question

The Revolution Question

FEMINISMS IN EL SALVADOR, CHILE, AND CUBA

JULIE D. SHAYNE

RUTGERS UNIVERSITY PRESS
New Brunswick, New Jersey, and London

LIBRARY OF CONGRESS CATALOGING-IN-PUBLICATION DATA

Shayne, Julie D., 1966–
    The revolution question : feminisms in El Salvador, Chile, and Cuba
Julie D. Shayne.
        p.   cm.
    Includes bibliographical references and index.
    ISBN 0-8135-3483-6 (hardcover : alk. paper) — ISBN 0-8135-3484-4 (pbk. : alk.
paper)
    1. Feminism—El Salvador.   2. Feminism—Chile.   3. Feminism—Cuba.
4. Women revolutionaries—El Salvador.   5. Women revolutionaries—Chile.
6. Women revolutionaries—Cuba.   7. El Salvador—History—1979–1992.
8. El Salvador—History—1992–   9. Chile—History—20th century.
10. Cuba—History—20th century.   I. Title.
HQ1460.5.S53 2004
305.42—dc22   2004003816

A British Cataloging-in-Publication record for this book is available
from the British Library

Manufactured in the United States of America

Dedicated to my beloved father Barry

Contents

Acknowledgments

THERE ARE MANY, many, many people who deserve a heartfelt thanks for all of the support they offered me throughout this project. First, the many people who provided me the initial contacts that enabled me to start my research: In El Salvador, Leslie Schuld and the Center for Exchange and Solidarity; in Chile, Lois Oppenheim and Robert Austin; and in Cuba, Margaret Randall, K. Lynn Stoner, and the Latin American Scholars Program of Arizona State University.

There are also many people whom I wish to thank for reading all or parts of this manuscript in its various stages and providing me incredibly insightful and helpful feedback, including: John Foran, Karen Kampwirth, Barry Levitt, Irene Browne, Ilja Luciak, Susan Franceschet, Donna Murdock, Val Moghadam, Eric Selbin, Kum-Kum Bhavnani, Rich Applebaum, Tim Harding, Linda Klouzal, Mina Caulfield, and my wonderful editor, Kristi Long.

There are no words to adequately thank Anna Sandoval, who has worked with me for three years on this project, getting to know the women almost as intimately as I did, through her meticulous translating. I also want to thank Lisa Dillman for stepping in in a pinch to translate, and for letting me treat her as if my deadlines were more important than her own. Thank you is also in order to my research assistants, Courtney Rivard, Heather Jamerson, and Erin Tunney, for pulling things together at the end.

I also want to thank Manuel Llaneras for taking transcripts to and from Cuba for me, and Daimin Menocal for her invaluable assistance in making sure that her mother's interview transcript accurately reflected our conversation. And thanks are due also to the Institute for Comparative and International Studies at Emory University for the funding necessary to finish this project. A passionate thank you is also in order for the revolutionary and feminist women who graciously opened their homes and histories up to me and have provided me permanent political, intellectual, and feminist inspiration.

I thank my family from the very bottom of my heart. My mother and stepfather have always treated me like I can do anything, and that was certainly an invaluable message to receive when trying to get through the seemingly endless process of writing a book. There is simply no way that I would have been able to embark on this project were it not for the unwavering love and support of my beloved father. Sadly, his early passing means that he will never be able to see, or hold, or read this book. Fortunately my heart and mind can envision the glow of pride and ecstasy on his face were he able to have done just that. Credit also must go to my precious daughter for her amazingly easy disposition, which allowed me to work regularly and intensely on this book during the first sixteen months of her life. Her support became wonderfully obvious when the first word out of her mouth—after *Mama* and *Dada*—was *book*! And finally, I must thank my absolutely wonderful husband Dave, for being my everything.

List of Acronyms

AMD	Association of Mothers Seeking Child Support (Asociación de Madres Demandantes)
ANDES	National Association of Salvadoran Educators (Asociación Nacional de Educadores Salvadoreños)
ARENA	National Republican Alliance (Alianza Republicana Nacional)
CNR	National Coordination for Repopulation (Coordinadora Nacional de la Repoblación)
CO-MADRES	Committee of Mothers and Relatives of Political Prisoners, Disappeared, and Assassinated of El Salvador (Comité de Madres y Familiares de Presos, Desaparecidos y Asesinados de El Salvador)
CONAMUS	The National Coordinating Committee of Salvadoran Women (Coordinadora Nacional de las Mujeres Salvadoreñas)
CRIPDES	Christian Committee for the Displaced People of El Salvador (Comité Cristiano Pro-Desplazados de El Salvador)
DIGNAS	Women for Dignity and Life "Breaking the Silence" (Mujeres por la Dignidad y la Vida "Rompamos el Silencio")
FMLN	Farabundo Martí Front for National Liberation (Frente Farabundo Martí para la Liberación Nacional)
FPL	Popular Forces of Liberation (Fuerzas Populares de Liberación)
MAM	Mélida Anaya Montes Women's Movement (Movimiento de Mujeres Mélida Anaya Montes)
ONUSAL	United Nations Observer Mission in El Salvador (Observadores de las Naciones Unidas en El Salvador)
PDC	Christian Democratic Party (Partido Democrático Cristiano)

PRTC   Revolutionary Party of Central American Workers
          (Partido Revolucionario de Trabajadores
          Centroamericanos)

CHILE

AFDD   Association of Relatives of the Detained and Disappeared
          (Agrupación de Familiares de Detenido y Desaparecido)
MAPU   Movement for United Popular Action
          (Movimiento de Acción Popular Unitaria)
MEMCH '83 Movement For the Emancipation of Women '83
          (Movimiento Pro-Emancipación de la Mujer '83)
MIR   Revolutionary Movement of the Left (Movimiento de
          Izquierda Revolucionario)
MOMUPO   Movement of Shantytown Women (Movimiento de
          Mujeres Pobladores)
SERNAM   National Women's Service (Servicio Nacional de la Mujer)
UP   Popular Unity (Unidad Popular)

CUBA

FEU   Federation of University Students (Federación Estudiantes
          Universidades)
FMC   Federation of Cuban Women (Federación de Mujeres
          Cubanas)
MR-26-7   Revolutionary Movement of 26 July (Movimiento
          Revolucionario 26 de Julio)

The Revolution Question

Introduction

FEMININITY, REVOLUTION, AND FEMINISM

> We did not have a gender consciousness, before and during the
> war, but unconsciously we hoped that with change in society
> and from the class struggle, there was going to be a situation of
> equality for women. Unconsciously that was the feeling. . . .
> They [the men on the Left] always said that this [the women's]
> struggle was secondary; always they said the problem was cap-
> italism and I think we believed that because we didn't know
> the depth of our situation.
>
> —Lety Mendez, 1998

WHILE IN EL SALVADOR in 1998 I spoke with Lety Mendez,[1]
a Salvadoran ex-guerrilla and former head of the women's secretariat of the
Farabundo Martí Front for National Liberation (Frente Farabundo Martí para
la Liberación Nacional, or FMLN). Lety explained that women were of strategic significance to the Salvadoran revolutionary movement. She astutely noted
that it was the work of women guerrillas that fostered a political openness that
was partly responsible for developing support for the Left. It was women, Lety
argued, who made it possible for the guerrillas to move more freely in an
extremely hostile terrain. During the revolutionary struggle however Lety
experienced her own and her *compañeras'* (comrades') contributions continu-
ally undervalued and unacknowledged. Such frustrations eventually fostered
Lety's feminist consciousness.

My conversation with Lety complements another lengthy interview I did
with Miriam Ortega Araya in Santiago, Chile, in March 1999. Miriam is a
labor organizer. I spoke with her in an office walled with posters from International Women's Day celebrations, the Latin American and Caribbean feminist *encuentros* (gatherings), statements against domestic violence, and other
feminist issues. She graciously offered me her time, explaining in scrupulous
detail the ins and outs of the Chilean Left, feminism, and her experiences
with both. She was active in the trade union movement during the tenure of

Salvador Allende, as well as the Revolutionary Movement of the Left (Movimiento de Izquierda Revolucionario or MIR), a guerrilla organization that maintained, as did Fidel Castro's movement in Cuba, that true revolution could only come about through armed rather than political resistance. She explained her process of exile, clandestine return, subsequent twelve years of incarceration under dictator General Augusto Pinochet, and current commitment to feminism in her South American nation. As Miriam struggled for justice for the workers in Chile she began to notice gender inequities. This imbalance eventually led to the disappearance of the already deprioritized political demands of women. Upon returning to Chile her commitment to feminism came to fruition, ironically, while in prison. Initially, as a way to pass the time, the women political prisoners organized educational workshops, which they each alternately facilitated based on their own intellectual training (for example, one discussion focused on biology since one of the women was a trained biologist). Eventually, feminists outside of the prison brought in theoretical pieces by, among others, Chilean feminist Julieta Kirkwood.[2] These were then circulated among the women who usurped this space that was intended to squelch their leftist spirit and they thus transformed it into a locale of feminist empowerment.[3]

In the summer of 1999 I traveled to Cuba, where I had the opportunity to meet with a diverse collection of revolutionary and/or feminist women. One such woman, María Antonia Figueroa, recalled her and her mother's participation alongside Castro in the struggle against infamous dictator Fulgencio Batista. María Antonia, former head of the Revolutionary Movement of 26 July (Movimiento Revolucionario 26 de Julio, or MR-26-7) finance committee, spoke to a colleague and myself through the relentlessly thick Havana humidity. As she comfortably swayed back and forth in her rocking chair, María explained that women were a fundamental sector in the Cuban Revolution. Her humble apartment walls were covered with pictures of her martyred and deceased relatives as well as Castro, whom she described as a brother of sorts. She discussed the canonical Cuban women revolutionaries,[4] but was also meticulous in reminding us that women participated from all walks of life, in a variety of tasks. Some lived and some died in the struggle but all were united in their revolutionary commitment to a society free of Batista's dictatorship. Similar to Lety, María noted that the roles women played were strategic specifically due to their gender. María explained that despite the importance of women to what was seen as "the people's struggle," women revolutionaries were still confronted with formidable obstacles.

A THEORETICAL OVERVIEW

I have been thinking about questions regarding the relationship between revolution and feminism since 1994, when I returned to El Salvador for the fourth time and started speaking with ex-guerrillas/feminists like Lety Mendez. Those discussions led to my first project in which I argued that women's experiences in revolutionary El Salvador were both central to the resistance movement and inseparable from the emergence of feminisms (Shayne 1995). Since then, I have continued to pursue these questions through the cases of Chile and Cuba and address more specifically: What was it about the roles of women that made them so important to revolutionary movements, and how exactly did these experiences lead to feminism? For decades, Marxists and feminists have attempted to answer the "woman question": What can revolutions do for women? Or, what do women need from revolutions? Complicating this a bit, I pose the "revolution question(s)": What do women do for revolutions and how does revolution relate to feminism? In this book, I attempt to answer these questions through a comparative analysis of El Salvador, Chile, and Cuba.

Scholars of the Americas have taken various approaches in understanding feminism, gender, and the Left in Latin America, as well as their complicated relationships to one another. Nearly all such discussions are grounded in Maxine Molyneux's (1985) concept of practical gendered versus strategic feminist interests. Molyneux argues that a distinction exists between women organizing to meet basic needs that are the result of a gendered division of labor (i.e., child care) or what she calls *practical interests*, and those explicitly organizing to counter systems of patriarchy (i.e., safe and legal access to abortion), or *strategic interests*. Both types of struggle are common for women in Latin America. Molyneux does not suggest that one type deserves priority over the other, but rather that a theoretical distinction does exist. She also suggests that struggles that strive to meet practical needs—for example, a collective soup kitchen— may eventually lead to those of a more strategic or feminist nature. When women spend time together outside of the home they tend to share stories of their personal experiences with sexism, including domestic violence, only to find that such events are hardly unique. At the same time, these women become comfortable with their more independent lives outside of the home. We will see this in the case of revolutionary Chile, where women participated in government organized mothers' centers. Together these factors may, in Molyneux's estimation, enable strategic (feminist) mobilization.

In this book we will see a different but related phenomenon: women who originally became involved in revolutionary movements in order to meet practical needs, albeit of another sort. In the case of El Salvador, women noted a variety of reasons for getting involved—most often, a sense of fear for their lives (Luciak 2001, 70). In other words, participation in the revolutionary struggle was seen as a means toward survival, certainly a practical demand. Though such demands were completely ungendered, a collective consciousness among some women was fostered through common experiences with sexism that would later serve as an impetus to struggle for strategic needs. We will also see, specifically through the case of Cuba, that when women's practical needs are met, the likelihood of feminist mobilization is decreased.

Similarly, Temma Kaplan suggests that there is a distinction between what she calls female consciousness and feminist consciousness. Female consciousness, according to Kaplan is the "recognition of what a particular class, culture, and historical period expect from women, [which] creates a sense of rights and obligations that provides motive force for actions" (Kaplan 1982, 545). This female consciousness is the bedrock of feminine mobilization, or that which strives to meet what Molyneux calls the "practical" needs of women. On the other hand, feminist movements contest patriarchal relations in any given structure, thus focusing upon strategic demands. For example, the only women's organization that currently exists in Cuba, the Federation of Cuban Women (Federación de Mujeres Cubanas, or FMC), is explicitly feminine and not feminist. The federation works to assure that women are integrated into Cuban society in its current form, whereas the Salvadoran feminist organization Women for Dignity and Life "Breaking the Silence" (Mujeres por la Dignidad y la Vida "Rompamos el Silencio" or DIGNAS) challenges the patriarchal structure of the society that is responsible for inhibiting the full integration of women. Kaplan also argues that women's public protests, even when framed in entirely traditional notions of femininity, convey important political messages about the strength of women. We will see this throughout the book, especially in the many examples of women organizing as mothers.

Some organizations of women are more difficult to identify as either strategic or practical, or feminine or feminist. A common critique of Molyneux's work is the implication that practical demands are apolitical (Lind 1992).[5] However, participating in a collective soup kitchen tends to be an action in response to an unequal distribution of wealth, most certainly a political circumstance. Additionally, women fighting for the respect of human rights are certainly in the throes of a political movement, but one that cannot be identified as either practical or strategic, feminine or feminist. The groups of mothers of the disappeared throughout Latin America fall into this gray area. As such, they are of particular interest to scholars (Acosta 1993; Arditti 1999; Chuchryk 1989b; Fisher 1993; Schirmer 1993a; Stephen 1994, 1997). Throughout the bloodier parts of Latin American histories the "disappearance" of civilians was normal procedure. Suspected leftists, their sympathizers, and even their family members were kidnapped (generally in the middle of the night), later tortured, and never seen again, dead or alive. The prevalence of such violations to human rights brought Argentinean women together as they demanded to know the whereabouts of their "disappeared" loved ones. As parallel situations consumed Latin America, such committees were organized in Chile, El Salvador, Guatemala, Honduras, and Peru (Muños and Portillo 1986). (When I was in Cuba one of the women with whom I spoke also explained that mothers in her country organized a similar campaign to protest the brutality of Batista's dictatorship against their children.) Despite the fact that political activity had been forced underground, almost immediately the mothers of the disappeared played a public role in politics. In each country the mothers would take to the streets and publicly display their grief as a way to protest the systematic human rights violations that dominated their countries. In addition to their shared experiences with deep personal loss, these women's gendered life experiences were the bond that held them together. The committees eventually became central to fostering women's empowerment. In this case gender roles were significant as the women organized as mothers, grandmothers, wives, and the like, fully embracing rather than contesting their feminine roles. Their political personas were indisputably feminine providing a new face to nonviolent militant politics. In this case, however, the sociopolitical unity of these women is in no way indicative of feminism and in some cases even quite opposed to it.

In addition to inadvertently offering an example of a social movement comprised solely of women, the mothers of the disappeared also utilized their femininity to gain entrance into politically hostile territory likely to be closed to men. The safety provided to the women was short-lived, however. This presumably apolitical group of women—mothers, wives, and grandmothers— became a regionally significant political actor totally separate from feminism. In a far different context, women guerrillas also manipulated femininity toward political ends. For example, in both El Salvador and Cuba, women guerrillas posed as wives to their male *compañeros* in order to enable male guerrillas to move more safely without drawing attention to themselves. Like the mothers of the disappeared, the Salvadoran and Cuban women used femininity in order to advance a very political project. In this book I will show that such manipulation of assigned gender roles has been central to advancing revolutionary movements.

As all of this suggests, the distinctions that Molyneux and Kaplan offer between strategic and practical demands and feminine and feminist movements, respectively, are not entirely parallel to the discourse and ideology advanced by the women we will meet in this book. What they do offer however is a way to identify theoretical distinctions that can be useful in avoiding the tendency to categorize all women activists as feminists. For example, many of the extremely militant and armed revolutionaries I spoke to in El Salvador and Cuba saw their actions as completely disconnected from feminism. On the other hand, as I will discuss in chapter 2, women in El Salvador have organized around their identities as mothers (some might argue, the epitome of femininity) for the seemingly practical demand of child support, yet have very much framed their movement as one that is feminist. Assumptions about who is a feminist and who is not are a bit counterintuitive in the case of Latin America. For example, women who demonstrate political militancy as guerrillas or union activists are not necessarily feminists. Similarly, women who politically embrace their identities as mothers are not necessarily antithetical to feminism. Regionally these distinctions continue to be debated among Latin American and Caribbean activists and academics in hopes of moving toward more fluidity within these seemingly polemic models.

Such regional coordination of women has also been of great interest to scholars of Latin American feminism (Alvarez et al., 2003; Sternbach et al., 1992). The Latin American encuentros began in July of 1981, with two hundred women from fifty organizations convening in Bogotá, Colombia. The numbers of attendees have multiplied exponentially throughout the years; at the 2002 meeting in Costa Rica, 850 women attended, representing nearly every country in the region. For the past two decades women attendees have represented a plethora of types of organizations: women union activists, ex-guerrillas, lesbians, women of color, leftist party members, religious organizations, members of autonomous feminist organizations, representatives from nongovernmental organizations, and human rights organizations. According to Alvarez and colleauges these meetings have inspired "numerous intraregional issue- and identity-specific networks as well as advocacy coalitions on a range of issues such as women's health and sexual and reproductive rights, violence against women, and women's political representation" (2003, 539). Such networks are the result of intense and often ugly debates. Divisions persist though the protagonists continue to grow and change. One of the earlier conflicts particularly relevant to my study is the tension between women who identify as *políticas* (women of leftist parties) and those who are *feministas*. Políticas argue that the goal of women's liberation is most likely to be met by women working within their leftist parties. On the other side of the debate, feministas argue that the parties are too restrictive with respect to the realization of feminist goals, and therefore autonomous organizations are necessary. This division reflects the sectarianism that was present in the leftist organizations in which most of the women started their political activism, as we will see in the cases of El Salvador and Chile. Many women, however, fell outside of this debate by embracing a practice of *doble militancia* (double militancy), thereby prioritizing their commitments to neither feminism nor their leftist parties. Recently this division has been exacerbated by a split between institutional and autonomous feminists,[6] as well as *históricas* (older feminists) and younger women (Alvarez et al., 2003; Acuña interview 1999). Though the demographics of the attendees has diversified significantly, conflicts continue to percolate surrounding the hegemony of white/*mestiza*, heterosexual, middle-class, and Spanish-speaking women. These tensions are as far from resolution as the "woman question" is from being answered. Despite the persistent conflicts, the exchange of, and exposure to each other's revolutionary, feminist, and other political experiences have served in strengthening regional and local feminisms.[7] The encuentros have been the locale for most second-wave feminist dialogue in Latin America and the Caribbean.

Another way in which second-wave feminist ideas found their way to the region was through the travel of Latin American and Caribbean women to Europe, the United States, Mexico, throughout the rest of the region, and vice versa. Exiled leftist women, mainly Chileans, arrived in Europe when second-wave feminism was flourishing. (The U.S.-sponsored military coup against democratically elected socialist Salvador Allende happened in 1973, forcing leftists into exile.) Feminism was a theory easy for these women to assimilate into their own worldviews, as oppositional thinking and actions were precisely the reason for their exile. Eventually the Chilean women returned home, bringing their expanded political ideas and agendas with them. The sentiments were well received as their return corresponded with the beginnings of a parallel second wave feminist boom in their home nation (Frohmann and Valdés 1995; Matear 1997; Palestro 1991). A similar pattern has been noted with respect to El Salvador. Some female members of the FMLN spent time in Mexico doing political work, which was to eventually expose them to international dialogues regarding women's rights (Luciak 2001, 14). Additionally, solidarity activists from the United States and Europe traveled to El Salvador, where the cross-national dialogues led to rich exchanges between leftist and feminist ideologies, each enhancing the other (Chinchilla 1992; Meyer 1994; Stephen 1997). Cuba's isolation from the world impeded transnational feminist exchanges for most Cuban women, however. Leaders of the FMC, an organization that has, since 1960, functioned as the state-supported women's commission, were indeed exposed to international dialogues about feminism. They chose, however, not to share those discussions with Cuban women at large, ensuring that conversations about feminism remained inaccessible to the average Cuban woman. (The FMC will be discussed in detail in chapter 6, which offers insights into such practices.)

The scholarship about women, revolution, and feminism creates dialogue among the above theoretical ideas. In the past twenty or so years the numbers of women have increased significantly in Latin American guerrilla struggles.[8] Indeed, approximately 30 percent of the Salvadoran guerrillas were women. Political changes beyond the borders of Latin America, not the least of which was the rise of an international feminist movement, are in part responsible for creating a climate that facilitated such an increase (Luciak 2001, 2). Karen Kampwirth (2002) argues that the numbers have risen in part due to the prolonged nature of guerrilla struggle, changes in the economy (which have pushed women into the public sphere), and the increased participation of women in liberation theology. When Cuba is compared to El Salvador we will see how the passage of time reflects such changes. For the most part, the Cuban revolutionaries employed a *foco* strategy, one characterized by a series of small, focused attacks. In El Salvador, however, the guerrillas mobilized vis-à-vis what is known as the prolonged war strategy, or a longer and more relentless struggle of ongoing attacks. If nothing else, the length of this later strategy was in part responsible for increased participation of women in order to guarantee a consistent presence upon which the prolonged war strategy relies. In both types of revolutionary structure women played roles shaped by the assumptions surrounding what it means to be a woman. That is, a truly feminine being is expected to be apolitical, which was anything but accurate in the case of revolutionary movements (Kampwirth 2002; Shayne 1999; Stephen 1997). Similar to what we saw with the mothers of the disappeared, women guerrillas were also freer—at least initially—to move in hostile terrain as they aroused less suspicion. For example, in the cases of Cuba and El Salvador, women transported weapons, hiding them under their skirts.

Despite the increases in the quantity and quality of women's participation, social and structural obstacles remain (Lobao 1990). Revolutionary movements do not in and of themselves pose challenges to patriarchal structures, especially at the micro level of the family. Since women were expected to play the role of caretaker of the family, they were restricted in their options. Related to this, poor and working-class women had the onus of working to help make ends meet, which severely limited their time to participate in political events of any type. Because these restrictions were less prevalent among middle-class women they tended to be more able to participate in revolutionary movements than their working-poor counterparts (Jaquette 1973; Lobao 1990.) (This distinction was more apparent in the cities where women participants in the urban undergrounds tended to come from more privileged backgrounds whereas in rural combat peasant women tended to predominate.) All three cases help demonstrate this point as the few women who were able to elevate into leadership positions came from privileged class backgrounds. Revolutionary movements were then strengthened by the presence of these women because their class status resulted in cultural capital that was used to enhance the revolutionary movements. For example, in the case of Cuba, one of the top women leaders in the revolution was a lawyer and was able to provide very important legal skills to the revolutionary project. Unfortunately, this potential of women to add to revolutionary struggles was one of the many things overlooked by male leadership in these movements.

Though middle- and upper-class status often enabled women to join revolutionary struggles, sexist attitudes of male guerrillas have also played a significant role in preventing women guerrillas from taking on leadership positions. In addition to personally frustrating experiences with male leftists, women revolutionaries were potentially limited by the ideological structure of a revolutionary movement. Valentine Moghadam suggests that revolutionary movements are organized in one of two ways, "the 'woman-in-the-family' or patriarchal model of revolution, and the 'women's emancipation' or modernizing model" (1997, 137). The woman-in-the-family model of revolution tends to equate national liberation and discourse to patriarchal values, while the contrasting women's emancipation model postulates that the emancipation of women is a fundamental part of a socialist revolution. In the former, women are reduced to mothers of the revolution rather than actual revolutionaries, while in the latter women are often left with promises unmet. The sexism that leftist women experienced, combined with the organizational training they received, in part led many women ex-guerrillas to join and even lead feminist movements (Chinchilla 1992; Kampwirth forthcoming; Shayne 1995 and 1999). This is precisely what happened in El Salvador, as we will see in chapter 2. In short, together the above concepts help answer the "revolution question(s)": What do women offer revolutions, and how does revolution relate to feminism? We have seen that women's mobilization takes a variety of forms; sometimes organizing to meet basic needs, sometimes to explicitly challenge patriarchy, while in other cases, some combination of the two. I have also noted that femininity enabled militant (armed and peaceful) political action while providing a certain degree of safety. Additionally, national, regional, and international collaboration in the form of conferences and individual travel, especially in the context of second-wave feminism, enabled an exchange of ideas that further fueled feminism. And finally we saw that women's strategic, yet undervalued, contributions to revolutionary struggle served to both inspire feminist consciousness while training women to organize under this additional banner.

In the rest of this book I will address the complex interplay between revolution and feminism by analyzing and interpreting the roles women play in revolutionary movements, how gender is exploited and transformed through such participation, and the attendant feminist movements that grow from revolutionary mobilization. I find a helpful way of synthesizing all of the above is through a concept I call *revolutionary feminism*. Revolutionary feminism refers to a grassroots movement that is both pluralist and autonomous in structure. It seeks to challenge sexism as inseparable from larger political structures not explicitly perceived to be patriarchal in nature, but from the perspective of feminists, entirely bound to the oppression of women. In this sense, *revolutionary* literally refers to the type of historical process that enabled the development of the feminist movement. Some revolutionary feminists may be more centered on an ideology that sees the eradication of class and gender hierarchies as inseparable (a common theme in El Salvador), whereas revolutionary feminists in Pinochet's Chile saw democracy and feminism as one united struggle. What the feminists in El Salvador and Chile share is the fact that revolutionary movements provided the political, ideological, and logistical foundations for their feminisms. As we will see in the case of Cuba, a revolutionary movement in and of itself is not sufficient in leading to the emergence of feminism.

In this book I will argue that five factors need be present for the emergence of revolutionary feminism: The first factor refers to the process of women revolutionaries challenging socially prescribed roles reflective of femininity, or what is often called "gender-bending" (Lorber 1994).[9] To a certain extent, the mere presence of women in a revolutionary struggle is, in and of itself, a confrontation with gendered expectations of behavior (Jaquette 1973; Lobao 1990). What is significant to my model however is not simply the existence of women but in what capacity were they involved in revolutionary struggles. The staying power of such challenges to gender is not only related to the type of tasks, but also to the number of women performing such revolutionary work. (This distinction will become clear as we move through the cases).

The second factor is that of a logistical nature: women revolutionaries need to have received training as activists as a result of their experiences in a revolutionary movement. This factor is necessary as a social movement is not able to emerge if the actors are lacking the skills necessary to advance their agenda. The third factor is a sociopolitical cleavage in the postrevolutionary period, which provides the organizational and ideological space for mobilization. Sociologists call this space a political opportunity structure (Tarrow 1994).

The fourth factor is the sense on the part of women that their revolution remains incomplete. This can be the result of unmet practical needs, and/or they feel politically abused by the sexism to which they were exposed during the revolutionary struggle. This factor is crucial as it is indispensable to the development of a collective feminist consciousness, the fifth and final factor. To determine the strength and presence of a revolutionary feminist movement three things need be considered: (1) Is the movement politically autonomous from larger social institutions? (2) Is the movement significantly empowered to bring about measurable sociopolitical change? (3) Is the movement structured in a pluralistic fashion? In the rest of the book I will look at the cases of El Salvador, Chile, and Cuba to further explore these ideas.

WHY EL SALVADOR, CHILE, AND CUBA?

Why such an eclectic and seemingly asymmetrical group of countries? I chose these three countries for a variety of reasons.

Each has a unique revolutionary history allowing for a more textured discussion. In 1959, armed Cuban guerrillas (the MR-26-7) under the leadership of Fidel Castro ousted U.S.-backed dictator Fulgencio Batista from power through a successful revolutionary insurrection. Two years later Castro declared Cuba a socialist state and has been leader of the country ever since. In Chile we have a rather different scenario. In 1970 socialist Salvador Allende was elected president through open and democratic elections inaugurating the beginning of what was to be a "partial revolution."[10] Allende had held office just under three years when he died in a U.S.-backed military coup led by army general Augusto Pinochet. From 1973 to 1989 Pinochet militaristically ruled the country. In 1990 he stepped down after the Chilean people registered a no vote in a plebiscite that asked if they wanted Pinochet to continue ruling the country. In 1990 a transition to democracy began in Chile. In El Salvador, we have yet another scenario. In 1980 a coalition of five guerrilla organizations joined together as the FMLN. They fought a war against a series of fraudulently elected, and U.S.-supported, militaristic rulers. The war was largely about unequal distribution of wealth, specifically land. The FMLN was not militarily victorious but in 1992 peace accords were signed resulting in what has come to be known as a negotiated revolution. In other words, we have three different types of revolutionary experiences: negotiated (El Salvador), partial (Chile), and successful (Cuba).

Analytically there are several reasons why I chose these three countries: Despite the differences in outcomes and strategy, parallels exist. The most significant parallel to this book is that each country had militant, though not necessarily armed, leftist revolutionary movements. The different structures and results of the revolutions offer a more complex and theoretically diverse background from which to analyze issues of feminism and their relationship to armed versus electoral struggle and complete versus partial revolution. Additionally, these three cases represent an evolving chronology (the 1950s, 1970s, and 1990s) providing the space to analyze how the passage of time affects sociopolitical events—a particularly important factor when assessing the progress of women and their attendant social movements. Another interesting comparison is illuminated through the inclusion of Chile in this project. Definite parallels existed between the status of, and program for women in Allende's Chile and Castro's Cuba. And, notably, parallels also existed between feminism under Pinochet and feminism in postwar El Salvador. These latter two cases, of course, differ dramatically in their political structures (military dictatorship versus democratic transition). However, we are still able to draw conclusions regarding feminism in nonsocialist periods. In other words, Chile becomes the theoretical bridge between Cuba and El Salvador.

METHODOLOGY

Data for the study is based on formal interviews with leaders in revolutionary and feminist movements, ex-combatants in revolutionary organizations, participant observation, and informal interviews with women from different parts of the revolutionary movements. Before reaching each country, I identified the organizations that I wanted represented and established contacts from those organizations. Once I was in the country, I used my initial contacts to develop a snowball sample. In many cases, finding respondents was not difficult, as many of the women I interviewed were still prominent in political and feminist organizations or had long histories with the Left.

My main questions focused upon the roles of women in revolutionary organizations and their relationships to feminism in the aftermath of such movements. I wanted to understand the ideology and structure of the various organizations and the experiences of women within them. My desire to understand the relationship between revolutionary and feminist organizations pointed me in the direction of women in positions of leadership. That is, in order to understand two simultaneous political histories (revolution and feminism) it made most sense to speak with the protagonists who were the most seasoned activists, which meant women in various levels of leadership. This meant that women with whom I spoke were quite savvy about politics. They understood how decisions were made, why outcomes looked as they did, and in some cases were quite central to making these important decisions. Additionally, women in positions of leadership were able to speak to the overall gendered division of labor within the revolutionary context, a question of great importance to my research, as they had a more comprehensive view of the organizational structures. Furthermore, in order to understand the organizational and ideological histories that were so central to my research agenda I needed to speak with women who had extended relationships with their respective organizations, making women in positions of leadership the most logical place to turn. And finally, women in leadership were the most plugged in politically, and were thus able to put me in touch with other women like themselves, which proved quite useful in facilitating my snowball sample. I turn now to the specifics of each country.

Though my formal research in El Salvador did not begin until 1993 and 1994 my participant observation of Salvadoran politics began in 1984 when I traveled to El Salvador for the first time. With the first four years of the Ronald Reagan/George H. W. Bush era completed and the Cold War peaking, the war in El Salvador was raging. It was from that trip that the depths of U.S. involvement, and the intensity of revolutionary opposition, became clear to me. From that point on, Latin America became a permanent feature in my intellectual and political curiosities. Ten years later I returned to El Salvador for the fourth time. In 1994 I traveled to El Salvador for two weeks as part of a women's delegation hosted by the Center for Exchange and Solidarity (Centro de Intercambio y Solidaridad, or CIS). During our stay the fifteen of us met with fourteen groups of women, including feminists, women's commissions of unions, indigenous women's groups, and representatives of political parties. I was also able to interview six women, mostly leaders in the feminist movement, and/or ex-combatants. I had easy access to these women as I had met most of them through the meetings organized by the CIS. In our meetings and interviews we discussed the history and future of the FMLN, the experiences of women in the various components of the Left, and the evolution, structure, and goals of the extremely nascent postwar women's movement. The women with whom I spoke were, on the average, in their mid-twenties to mid-forties. Their class backgrounds were slightly varied, spanning from *campesina* (peasant) to middle class, with the majority falling in what could be called the working middle class. The interviews and meetings were all recorded, and lasted between thirty minutes and three hours; some were in Spanish and others in English.

The year 1994 was a particularly exciting time to be in El Salvador. The "elections of the century" were happening,[11] and along with my group I served as an unofficial observer. As a result of the elections feminists unveiled their historic *Mujeres '94* (Women '94) platform (to be discussed in chapter 2) and had quite successfully pushed women's issues onto the national agenda. I also participated in the International Women's Day march, which provided me a look at the praxis of revolutionary feminist politics. Both before and after this trip I also conducted four interviews with Salvadorans who were in the United States for various political reasons, and I attended talks and group meetings with five Salvadoran feminists.[12] It was also at this same time that colleagues conducted four interviews for me using questions I wrote.

In the summer of 1998 I then returned to El Salvador for the fifth time. On this trip I did follow-up interviews with women that I had interviewed or met in 1994. Additionally, these women put me in touch with other feminists with connections to the revolutionary movement so I once again spoke with women ex-combatants, current feminist leaders, members of leftist organizations, or parties, and various combinations thereof. Through my questions I sought to understand the roles of women in the guerrilla and popular movements during the war, the ideology and structure of the current feminist movement, and the relationship between the two. The formal interviews lasted anywhere from one to three hours. The women I interviewed ranged from nineteen to fifty years in age. Their levels of education spanned secondary schooling to graduate school, and their social classes from campesina to middle-class backgrounds. The majority of interviews were conducted in Spanish and were tape recorded. While there I also collected organizational pamphlets, mission statements, and books, which helped to explain the self-perception of the activists and their organizations.

Just as in 1994, the political environment in El Salvador was quite ripe for conducting research. Preparation was underway for the upcoming elections and the FMLN was debating whether to advance a woman presidential candidate. While there I was invited to be an international observer at the Sixth National Convention of the FMLN. This was the FMLN's electoral primary, where the main topic on the agenda was the upcoming presidential elections. Feminists inside the party were pushing for human rights ombudswoman Dr. Victoría Marina de Aviles as the FMLN's presidential candidate. Just as in 1994, feminists once again placed women's issues onto the national political agenda. Though polls showed her to be the second most popular political figure in the country (second only to the former first lady) the FMLN eventually chose not to elect her as presidential candidate. The ticket they chose instead lost in the first round of elections. As a result of the political mood in the country and participation in these types of events I was also privy to much inside dialogue. In total, the data I collected between 1993 and 1998 consists of thirty-one formal, semistructured interviews, and nineteen group meetings.

I visited Chile for the first time in October of 1998 and stayed for seven months. I traveled to Chile with several very solid contacts from colleagues in the United States and was easily able to initiate a snowball sample that resulted in interviews with twenty-three Chilean women. Making contacts did not prove difficult, as the women were quite enthusiastic about committing their experiences to history and putting me in touch with their colleagues. The Chilean women with whom I spoke were similar to the Salvadoran women in that they held leadership positions of various levels in leftist parties and organizations, and/or the feminist movement. I interviewed women who were active during the Allende years as government functionaries and grassroots activists, leaders of the anti-Pinochet movement, feminist and otherwise, members of the contemporary women's movement, and various combinations thereof. Questions were designed to get a sense of how women felt about the Popular Unity (Unidad Popular, or UP) government of Salvador Allende and their positioning within it, the roles of women in the struggle against the dictator, and their ideas about the Left and feminism. I also spent time in the National Library of Santiago, which has an extensive collection of feminist newsletters from the 1980s and the gender studies library at the Latin American Faculty of Social Sciences (Facultad Latinoamericana de Ciencias Sociales). The women I interviewed varied in age from twenty-nine to seventy-eight, with levels of education that ranged from secondary schooling to Ph.D.s. As in El Salvador, their social classes spanned the spectrum, with the majority residing in the Chilean middle and upper middle classes. The interviews lasted between one and three hours, were cassette taped, and conducted in Spanish, in Santiago, Chile.

And, as in El Salvador, the political backdrop in Chile was quite ripe for research. A few weeks after my arrival, ex-dictator Pinochet was arrested in England on charges initiated by the Spanish government that he was responsible for crimes against its citizens during his dictatorship. The question of whether Pinochet would ultimately be held accountable for his crimes against humanity depended on the outcome of the appeals regarding whether or not he could be extradited. As the decisions kept changing there were ongoing anti-Pinochet rallies organized in large part by the Association of the Families of the Detained and Disappeared (Agrupación de Familiares de Detenido y Desaparecido or AFDD) as well as much smaller pro-Pinochet rallies. (Pinochet was ultimately returned to Chile and not tried for his crimes.) While I was in Chile, there were also presidential elections, and the Communist Party advanced a woman presidential candidate for the first time. Additionally, there were fairly regular street protests and strikes by university students, educators, and Mapuche Indians for their various political grievances. I was also an invited attendee of a cross-generational conference of approximately fifty Chilean feminists to discuss the history and future of their movements. Combined, the rallies, protests, and meetings provided me many opportunities to participate in the political events in Chile and informally interview countless more women.

In July of 1999 I then went to Cuba where I spent one month.[13] The political backdrop in Cuba was comparable to that of El Salvador and Chile, but in a distinctly Cuban way. That is, public grassroots events and dissent in Cuba are virtually invisible, and political organizations closed to "outsiders"— especially foreigners from the United States—so I was not privy to the same sorts of street rallies and planning meetings that I attended in El Salvador and Chile. However, I was in Cuba for the celebration to commemorate the birth of the the the MR-26-7, a date of great significance to Cuban revolutionaries. Huge flags with one red and one black stripe, bearing the MR-26-7 acronym hung from windows all over Havana, next to Cuba's national flag. Together the flags conveyed loyalty to and celebration of the Cuban revolutionary movement. Similarly, the absence of the flags offered a tiny glimpse into how and which Cubans feel connected to this historic date.

Cuba is an exceptionally challenging place for fieldwork, especially as a U.S. citizen. The group of scholars of which I was a part was denied institutional support for our various research agendas,[14] which meant that the Cuban Ministry of Culture did not endorse our projects. In other words, what I was doing was actually illegal in the eyes of the Cuban state. This presented an obstacle in Cuba, which I had not encountered in either El Salvador or Chile. When attempting to set up interviews in Cuba, potential interviewees would often ask me who was sponsoring the project and some, upon hearing that I had no sponsorship, opted not to be interviewed. In the Cuban context the lack of institutional support implied that speaking to a researcher could be construed as a breach in national unity, a legal violation in revolutionary Cuba. Out of respect for this law (and perhaps out of fear of repercussion) it was often the more stalwart supporters of the revolution who declined interviews. This is not to say that all interviews presented obstacles. Many women were very excited about recalling their histories and committing and entrusting them to a project such as this. Just as in El Salvador and Chile, in Cuba I interviewed women in relatively high positions in the revolutionary movement and those with varied relationships to women-focused projects. All together I was able to interview nineteen women that were participants in the anti-Batista movement, members of the FMC, professors and researchers of gender studies, filmmakers, and women from a now defunct feminist organization. Through my questions I attempted to understand the roles of women in the insurrection, their beliefs about feminism, how gender and gendered roles had changed through the revolution, and how women felt about their positions in postinsurrection Cuba. The women ranged from forty-four to eighty years in age, and were a highly educated group with nearly half holding Ph.D.s and the rest a minimum of a high school, if not university, education. Social class, like everything in Cuba, is exceptionally complex and neat categories become slippery the moment one attempts to apply them. That said, the women in my sample ranged from working- to middle-class positioning, which is determined in part by their upbringing before the revolution (or their parents' status), as well as their position in contemporary Cuban society. Interviews lasted anywhere from two to four hours, and were generally conducted in Spanish, save a few with women who were, at minimum, bilingual.

In addition to my interviews I spent time in the Cuban National Library as well as archives maintained by the FMC. I complemented the interviews I conducted in all three countries, the documents the women I interviewed provide me, and some historical texts from the few collections I had access to, with secondary publications by other U.S. scholars of Latin American revolution and feminism.

THE ORGANIZATION OF THIS STUDY

Though I will only be looking at three countries I will be analyzing and comparing six cases that are central to this project: revolutionary war El Salvador (1980–1992); postwar El Salvador (1992–1999); Allende's Chile (1970–1973); post-Allende/Pinochet's Chile (1973–1990); the Cuban anti-Batista movement (1952–1959), and Castro's Cuba (1959–1999). I have divided each country into two periods, revolutionary and postrevolutionary, though I must warn the reader of the potential limitations of such a categorization. To refer to the civil war in El Salvador as the revolutionary period contradicts most scholarship on revolutions that identifies El Salvador as a "failed revolution." Similarly, to call the period after 1959 in Cuba the postrevolutionary period is inconsistent with how Cubans understand their situation. That is, the postrevolutionary period does not yet exist and will not

Historical Periods in Question

	Cuba	Chile	El Salvador
Revolutionary Period	1952–1959	1970–1973	1980–1992
Phase	Insurrectionary guerrilla struggle against Batista	Tenure of Salvador Allende	Antigovernment guerrilla struggle
	Led by the MR-26-7	Led by the UP coalition	Led by the FMLN
Postrevolutionary Period	1959–1999	1973–1990	1992–1999
Phase	The period immediately following the insurrection	The period immediately following the presidency of Salvador Allende (the Pinochet dictatorship) until the initiation of the transition to democracy	The period after the war ended vis-à-vis a negotiated settlement and peace accords

until the Communist Party is no longer in charge of the country. Rather, Cubans would call the period immediately following the ousting of Batista the "revolutionary period." And Chile is also complicated, as the tenure of Salvador Allende is not entirely revolutionary but what I am calling a partial revolution. Despite the fact that these labels could be contested I think analytically and organizationally it is a useful way to structure the comparison. If we think of the terms as a descriptive way to identify chronological periods their utility becomes apparent. Despite debates over terms, it will become clear as we move through the different cases that in all three countries some sort of revolutionary transformation took place.

As I will explain in this book, feminist movements developed in the aftermath of the revolutionary struggles in El Salvador and Chile, whereas in Cuba that was not the case. Because the case of Cuba is unique in its lack of feminism, I have chosen to organize this book in reverse chronological order. Chapter 1 explores the roles of women in the Salvadoran revolutionary war and the relationship of their roles to gender. It is in this chapter that I introduce a concept I call *gendered revolutionary bridges*. Chapter 2 looks at the revolutionary feminist movement that emerged in postwar El Salvador and the relationship of its members to the revolutionary struggle that preceded it. Chapter 3 moves south to Chile, and discusses the radical sociopolitical experiment vis-à-vis the democratic election and tenure of Salvador Allende. In that chapter I analyze the roles of women in the Allende government and the effects of his policies upon women. Chapter 4 examines the subsequent Pinochet regime in Chile, and the militant and/or feminist actions that Chilean women organized in opposition to the dictatorship. Chapter 5 moves on to Cuba and, as in El Salvador, explores the roles that women played in the insurrection against Batista and the significance of gender to those roles. Chapter 6 discusses questions of gender politics and feminism in postinsurrection Cuba. I conclude the book by revisiting my conclusions and offering an analysis of their implications.

CHAPTER 1

Gender and the Revolutionary Struggle in El Salvador, 1979–1992

I could say that as women we could have given more and we could have had a more coherent space for our strength; women [participated], and like statistics indicate, it was in quantity as well as quality. But we [were part of] the process of the party within an historical framework. We could not ask "for pears from an apple tree"; we [women] could not, at that point in time. When organizations emerged, nobody really, very few people, fought for women. All of us women threw ourselves into the struggle for the goals of the people and other goals. That participation was very important because we regained women's participation, and even though it was not for our own rights, it was important.

—Lety Mendez, 1998

THE TINY CENTRAL AMERICAN nation of El Salvador has a history plagued with violence, inequitable distribution of wealth and land, and political structures which have been manipulated by the oligarchy and military in order to maintain these deeply skewed power relations. Unlike Chile, El Salvador does not have a history of democracy of which to boast. In contrast to Cuba, El Salvador's prerevolutionary status is not one of a personalistic dictator, but rather of a series of often short-lived, militarily controlled juntas who usurped power under the pretext of "free" elections. By 1980 the Farabundo Martí Front for National Liberation (Frente Farabundo Martí para la Liberación Nacional, or FMLN) united and declared war against the Salvadoran government and military. The attempted revolution was long and costly by all measures: during the twelve years that the war officially raged, seventy-five thousand people were killed, two million displaced, an estimated one million people became war refugees, and eight thousand disappeared; this was compounded by billions of dollars in economic losses (Keen and Haynes 2000, 499; Stephen 1994, 196). Of these deaths a significant majority have been found by the United Nations to be the result of the Salvadoran military.[1]

In 1992, the Salvadoran government/military, upon realization that they were unable to defeat the guerrillas militarily, finally came to a UN-brokered settlement, or what has since been considered a "negotiated revolution."[2] In this chapter I will begin answering the first part of the revolution question—What do women do for revolutions?—by focusing on the specific roles of women in the Salvadoran revolutionary movement.[3] Using a concept I call *gendered revolutionary bridges*, I will argue that the contributions of women to both the popular and guerrilla movements were largely enabled and dictated by traditional notions of femininity, and that these contributions were fundamental to the development of the Salvadoran revolutionary project.

A BRIEF HISTORY OF EL SALVADOR

Just as the nation of El Salvador has been subjected to the hegemonic dominance of colonial and neocolonial powers, so too have Salvadorans at the individual level been restricted by a repressive triple alliance of the military, government, and economy.[4] By the late nineteenth century the oligarchy had firm control over the social and economic autonomy of Salvadorans. In the case of El Salvador, the oligarchy was a tiny group of families infamously known as the "fourteen families." They acquired this name because—geopolitically—El Salvador is divided into fourteen departments, and each one was said to be controlled by an individual family. The power inequities were legally sanctioned through laws that made it illegal for indigenous peoples to collectively own land. The ramification of this was quite extensive, as El Salvador's economy was, and remains, agriculturally based. As a result, the oligarchy was able to gain control of the majority of arable land, leading early on to the structural maintenance of race and class stratification, something that is still present in El Salvador today. By the mid-nineteenth century necessity and entrepreneurial savvy led to the discovery of a lucrative commodity for the world market: coffee. The development of coffee contributed to El Salvador's economic strength on an intranational level. In addition to the best land being concentrated in the hands of the oligarchy, most presidents at this time were also both military generals and coffee growers. Once the coffee industry began to emerge as the dominant economic force in El Salvador, the government usurped land from indigenous peoples and peasants. As a result, they would eventually become the laborers on what had formerly been their land. During this same period, 1821–1898, the attempted disenfranchisement of the peasantry spawned five uprisings in the coffee growing region of the country. By 1912 the National Guard was established and typically based in close proximity to major farms. First and foremost, the Guard became accountable to land owners rather than the military, further solidifying the concentration of power within the triple alliance. Such lack of clear boundaries among the economic elite, governmental structures, and military powers would prove decisive in inspiring the revolution of the 1980s.

Perhaps the development that had and continues to have the most profound impact on El Salvador occurred in the early twentieth century, when the United States emerged as a leading world power. One of the earliest examples of U.S. hegemony in the region occurred in 1914, when Panama lost control of its canal to the United States. The canal enabled the development of an export economy which has since caused underdevelopment in much of Central and South America. Additionally, Panama has proved a strategic site for the launching of U.S.-directed military operations.[5] The politically vulnerable position of El Salvador was not solely the result of outside forces. For nearly the first twenty-five years of the twentieth century (1907–1931), political power within El Salvador was concentrated in the hands of a single family—the Meléndez clan. In 1929, during the rule of the Meléndez family, the stock market crash occurred, further exacerbating the egregious living conditions of the majority of Salvadorans. El Salvador, like many single-export based economies, found itself in dire straits as coffee prices dropped dramatically on the world market and former importers of coffee (namely the United States) had far less surplus to spend on luxury goods. In short, material living conditions deteriorated in tandem with the intensification of dictatorial rule.

As the standard of living grew progressively worse, people began to organize. As early as 1925, a small Communist Party, under the leadership Augustín Farabundo Martí, began its clandestine organizing. As a university student Martí was introduced to the radical theories of Marxism, which he eventually translated into political action, leading to his expulsion from El Salvador in 1927. Upon his return in 1930 he resumed his political organizing, this time with the support of other university students, taking his message to the peasants in the countryside. Again, the government attempted to stop Martí by incarcerating him, but it was unsuccessful, as a hunger strike led to his eventual release. Such was the context that led to a free election in El Salvador with a victory for Arturo Araujo, wealthy landowner and liberal. Upon election, Araujo pledged to create social harmony through a series of basic reforms, like education, while also announcing that the newly formed Communist Party would be able to participate in the upcoming municipal elections. This unprecedented political openness prompted a military coup and a period of military rule led by General Maximiliano Hernández Martínez, who stayed in power until 1944. This new development resulted in the transference of power from the oligarchy to the military—a period in Salvadoran history that would not subside until the signing of the peace accords in 1992.

It was in this context in 1932 that Farabundo Martí led an historic insurrection in both San Salvador and the western regions of the country. When the legislative elections were yet again marked with fraud, Martí and others realized that the Martínez regime was not going to permit them to participate democratically so they set a date for an insurrection—22 January. The plan was discovered, however, and Martí was captured on 18 January. The insurrection turned into an unorganized uprising met by what has become infamously brutal repression; entire villages were razed and liquidated, causing deaths in the tens of thousands—the most common estimate is thirty-thousand people, fewer than 10 percent of whom even participated in the action. Additionally, this uprising proved the catalyst for the virtual elimination of El Salvador's indigenous population. Thomas Skidmore and Peter Smith suggest that several messages emerged from this insurrection. First, peasants learned to distrust city revolutionaries who, as evidenced by the 1932 slaughter, could lead them to destruction. Second, indigenous peoples began to protect themselves by hiding their traditional habits, including their clothing and customs. Third, leftists concluded that there was a potential for opposition in the rural areas. And fourth, the Right concluded that the way to deal with popular agitation was through repression (Skidmore and Smith 1997, 348). Symbolically, this insurrection has stayed with Salvadoran leftists, as the former guerrilla organization (now leftist political party) took its name from the fallen revolutionary—the Farabundo Martí Front for National Liberation.

Another development significant to Salvadoran history was the triumph of the Cuban Revolution in 1959 for its effects upon U.S. policy toward the region. As the United States sought to avoid "another Cuba" and thus lose its political and economic influence upon other countries in the region, it created the Alliance for Progress program, which aspired to be an alternative to right-wing dictatorships and left-wing guerrillas. The military dimension of this policy focused upon counterinsurgency, while the political side focused on the institutionalization of centrist parties whose economic focus was capitalist development. It was toward this end that the United States unsuccessfully continued to exert pressure on the Salvadoran government to hold what could be marketed as free elections.

In 1972, José Napoleón Duarte, founder of the Christian Democratic Party (Partido Democrático Cristiano, or PDC) and favorite of the United States, mounted a reformist challenge. The moderate coalition, of which the PDC was the largest part, pledged a commitment to peaceful reform through electoral means. Duarte won the elections in 1972, but the military ignored this victory and turned power over to their own colonel. Duarte was subsequently arrested, tortured, and exiled. As the Cold War continued to intensify, the United States clung to a political rationale that justified massive military support for—at best—pseudodemocracies in exchange for a commitment to ending any form of leftist organizing. This policy facilitated civilian-military juntas ruling El Salvador throughout the 1970s. Leftists responded to the escalating repression by organizing five individual political-military organizations, which, in 1980, would eventually band together to make up the FMLN. The FMLN declared war against the corruption and violence perpetuated by its own government and, by extension, the interventionist policies of the United States. One of the most infamous acts of government-sponsored violence to precede the FMLN's official declaration of war was the assassination of the revered Archbishop Oscar Arnulfo Romero while celebrating mass in the Cathedral in San Salvador. Archbishop Romero was the pure embodiment of liberation theology, the Catholic-inspired teachings of economic social justice for all peoples (particularly the poor). Liberation theology would prove extremely influential in the revolutionary movement in El Salvador,[6] particularly for women, as it was typically the first place where women were exposed to leftist politics. The intention of the government was to silence one of the most admired leaders of the struggle for social justice in El Salvador. It was against this already bloody backdrop that the war officially began.

In 1981 the FMLN launched a highly premature and unsuccessful final offensive. Despite this setback, and much to the surprise and dismay of the military and government, the guerrillas were not fully eliminated. Eventually Duarte, who was undeniably conservative, took over as head of the government, announcing a plan for land reform. The administration of Ronald Reagan pressed for elections in early 1982, the goal being to elect an assembly that would select an interim president. The election was tainted from the beginning—the right wing was led by the infamous ex-major Roberto D'Aubuisson, whom even former U.S. ambassador Robert White had referred to as a "pathological killer" (Dunkerley 1982, 203). Duarte represented the center/center-rightist coalition while the leftists boycotted the elections; the FMLN argued that elections would be anything but transparent in such a climate of repression, especially since the leftist candidates could not even be guaranteed safety. Washington had high hopes for Duarte and his reformist programs to undermine the guerrillas. Duarte's government redistributed significant chunks of farmland, but he could not remove the oligarchy's hold on power, which had made the gap between the rich and poor the largest in nearly all of the third world. Few observers have doubted that without U.S. aid the Salvadoran government would have collapsed. Indeed, throughout the administrations of Reagan and his successor, George H. W. Bush, anticommunist rhetoric was accompanied with between 1.4 and 1.5 million U.S. dollars per day in aid. The civil war was brutal by all accounts. The government waged an intense counterinsurgency campaign characterized by paramilitary death squad militias in the cities and aerial bombing campaigns in the countryside. Death squads targeted suspected members of the popular movement and their families through kidnapping, assassinations, "disappearances," and/or torture. Their goal was to psychologically intimidate the opposition from organizing. For the most part they were unsuccessful. In the countryside the Salvadoran military carried out a scorched-earth campaign that sought to eliminate the popular support for the guerrillas by waging war against civilians. The most effective tool that the military had to accomplish its goal was an air force plentifully stocked by the United States. Bombing campaigns were central to its plan. In response, the FMLN guerrillas organized an ongoing military campaign with the goal of limiting the military's access of the countryside by destroying bridges and other acts of sabotage. The war persisted for twelve bloody years, with the human casualties and economic destruction reflecting that length: there were seventy-five thousand dead, two million displaced, an estimated one million war refugees, and billions of dollars of economic loss to a country that had anything but a budget surplus.

Finally, in 1992, the National Republican Alliance (Alianza Republicana Nacional, or ARENA) government (known by some as the party of the death squads), agreed to negotiate an end to the civil war. Tommie Sue Montgomery suggests that the objectives of the peace accords—that is, to promote democracy, guarantee absolute respect for human rights, and move toward the unification of Salvadoran society—were unprecedented, as no previous civil war ended in an agreement to not simply stop the fighting, but, as she notes, to restructure society (1995, 226). Significantly, the FMLN is a freely operating political party; it currently represents thirty-one of the eighty-four deputies in the National Legislative Assembly, and has more seats than any other party. At the municipal level, the FMLN now governs 60 percent of the country, including the capital city and largest municipality, San Salvador (Stewart 2003). The FMLN has lost all bids at the presidency since the signing of the peace accords, but is far from abandoning the electoral route. Unfortunately, the ARENA has yet to fully prove that the peace accords were more than a political gesture to alleviate social pressure from the opposition movement. The future of El Salvador and its relatively nascent democracy is still quite ambiguous. To understand the roles that women and feminism will play in that future we must first look back to their history of resistance within the attempted revolution of the 1980s.

FEMININITY AND THE SALVADORAN REVOLUTION

The concept of a feminine guerrilla is seemingly antithetical; after all, guerrillas are bearded, cigar-smoking men in heavy-duty military fatigues. In the case of El Salvador this image tells only part of the story. In the rest of this chapter I will draw from the case of El Salvador to begin answering the first part of the revolution question: What do women offer revolutions? Specifically, I will discuss the roles of women within both the armed and unarmed sectors. I will focus this discussion on three sectors of the opposition movement: (1) the union sector, through a discussion of the teachers union, the National Association of Salvadoran Educators (Asociación Nacional de Educadores Salvadoreños, or ANDES); (2) the human rights sector, as embodied by the Committee of the Mothers of the Disappeared (Comité de Madres y

Familiares de Presos, Desaparecidos y Asesinados de El Salvador, or CO-MADRES) and the Christian Committee for the Displaced Peoples of El Salvador (Comité Cristiano Pro-Desplazados de El Salvador, or CRIPDES); and (3) the guerilla sector, via the FMLN. I have chosen to focus on ANDES, the CO-MADRES, and CRIPDES because all three organizations are largely comprised of women. In each of these organizations, the gender composition was not intentional but rather happened by default: in El Salvador school teachers and refugees were largely women, as are, of course, the mothers and wives who make up the CO-MADRES.

Popular imagination (and some older scholarly work) offers the image of a revolutionary as an armed male peasant. What this and similar studies hope to do is offer a more expansive notion of who "the" revolutionary is in order to explicitly include women (Kampwirth 2002; Luciak 2001). In short, not all revolutionaries are men, nor poor, nor even armed. As such, attention to the popular movement is particularly crucial to feminist analyses of revolution as the organizations that make up such a movement (student, union, or human rights organizations, etc.) are typically underacknowledged for their revolutionary contributions. Furthermore, these types of organizations are often where women were overrepresented. It is for this reason that I begin with brief discussion of the popular movement.

Women and the Popular Movement

According to Salvadoran social scientist Mario Lungo Uclés, the *popular* in *popular movement* is characterized by "an identification with social transformation in economic, political, cultural, and social terms that benefits the marginalized. . . . Popular organizations are the organized representation of the interests of the poor and working classes" (1995, 153). Lungo Uclés explains that during the war in El Salvador the popular movement was understood to be part of the revolution, closely identified with the FMLN. He notes, however, that understanding the popular organizations solely "as appendages of the guerrilla groups" does not adequately represent the wartime reality. Indeed, the popular movement, according to Lungo Uclés, is better understood as the "broad-based political expression of the revolution" (155), which maintains a common political project through a close yet distinct relationship with and from the FMLN. The main thing that differentiated the popular and guerrilla movements was the fact that the popular movement relied largely on nonviolent tactics, whereas the FMLN's strategy revolved around armed insurgency. In tracing the evolution of the political and organizational ebbs and flows of the Salvadoran popular movement, Lungo Uclés notes that at certain historical moments (namely, 1980–1982), the repression of the government and military became so intense it forced the popular movement underground, and/or into the mountains with the guerrillas. By mid-1983, the popular movement eventually rebuilt itself in order to show its presence through what was to be a prolonged struggle and, as we will see below, the women of the mothers of the disappeared (CO-MADRES) were central in revitalizing the popular movement. From Lungo Uclés's perspective there are several reasons why the popular movement was important: its breadth, its flexibility, its ability to mobilize rural communities, its quasi-autonomy from the FMLN, its ability to foster coalition and incorporate new sectors, and its ability to reduce the fears of unincorporated sectors. In Lungo Uclés's otherwise detailed account of the popular movement he makes no mention of women. In the sections that follow I will draw from Lungo Uclés's conclusions to discuss some of the contributions of women-centered organizations to the popular movement.[7]

The National Association of Salvadoran Educators (ANDES). One such organization is ANDES, which was founded by Dr. Mélida Anaya Montes in 1965, a woman recognized as heroine and martyr to women and men of the Salvadoran Left.[8] At the time of her assassination in 1983, she was second in command of the Popular Forces of Liberation (Fuerzas Populares de Liberación, or FPL), one of the five political-military organizations that made up the FMLN; her position was one of the two highest positions in the FMLN ever held by a woman (Golden 1991, 166). Due to the fact that the great majority of educators in El Salvador are predominantly women, ANDES' membership is 90 percent women (Thomson 1986, 72). The name ANDES "21 de Junio," by which it is also known, comes from the first demonstration, which took place on 21 June 1965, fifteen years before the war was officially declared. At that march, twenty thousand people—both teachers and other workers who were there to show their solidarity—marched through the streets of San Salvador. They surrounded the presidential palace in order to announce the formation of their union and demand that the government grant it legal status. In a 1995 interview, Esperanza Ramos,[9] the president of the Women's Secretariat of the National Association of Salvadoran Educators (Cooperativa Asociación Nacional de Educadores Salvadoreñas), recalled, "This march was just huge; it was blocks and blocks, thousands of teachers who just threw themselves into the streets under an executive council of which Dr. Mélida Anaya Montes was an integral part. Basically, from the necessities of health [care] and economic conditions we came together to form ANDES '21 June.'"

In 1967, also under the leadership of Anaya Montes, the women of ANDES took to the streets again to celebrate their legal status and press for a national board to listen to their grievances (NAP 1989, 50). ANDES then held two more major strikes organized by Anaya Montes, one in 1968 and one in 1971, the latter being one of the most massive women organized national strikes ever held against the government (Golden 1991, 166). In 1975,

ANDES helped to expand the popular movement by assisting in the formation of the Popular Revolutionary Block (Bloque Popular Revolucionario, or
BPR), a broad-based coalition that represented peasants, workers, students,
and shantytown dwellers who opposed the government.

As early as 1968 the teachers were physically attacked in response to their
protests. Throughout the 1970s the leaders of ANDES were detained, their
offices bombed, and their street protests fired upon. Such attacks were part of
the government's psychological war against the civilian population. In one
particularly egregious attack, young students in a rural school entered their
classroom and were greeted by the severed head of their teacher sitting upon
the desk (Thomson 1986, 74). Esperanza Ramos and Alicia de Astorga were
both captured and tortured. Ramos explained the gruesome scenario and
how their detention, abuse, and exile served to deepen their commitment to
struggle:

> In 1982 we were a team of collaborators and at this time the executive
> council was [coordinating] support for our work . . . in secretive ways
> because in that year there was intensive repression against the teachers.
> They had already assassinated three or four hundred teachers. . . . People
> were disappeared or forced into exile. By the fourteenth of August we
> already had three unions, and on that day they captured us. First men
> came in civilian clothes, heavily armed, but when they realized our num-
> bers, which were twenty-three teachers, we were in the school . . . they
> suddenly did not appear to be civilians; they were uniformed. They took
> us in a huge truck and they stepped on us, and pinned us down, they tied
> our hands and then they took us to the Hacienda [Treasury] Police. They
> took pictures of us in all sorts of positions, they interrogated us, and they
> took us to a place and they separated us, the men in one room the women
> in another. And then four of [the women] they took to another place, and
> Alicia was one of them. On the four they used the *capucha*,[10] etcetera. They
> tortured us . . . in all sorts of ways, [including] damag[ing] our morale. . . .
> They gave us electric shocks, they put us in rooms with bright reflective
> lights, they would not give us water or any food, they kept us standing up,
> they would not let us sit down, or lie down, not even to rest. In total we
> spent nineteen days. But after seventeen days they stopped torturing and
> interrogating us because they said they could not rip out our tongues and
> we would not talk. . . . [Because of international pressure] they delivered
> the men to Mariona Prison and the women to the women's prison. When
> they delivered us they were saying that we were the top commanders of
> the FPL. . . . The treatment was a little better in the political jails because
> the female political prisoners organized and networked. . . . So they con-
> signed us to the political prisons for eleven months and then they gave us

amnesty. After the amnesty we were released. Some were killed upon release and some were forced into exile.

Esperanza continued, explaining the farce of amnesty in such a political climate. She and Alicia fortunately lived to recall these horrific experiences. They were escorted by the International Red Cross to Mexico and remained in exile for eleven months where, she explained,

> everyone decided on their own whether to go farther away or back to El Salvador. In the case of Alicia and myself we decided to go back to our country and continue the struggle and fight for the literacy campaign and for our people. We came back with more conviction, more force, more vindication, more will to continue to deepen ourselves in the struggle. What we didn't do before the arrest we decided to do now. In my case, I became more militant with the FPL, the FMLN, and engaged in activities that we needed to engage in in order to achieve the peace accords.

In short, the women of ANDES were militant union activists, and some members eventually became members of the FMLN. Ramos discussed ANDES' ideological vision and relationship to the overall struggle:

> With respect to the struggle of the people, the feeling of ANDES was to be sensitive, to become closer with the people, with the students, with the parents of the families, with the communities; and we always felt this pain, the human pain of social change. . . . We saw the initiative we needed to take to be part of the general struggle . . . and some of us were in the FMLN. . . . We have examples of women who were on the front lines of the war, teachers, and we have stories of teachers who made that great jump, that special jump, after working with ANDES in the zones controlled by the FMLN they took up arms and also took up their pencils and went to teach the combatants and guerrillas how to read and write as they were side by side with them.

Ramos's words reflect the commitment of ANDES to the revolutionary movement as well as the particularly fluid boundaries between the popular and armed movements. It was this blurriness that the military and death squads used as their rational to carry out their terror campaigns against civilians and unarmed activists.

THE HUMAN RIGHTS SECTOR

THE COMMITTEE OF MOTHERS AND RELATIVES OF POLITICAL PRISONERS, DISAPPEARED, AND ASSASSINATED OF EL SALVADOR (CO-MADRES). The women of the CO-MADRES both responded to the violence perpetrated by the military and eventually were added to its list of targets. As I discussed in the introduction to this book, the committees of the mothers of the disappeared in Latin America have played a leading role in the struggle for human rights and social justice, and El Salvador was no exception. Due to the severity of human rights violations before and during the war, the undertaking of these mothers was massive. Like their counterparts in much of Latin America,[11] they repeatedly bumped into each other in their relentless attempts to locate their disappeared loved ones.

In 1977, twelve women sharing a Christmas Eve dinner provided for them by Archbishop Romero joined together to form and lead the CO-MADRES. Before and during the war, at least four hundred mothers risked their own safety and openly affiliated themselves with this organization (Thomson 1986, 109).

In the beginning, the women of the CO-MADRES were motivated to act by their individual and collective pains. It did not take long for their demands to move beyond their own families. In 1978 they staged their first hunger strike and subsequent three-month occupation of the Red Cross, where they demanded the immediate release of political prisoners. Also that year, the CO-MADRES attracted international attention in order to pressure the Salvadoran and U.S. governments by holding a peaceful occupation in the office of the United Nations in El Salvador. In October of 1980, after the women were forcibly prevented from holding a public vigil in San Salvador, members occupied the offices of the Ministry of Justice until the National Guard forcibly removed them a week later.

In order to reach other Salvadoran women, especially mothers like themselves, the CO-MADRES would occupy Catholic churches. Their actions were in part legitimated by the special social positioning of mothers accorded by Catholic discourse and ideology.[12] Once inside the churches, the CO-MADRES called upon mourning women just like themselves to demand that the Salvadoran government return their children. Additionally, throughout the 1980s they traveled to Australia, Canada, the United States, Europe, and the rest of Latin America to make heard their demands for peace and justice in their nation (Stephen 1994, 2; Thomson 1986, 109).

As the repression increased in the country the women of CO-MADRES became more familiar with the attacks against those outside of their families. María Teresa Tula, longtime CO-MADRES activist, recalls the increase in repression in 1979 and 1980:

> During this time many people had to leave El Salvador and go into exile in other countries. We were moving around too. . . . Right around this time Silvia Olán was disappeared. . . . She was secretary of the SLES (Electrical Workers Union of Sonsonate). Two members of a death squad arrived and abducted her from her office. . . . CO-MADRES took up the

search for her body along with . . . two young men who [also] disappeared. . . . Two days later, the body of Silvia Olán was found by a group
of campesinos in a place called La Laguna in the town of Coatepeque.
There was evidence that she had been raped before she died. They had cut
off part of her genitals and stuffed them into her nose. They cut off her
breasts and her fingers as well. They had burned her eyes with acid, pulled
out her tongue, and strangled her. You can't imagine how terrible it is to
find someone like that, especially someone you admired and cared for
(quoted in Stephen 1994, 79–80).

As a result of this and countless other similar attacks, the women of the CO-
MADRES expanded their mothering energies toward the entire country.
They used their culturally acquired and sanctioned status of mothers to mobilize from a position of morality, implicitly urging the military and government
to respect the Catholic order of Salvadoran society. Rather than heeding their
call the military instead psychologically abused and violently punished them
for their actions. In the early 1980s, the death squads published a statement in
which they claimed that they would cut off the heads of every member of the
CO-MADRES (Thomson 1986, 109). In 1982 (the same year that the
twenty-three ANDES members were abducted) the first member of the CO-
MADRES was captured and jailed:

> They set her free after 18 days. . . . She was left on the railroad tracks with
> her hands tied behind her back and a gag in her mouth so that she
> couldn't scream for help. . . . Her face was completely swollen and her
> teeth were broken where they had smashed her mouth in with the butt of
> a rifle. . . . They had burned her body with cigarette butts. . . . [T]hey beat
> her. They rammed their rifle butts into her breasts and burned her. They
> took off all of her clothes and she was raped by seven men. Then they
> burned her body some more (Tula, quoted in Stephen 1994, 111).

By 1989 the CO-MADRES office had been bombed five times. Since 1977
forty-eight members have been detained, five assassinated, and three disappeared (Stephen 1994, 3). As I noted above, due to these types of incidents,
public protests from a wide range of sectors had ceased in the early 1980s. In
1984 the CO-MADRES contributed to breaking this silence by marching
directly to the U.S. embassy to demand an end to the military aid, a popular
demand that catalyzed the mobilization of a cross-section of society. The
impact of the CO-MADRES upon the popular movement and struggle for
human rights was not overlooked by the government as indicated by the
increased oppression of its members. As we have seen, the government and
military tried repeatedly to thwart this curiously demure yet threatening sector of the human rights movement, but on all accounts were unsuccessful.

THE CHRISTIAN COMMITTEE FOR THE DISPLACED PEOPLE OF EL SALVADOR (CRIPDES). Another organization comprised and led predominantly of women and on the surface appeared benign and unthreatening was CRIPDES. As a result of the war there were two million internally displaced people and one million war refugees (Keen and Haynes 2000, 498). These staggering numbers are in great part the result of the U.S.-directed "scorched-earth" policy. In practice, this meant "killing any person or animal left behind and burning houses and crops. . . . [the military targeted civilians because it] wanted to eliminate the social base for the FMLN" (Thompson 1995, 112). As such, the essential part of the military strategy was depopulating the areas where the FMLN operated. In addition to fleeing the country to the United States, refugees were dispersed throughout El Salvador and Honduras in various types of refugee camps. Some were sponsored by the United Nations, and some by churches, while others ended up in areas controlled by the military and thus dependent upon the government.

The refugee camps were structured in such a way as to facilitate the creation of participatory democracy. The majority of the refugees were women who, as a result of the absence of the men in their lives, learned skills previously foreign to them, like carpentry, mechanics, general leadership, and administration of community resources. Through a variety of experiences, not the least of which was the contact with outside aid and solidarity organizations, the refugees came to "recognize themselves as human beings with full rights and capabilities" (Thompson 1995, 122). In 1984 the Catholic Church began talking about closing San Salvador–based refuges and relocating refugees to the countryside so that they could reconstitute new "homes." In response to this plan the refugees organized a forum of four hundred families, all refugees, and decided to form their own organization to address these and related issues. As a result, in the summer of 1984, CRIPDES, the first organization of displaced persons and refugees was formed. The church did end up closing the refuges in the city and helped to relocate the refugees to communities in the zones of conflict (areas that were neither controlled by the FMLN nor the army). In each of these resettlements CRIPDES committees existed. They helped to organize petitions for food, health and literacy training, and medicines. They also worked collectively to denounce human rights violations. By 1986 CRIPDES coordinated work in twenty-seven communities in four different departments in El Salvador (Thompson 1995, 124). What all of this meant, beyond the immediate attention to basic needs, was that CRIPDES was in direct opposition to the Salvadoran military's strategy of low intensity conflict.

While in El Salvador in 1998 I spoke with María Mirtala López Solorza. Mirtala, as she is known, at nineteen became part of the leadership of CRIPDES. At the time of our interview she was a substitute congresswoman for the FMLN in the National Assembly and worked in the area of public relations and media. She recalled the role of CRIPDES in the revolutionary movement:

> I believe it was extraordinary work. CRIPDES was one of the few, or the only, movement that confronted the repression on a daily basis. It confronted the police, demanding that bombings cease, demanding a stop to military operatives, a stop to the war, so that people could return home. . . . It was those of us that had nowhere to live that got involved. There were thousands and thousands of refugees without hope of returning and no one spoke for us. There was no reason for what was happening to us. We had to do things for ourselves. It was us that had to fight for our demands and our needs. If you ask other groups and social movements about the organizations that worked the most and put themselves in danger during the war, they will all mention CRIPDES.

As CRIPDES politically and physically challenged low-intensity conflict, the military stepped up a bombing campaign against the civilians in the zones of conflict, to where many of the refugees had returned. By January 1986, the number of displaced had risen to 500,000. In response to the initiative of the Catholic Church and the Salvadoran Foundation for Minimal Housing, CRIPDES established an organization, the National Coordination for Repopulation (Coordinadora Nacional de la Repoblación, or CNR) that was to facilitate the repopulation efforts. Between August of 1986 and April of 1992, through the organizing efforts of CRIPDES and the CNR, approximately sixteen thousand refugees returned to their homes (Thompson 1995, 130). In many cases their villages had been completely leveled and the refugees were forced to rebuild them from scratch; but they rebuilt with attention to health and education and, in some cases, strategies of collective organizing. The repopulation efforts were largely contingent upon international support and solidarity but they were organized in accordance to terms outlined by the refugees As the communities to which they repopulated were zones of conflict, largely controlled by the FMLN, the former refugees tended to be in support of and protected by the FMLN. However, for the refugees the motivating factor for the repopulations was to return to their homes, not to return to the FMLN. Mirtala explained the determination of CRIPDES and the subsequent response of the military to the leadership of CRIPDES:

> We were solely a peasant movement, but a strong movement; a movement that did not allow anyone to hold us down. Some of the *compañeros* [comrades] would be arrested one day and we would hold a march the next day. And then, at the march, we were assaulted. We would then organize a hunger strike. We were constantly organizing actions during the war. In

1989 almost all of the governing board was captured. We were imprisoned for almost six months. We were beat up. They did all sorts of things to us except for rape. We were accused of being the bases and members of the guerrilla when in reality our work was strictly a demand for the return of refugees and displaced to rural areas.

In other words, as was the case with the military and death squad attacks against ANDES and the CO-MADRES, the intimidation tactics simply did not work; not only was the military's brutal attempts of separating the base communities from the FMLN a failure, it was also unable to squelch the actions of CRIPDES.

I asked Mirtala about the gender composition of the movement, to which she answered, "I would dare to say that it was primarily women, children, and the elderly because many of the men were already in the war. We were exemplary women; brave women that showed that women are capable of surviving and supporting our children." Indeed, the majority of refugees were women. Not only did they become the heads of households when their husbands went to war or were disappeared, they also ended up being the leaders in these repopulation efforts. From 1988 on, 90 percent of the leadership of the CNR were young women just like Mirtala López (Thomson 1995, 144). The presence of women in this movement, just as in the ANDES and the CO-MADRES, occurred by default. As Mirtala notes above, the men tended to be fighting in the war. Despite the preponderance of women in each of these organizations they should not be considered women's organizations, and certainly not feminist in nature, but rather organizations in the popular movement largely comprised of women. In the case of CRIPDES/CNR and ANDES, the activities of the women were not even gendered; that is, union activists and refugees are gender-neutral categories. The members of the CO-MADRES and their efforts were, of course, gendered as they organized as mothers, wives, grandmothers, and so on. The result in all three cases, whether gender existed explicitly as in the CO-MADRES or implicitly as in CRIPDES/CNR and ANDES, the organizations played a special role within the popular movement.

Despite the fact that members of neither ANDES nor the CO-MADRES marched through the city streets with weapons, nor did the members of CRIPDES/CNR trek through the countryside in guerrilla fatigues, their actions were very significant to the revolutionary project. A group of women schoolteachers, mourning mothers, or war refugees—the quintessential victims of war—were all presumably benign sectors of the population. All three organizations worked within the popular sector, fostering needed political support for an oppositional movement, both in the capital and countryside. In the case of CRIPDES and the CNR, the members actually provided

logistical support as well once they were able to repopulate to guerrilla controlled territory. All three organizations challenged the injustices of their government. All three were largely comprised of and led by women. All three
utilized nonviolent tactics. And all three, I would argue, because of all of this,
were more accessible to those—especially women—who were frustrated by
the repression but alienated by guerrilla tactics. As I noted above, Lungo Uclés
suggests that one of the strengths of the popular movement rests in the fact
that nonviolent movements were more likely to reduce the fears of those
members of the population in opposition to the repression perpetuated by
their government but intimidated by the option of armed resistance (1995,
155). Assuming this was in part the case, I would argue that these women of
the popular movement were significant in mobilizing the base communities in
support of the revolution, and as such had the power to bridge the gap
between unincorporated civilians and the armed resistance.

The alliances these organizations had with the guerrillas were not always
clear, particularly during the war. Indeed, some of the activists themselves did
not always know such partnerships existed. As evidenced by the detention and
torture of these women, the government and army were not oblivious to the
strength of these organizations and their actions. I would even suggest that
the women of these groups were taking risks perhaps more dangerous than the
actual combatants, since they themselves were unarmed yet were met with the
same military tactics that the armed guerrillas were. This lack of clear boundaries further complicates the question: Who is a revolutionary?

Women and the Guerrilla Movement: The Farabundo Martí Front for National Liberation (FMLN)

Dividing this discussion into the popular movement and the guerrilla
movement is a bit problematic. This is in large part, as discussed above, due to
the fact that most (if not all) of the organizations of the popular movement,
despite the fact that they didn't carry weapons, were in one way or another
tied to the political-military organizations that made up the FMLN. That said,
in this discussion I will focus on those structures explicitly considered to be
within the FMLN: combatants, urban underground, politicos, and their logistical support networks.

From the perspective of some feminists, the ideological and thus organizational structure of the FMLN was rigidly patriarchal and hierarchical
(Vasquez 1996). Drawing from the Marxist-Leninist, as well as Guevaraist,[13]
theories of revolution to which the FMLN subscribed, the most central part
of a guerrilla movement is the vanguard, which is imbued with, and entitled
to, unchallenged authority to lead. The vanguard, from this perspective, is considered the "brain" of the movement. This is in contrast to the "masses," or
members of the actual communities intended to be the recipients of the

improvements resulting from triumphant revolutionary struggle. The masses function as the "eyes and ears" of the struggle and as such are also indispensable to defeating the enemy. As a result of its perpetuation of the public-private polemic, this structure, Vasquez and other feminists argue, proves significant in the maintenance of the gendered division of labor and larger social structure. The vanguard is understood to participate in the public realm, whereas the masses are relegated to the private. As a result of the leadership being predominantly male, men then became the public figures responsible for directing and representing the revolutionary struggle. The masses, on the other hand, who were largely comprised of women, remained in the private or hidden sphere of revolutionary struggle. In short, feminists argue, "conception, strategy, and political practice merged together to develop a revolutionary project that reproduced one of the strongest divisions of the system that they wanted to destroy: the division between women and men" (Vasquez 1996, 23).

The lived reality reflected this. In his comprehensive study of women in guerrilla movements and democracy in Central America, Ilja Luciak (2001) analyzed and synthesized the data generated from the United Nations Observer Mission in El Salvador (Observadores de las Naciones Unidas en El Salvador, or ONUSAL) which supervised demobilization of the FMLN. Per the 1992 peace accords, the FMLN forces were to demobilize in a five stage process to begin on the first of May and be completed October 31, 1992. Members of the FMLN were processed and registered by the ONUSAL according to their status as combatants, wounded noncombatants, or *politicos*— that is, militants that were engaged in political work on behalf of the FMLN both within and outside of El Salvador. As reported by Luciak, 1994 data collected by the ONUSAL indicated that a total of 15,009 members were registered. Of those, 8,552 were combatants, 2,474 wounded noncombatants, and 3,983 political cadres. Of these combined totals, 4,492 were women.[14] When looking at the specific categories, women made up anywhere between 27 to 34 percent of the membership of the five armies that comprised the FMLN, and of the three categories they were the most heavily represented in the category of political cadre, comprising 36.6 percent of the total. With respect to combatants, women represented 29.1 percent, or 2,485 of the 8,552. And in the final category of wounded noncombatants, of the 2,474 that were registered, 549, or 22.2 percent, were women (Luciak 2001, 3–6). Though all of the women with whom I spoke did not explicitly identify their positions within the revolutionary struggle in the context either of the aforementioned categories or as part of the guerrilla body (brains, or eyes and ears), their experiences very much fit into these two frameworks.

As articulated to me through various interviews, there were a variety of ways and reasons why women became involved with the FMLN: some came from active leftist families, many were initially involved with the Christian

Base Communities; some were involved with student (high school and university), peasant, or union organizations; and others acted out of fear and simply felt as if they had no other choice. As a woman named Elsy whom I interviewed in 1994 explained, "[W]e realized that the Frente was there to protect us, so for many of us, our aspiration was to incorporate and join the Frente." Once members of the FMLN, women played a variety of roles, nearly all considered to be support oriented. They worked in logistics, communication, food distribution, and health and first aid services; on the rearguard and on the front lines; and in political and diplomatic work. Lety Méndez, Salvadoran ex-guerrilla and former head of the women's secretariat of the FMLN, explained in our 1998 interview the variety of roles she played with the FMLN:

> I was trained to make explosives and we worked in a team for two years (1978 to 1980) and in 1981, after the offensive, we moved to the war fronts. Most of the time I was very lonely, I was in the south of San Miguel and at the beginning I was the coordinator of the explosives school. Then I transferred to communications and I worked as the person in charge of the area for a long time. I [also] worked as an organizer, responsible for one of the units that had to work in two municipalities. . . . After that, for three years, more or less, I worked as coordinator of the press and propaganda workshop, and then I [was] transferred [again] and there I finished the last years of the war, coordinating the communications and finances of the region. Throughout these processes I participated as a combatant [just like] other people that were on the radio. In that way I participated directly in the actions. But in general my efforts to develop, were in the intermediate structures, that is where most of my development took place. At the end, when they gave us a graduation from the military army, they put me as a captain. Mostly that is where my main experience was, like many women. We had little space to occupy higher positions, we were always left at the intermediate structures and in support work.

Ana Matilde Rodar, known as Mati, is currently active with the feminist movement. She shared virtually the same experience as Lety Mendez, with a slight variety in the tasks that she performed; Mati fought in San Salvador, as Lety eventually would, with the FPL. In my 1994 interview with her, Mati recalled her own and other women's roles within the FMLN:

> [W]omen had the role of cooks, as radio operators, working hospitals, doing a lot of work with the population, and doing a lot of running from one place to another. Many women died when they left to deliver messages to the cities. I fought here in the metropolitan area [San Salvador] and my job was as a nurse. I "passed" as a student of medicine, so when the

compañeros, the combatants, would come down from the mountains wounded, I would also arrange for them to be admitted into the hospital. I also had the job of hiding arms in houses, also to arrange the arms so that they were hidden in cars so that they could be carried up to the mountains. It was logistical work, as they say.

In other words, we can see the significance of this work as the guerrillas clearly needed both weapons and access to medical treatment. Similarly, Marina Ríos, former noncombatant with the FMLN and current member of the feminist movement explained in my 1998 interview with her the variety of tasks that she performed:

> I am going to tell you something: I do not think my participation was that unique. It was the same as other women involved in the war. I remember my first activities. . . . My first actions were always in the service area. I was the one that delivered the medicines; I would go buy the medicines; I would make sure that there was food in the camp; I would also work with the support networks. There was a network that we had created, and since I knew the people in the community, I would go talk to them and see if they could be a bit more open. This was also the sort of work [I did]—the work of creating a network of supporters. At the time, it was considered support with respect to food, services, and information. I would go back and forth from the towns. . . . In this sense [as part of the FMLN], this is what I did at first. We also looked for houses for people to stay and the supporters would send corn, meat, etcetera. This is the kind of work I did. I was never in the front. In other words, I was not in battle.

Marina went on to explain to me that she wanted to go to battle, but because she had four daughters that option was not available to her. As Marina suggests, much of the work that women in the FMLN performed necessitated mobilizing the base communities to show their support for the guerrillas. It was typically women who established the links that resulted in—when available—food, shelter, and medical care for the FMLN. That is, women performed the typically feminine role of caretaker even in the context of guerrilla struggle.

I asked all of the women with whom I spoke not only what they did during the war but what they saw other women do. There was virtual consensus that women did perform important and dangerous tasks but their work was largely considered to be logistical in nature and therefore less important. From the perspective of Irma Amaya, ex-combatant, elected representative of the FMLN, and feminist activist

> [Women did] a little of everything; from the woman who lived at the edge of the guerrilla camps and who took a basket and went to the market to

buy or sell things and hidden inside her basket took messages, or took money that other people gave, or brought food; from these seemingly insignificant acts that really showed women's heroism even though the importance of those tasks wasn't recognized at the time and is still not recognized today. To combat in guerrilla squads, as they called them, to being a squad leader of a group of guerrillas, to being the nurse who took care of the combatants, who went with them to the front, to the trenches, who came for the wounded, who cured them, to those who wore radios on their shoulders to be in communication within the trenches and with other groups of comrades, or in other areas, or in the city. Those women also did political work in the zones of conflict and the expansion zone, winning over people, raising consciousness, explaining that the struggle was just. (Personal interview, 1998)

Two things are implicit in Irma's assessment. First, one of the reasons women were able to offer their support to the guerrillas was due to the fact that stereotypical notions of femininity allowed women to perform dangerous tasks partially protected by their femininity. For example, she refers to the woman who lived close to the guerrillas and delivered messages in her shopping basket. Certainly this sort of camouflage was not enough to remove women from harm's way but it did enable the completion of tasks that men would have found considerably more difficult to accomplish. A single man, bringing his basket to the market to shop would have been conspicuous in a way that women simply were not. Additionally, supporting what Marina Ríos explained about her own experiences with the FMLN, women often interacted with the bases to—as Irma noted—"win over the people." As I have suggested with respect to the CO-MADRES, despite the secondary status that women generally hold in Salvadoran society, they are also culturally endowed with a certain moral superiority. Additionally, teachers tend to be women. Perhaps it was this combination of moral righteousness and stereotypical ideas about women as educators that made the base communities more comfortable accepting revolutionary doctrine from women than they would have been were the same message communicated to them by men. In this sense women members of the FMLN were potentially able to inspire the base communities to hide guerrillas, provide food, and possibly even incorporate themselves directly into the struggle more effectively than were men. Because a woman was seen as timid and unthreatening it was less likely that her neighbors would feel intimidated by her revolutionary ideas. A man, on the other hand, would likely be more overpowering in similar situations, and that might cause unincorporated citizens to feel threatened by the FMLN in a way they might not when dealing with women. In short, women were able to minimize the intensity of the revolutionary rhetoric in a way that would prove effective in expanding their bases of support.

Logistical tasks in the context of guerrilla warfare are significantly more risky than their description may imply, and are literally indispensable to the success of a struggle. However, from the perspective of the FMLN, the real struggle was carried out by the armed combatants. As I discussed above, the FMLN advanced the strategy of armed struggle as it interpreted it to be the only option available. As we have seen, the fraudulent nature of Salvadoran elections superimposed upon a militaristic structure entirely unfamiliar with and uninterested in democracy ruled out electoral means as an avenue for political struggle. (We will see in the discussion of revolutionary Chile that electoral paths toward revolution are not impossible, at least in the short term.) As such, Che Guevara's revolutionary ideology that promoted the "new man" became the model from which the Salvadoran Left organized. His paradigm suggested that "the guerrilla soldier was an essentially masculine image, but the belief that armed struggle was the only possible path made many women regard the figure of the soldier and the possession of arms as actual possibilities to them" (Vasquez 1995, 21). Irma Amaya explained to me her decision to fight. She had been a student active in the popular movement advocating for the rights of campesinos and was eventually being pursued by the military. She recalled that

> practically speaking I had two or three options: one, renounce all of [my organizing], just stop, but that would not free me from being seen as dangerous, and yet I felt cowardly, too, because that would be like having learned my lesson and no longer believing . . . , so I said no, that's not the right choice. The second option was to flee inland, to go far from where I lived and hide from those who knew me, or even to leave the country altogether. I thought that those possibilities, leaving, . . . would not be an escape, and leaving the country was not an option because I had no way to do it. The third option was to become even more committed and involved and to fight to the finish, to see if there could really be positive outcomes, and that meant that I had to survive, to achieve change or to die trying, and I thought that regardless, I wanted to live, . . . but I thought that dying was not such a big deal compared to tolerating that situation, and that is where my decision came about. At sixteen I joined those clandestine organizations, I was part of what is known in this country as the Popular Forces of Liberation.

Conveying a similar sentiment, Maria Ofelia Navarrete de Dubon (known as Maria Seranno), former guerrilla leader and elected representative of the FMLN, has explained that "every time we got a little something together, the army came in and destroyed everything. Finally I thought, 'Well, if this is war, let's really fight back.' So in 1980 I joined the FMLN" (quoted in Cohen and Wali, 1990).

Though some women were able to become combatants, the barriers were formidable. Nearly all of the women I interviewed about this subject spoke of the phenomenon that women had to very much prove themselves in a way that was not expected of men. In many cases, familial obligations prevented women from pursuing that path, as the case of Marina Ríos suggests. Even if women were able to become combatants, those experiences were not automatically translated into positions of leadership. In my 1993 interview with her, María Morales—an ex-combatant, former FMLN candidate to the legislative assembly, and feminist activist—explained that the same cultural expectations surrounding familial obligations were also responsible for preventing women who were able to become combatants to emerge as leaders:

> At the opportunity of receiving military or any sort of training, those who would go were the men, because they had the space and the time and so women had to take care of the house, and if you were young you had to take care of your brothers and sisters. So the logical result was that men keep having more opportunities to advance, to obtain more capabilities, and because of these capabilities they are in commanding posts; they decide how a strategy is going to be defined and we are not there. That is, they do not take us into account.

Lety Méndez also explained that women were faced with the related obstacle of negotiating contradictory expectations surrounding gender, and, to be accepted, "a woman had to act the same way that a man did, but at the same time, you had the contradiction that if you acted the same as a man you were criticized. A man was not criticized for his attitudes, but if a woman wanted to imitate the way that a man acted, you were criticized. If you talked your way, like we women do, we were not accepted either, so it was a difficult contradiction for us." As the women I spoke to repeatedly explained, the results of all of this is that women had to work significantly harder to get the same recognition that men automatically received; Irma Amaya noted that

> those few women who managed to get important positions of leadership, like being commander, for example—that was not something many women achieved. It was something many men achieved and very few women [did], because being on the front to lead was never something people believed women were capable of until they had demonstrated it, proved themselves two or three times more capable than the men. . . . For a man it was easy, because just by the virtue of being a man, having a penis, that already earned him a vote of confidence to put them in charge. But being a woman, no; women had to prove two, three or more times, as many as necessary to demonstrate that they could do it, too.

Given these obstacles, how did women emerge into positions of leadership?

In El Salvador, as we will see in both Chile and Cuba, the handful of women who were able to reach high leadership positions during the war were generally those who came from more privileged backgrounds. This was in large part due to the fact that higher social class position translated to more advanced levels of education. In poor families money was so limited that, typically, not all children were able to attend primary school, let alone the university. When families did have enough money for any of their children to attend school it was a virtual certainty that the male child would be given that option; girls were expected to help out at home and/or would eventually leave their families when married and thus take their educational advantage with them. Universities are, typically, the nexus for the development of revolutionary ideals. Those submerged in such atmospheres would be privy to a political and intellectual climate that tended to foster a more critical consciousness. Additionally, access to the university community meant that women (and men of course) were part of the networks that would eventually make up the leadership of the revolutionary movement. Elevated class position also meant that the women were unencumbered with financial commitments to their families, as was the case for women from the working, poor, and peasant classes. If nothing else, this meant that these women had more free time to think about and act upon their convictions (Jaquette 1973; Lobao 1990). Similarly, access to the acquisition of skills that inadvertently became useful to the guerrillas proved helpful in climbing the revolutionary movement's hierarchy.

Lorena Peña Mendoza (also known as Rebecca Palacios), is a woman with a history of over thirty years with the FMLN. She was part of the urban underground, and served on the political-diplomatic commission as former deputy to the Legislative Assembly and as representative to the Central American Parliament. When I interviewed her in 1998, she explained why she had an advantage to be in the leadership of the FMLN. "Because I came from the middle class," she commented, "we had the advantage of having personal formation, that, from the start gives you other abilities. . . . At the beginning [of the war] that is an advantage, the advantage of an academic formation, on the one hand, [and] I had the advantage of my family; that is, a very liberal family and that marked in all three of us, my sisters and me, a self reliant attitude." All of Lorena's tasks—excluding her participation in the urban underground—necessitated a significant amount of cultural capital and ability to communicate effectively and articulately. For example, as a member of the political-diplomatic commission Lorena was expected to sound like a "professional politician," something that would have been impossible to do had she no access to the university. Similarly, Ana Guadalupe Martínez, another canonical (former) leader of the FMLN, gained her initial consciousness through her Christian upbringing. She also attended the University of El Salvador, where she became active in student politics over the university budget and its restrictions upon working-class students who could not afford tuition. Eventually Martínez joined the People's Revolutionary Army (Ejército Revolucionario del Pueblo), another of the five organizations that made up the FMLN, and since then she has held one of the two highest positions in the FMLN ever occupied by a woman.[15] Another respected high-level Salvadoran woman revolutionary is María Marta Valladares (known as Nidia Díaz), who in 1971 became active in the Salvadoran political struggle. By 1975 she was part of the leadership of the revolutionary movement. It was around that same time that she completed four years of advanced study in psychology. Similarly, her ability to pursue postsecondary education indicates options simply not available to poorer women. Valladares was a member of the Revolutionary Party of Central American Workers (Partido Revolucionario de Trabajadores Centroamericanos, or PRTC, another of the five organizations that made up the FMLN). In April of 1985 she was captured by a U.S. military advisor and after a major attack orchestrated by the guerrillas was eventually released in October of that same year.[16] Her work with the PRTC and FMLN shifted depending on the trajectory of the war, placing her at the UN-sponsored negotiation tables in Geneva in 1991, as well as in the position of FMLN vice presidential candidate in the 1999 elections. These two high-level positions also necessitated significant communication and professional skills simply not available to noneducated women.

As I have discussed, because of cultural, structural, and economic barriers, women were largely shut out of the top leadership positions. As Lorena Peña Mendoza explained, her experiences in leadership roles were not common. "Cases like mine are exceptions," she noted; "the majority of the compañeras were either combatants or in the service and support area. Of the 8,500 people that the United Nations verified as the army—not as militia, but army—35 percent were women; that is why our [FMLN] quota is up 35 percent to this day. One third of the [guerrilla] army was women, but most of them were in health, radio, and support posts."

In short, women participated in many capacities in the FMLN, but were confronted with a plethora of cultural and ideological barriers, which prevented the full revolutionary incorporation to which many of the women combatants strove. Despite the guerrilla glass ceiling, women's roles were fundamental to the revolutionary struggle, and as I suggested above, were useful in bridging gaps between the civilians and guerrillas. In some cases, as we saw with CRIPDES, the bridge resulted in bringing in new support networks in other cases that connection meant that women were able to enter hostile territory in order to do things like deliver messages. I elaborate this concept below.

CONCLUSIONS: SALVADORAN WOMEN AS
GENDERED REVOLUTIONARY BRIDGES

Through this brief discussion of Salvadoran history we have seen the evolution of a revolutionary movement in which women played very important, though not always visible or acknowledged, roles. We have seen that women were present in both the popular and armed struggle. Within the context of the popular movement, I have suggested that women organizing in their feminine capacity as teachers, mothers, and refugees had the potential to achieve certain fundamental alliances with the population that men were not as likely to foster. In the armed struggle, the tasks that women performed were in large part dictated by a traditional gendered division of labor, and/or their ability to move about more safely than men. Women typically performed the more feminine tasks of support—those of logistics, communication, and medical work. We saw that though these actions were fundamental to the overall military strategy of the FMLN and often quite dangerous for the women who performed them, they ranked lower on the guerrilla hierarchy than the public representation of revolution vis-à-vis armed combatants and leaders of the movement, positions most often held by men. Regardless of their placement on the guerrilla hierarchy, what this brief discussion highlights is the utility of femininity as a revolutionary tool.

Here I am suggesting that women bridged physical space in revolutionary exchanges and partially closed the gap between the organized left and unincorporated citizens. I have come to identify the women who have performed such revolutionary tasks as gendered revolutionary bridges. The gendered revolutionary bridge is a conceptual way of understanding the significance of women to revolutionary struggle. Literally, *gendered* refers to femininity, *revolutionary* to the type of social movement of which the women are a part, and *bridges* implies the strategic connections women make as a result and subversion of femininity within such a context. These links happened in the more literal sense as women guerrillas served as couriers and delivered messages in their shopping baskets, or in the equally important connections of working with the base communities to foster support that would eventually lead to food, shelter, and medical supplies. In the popular movement the bridges created could be better understood as strategic rather than literal. That is, women activists subverted prototypical images of femininity—of mother, teacher, and refugee—while transmitting highly militant messages. Though the explicit goal of the revolutionary movement was in no way to alter notions of femininity or masculinity, the implicit result of using familiar icons of femininity to communicate revolutionary sentiments was an expansion of the base of support for the movement, something absolutely fundamental to its growth. As I have suggested above, it is my contention that the presence of women in revolutionary movements served to minimize the apprehensions of unincorporated, but curious, civilians. In short, the work that women did for the Salvadoran revolutionary movement as gendered revolutionary bridges surfaced through their interactions with the population, both in the armed and unarmed movements.

Reflecting back on the discussion of the CO-MADRES, we can see that the mothers epitomized the notion of gendered revolutionary bridges. The morally elevated status of mothers meant that the CO-MADRES, at least in the organization's very nascent stages, did not carry the same stigma as a labor union while also bearing a certain moral authority independent of traditional political structures. As we have seen, this did not reduce government hostility toward the CO-MADRES's members. But because of their respected and even harmless demeanor as a group of mothers, grandmothers, sisters, and wives they not only served as bridges to legitimate the popular movement in the eyes of the unorganized, but also provided a minimal but needed amount of security; as María Teresa Tula has noted, "We participated in celebrations for international worker's day. . . . We were always invited to participate in the marches on this day. We would dress up in black and mingle with the workers and students in the march. The authorities usually respected us a little more than the young people and our presence could help keep them from being harassed" (quoted in Stephen 1994, 106). In the case of the teachers of ANDES and the refugees in CRIPDES, a similar phenomenon occurred. Certainly Christian women refugees were not the image of an armed resistance movement. Nor were female elementary school teachers the stereotypical representation of opposition. It is unlikely that these women-centered organizations were a conscious tactic that the Left designed to reduce the alienation resultant of the opposition. And as we have seen, this presumed passivity from which women, at least initially, gained some security is not something to which the military was to remain oblivious, as evidenced by the brutal repression brought upon some of these mothers, teachers, and refugees. Regardless of whether the expansion of notions of femininity was conscious or unconscious, however, women—drawing from their positions of moral authority and familial responsibility while militantly protesting as the mothers, teachers, and refugees that they were—proved to transform the traditional images of rebel and of woman.

In the case of the FMLN the potential of women to build bridges was slightly different. As we have seen, the gendered division of labor meant that women were much more likely to be intermediaries with the base communities. This was, more than anything, the result of sexism, and as such women militants often resented such positioning. That said, women were able to move about more safely as a result of their gender, which facilitated the transport of weapons, the delivery of messages, and even—while passing as nursing students—a guarantee of medical treatment for the guerrillas. In short, as a result of femininity and even sexism, women revolutionaries were able to create logistical support bridges, as well as bridges between the leftist movement and the masses.

What a feminist analysis such as this enables us to do is identify the centrality of women's revolutionary work within the population rather than further entrenching it as secondary to the guerrilla struggle, which was the typical perspective of the male leadership. Indeed, Che Guevara, the father of all guerrillas, is infamous for this oft-cited quote from his manifesto *On Guerrilla Warfare*:

> Women can play an extraordinarily important role in the development of a revolutionary process. This must be emphasized, for those of a colonial mentality tend to underestimate and discriminate against women. They are capable of the most difficult deeds, of fighting with the troops, and they do not cause sexual conflicts among the troops, as has been charged. Women, although weaker than men, are no less resilient. They can fight, and they have played an outstanding role in the Cuban war.
>
> Of course, there are not too many women soldiers. But they can be used in many capacities, particularly in communications. They should be entrusted with carrying confidential messages, ammunition, etc. If captured, they will invariably be treated better than men, no matter how brutal the enemy. They can cook for the troops and perform other duties of a domestic nature, teach the soldiers and the local population, indoctrinate the children, perform the functions of social workers, nurse the sick, help sew uniforms, and, if necessary, even bear arms. In Cuba, many successful marriages were contracted within the guerrilla forces (1962, 57–58).

As Ilja Luciak (2000) notes, acknowledging the potential of women in guerrilla movements was indeed forward thinking at the time of his writing; unfortunately, however, his words have more or less remained the manifesto that contemporary guerrillas continue to follow. The staying power of his words, and thus the ideological, political, and logistical implications for women, are inseparable from the emergence of feminism in postrevolutionary El Salvador, the subject of the next chapter.

CHAPTER 2

Feminism in Postwar El Salvador, 1992–1999

For me . . . if the feminism is not revolutionary, it is not feminism.

—Lety Mendez, 1998

ON NEW YEAR'S EVE, 1991, the war in El Salvador formally ended. The Chapultepec accords were signed and sought to address the fundamental causes of the war. The agreement mandated demilitarization, legalized the Farbundo Martí Front for National Liberation (Frente Farabundo Martí para la Liberación Nacional, or FMLN) as a political party, amended the constitution, reformed the electoral and judicial systems, attempted to settle the land distribution issue, established independent commissions to identify those responsible for the major human rights abuses, and purged the army of the most serious violators (Montgomery 1995, 226). With a background marred by civil war, grave human rights violations, severe inequality in land and resources, and a scant history of democracy, these advances were both ominous and inspiring; the Salvadoran people had to reconceptualize life and politics in a wholly new setting. As do all grand sociopolitical events, the peace accords have affected women in ways distinct from men. Indeed, it has been suggested by Salvadoran and North American feminists that the accords, beyond bringing desperately needed peace and the beginnings of democracy, have done little to change the lives of women. This reality is particularly conspicuous for, as chapter 1 demonstrated, women made substantial contributions to and took major risks for the revolutionary movement that was responsible for creating this new El Salvador.

In this chapter I will answer the second part of the revolution question: What is the relationship between revolution and feminism? By looking at three contemporary feminist organizations I will demonstrate that a revolutionary feminist movement is present in El Salvador. I will focus my discussion on three feminist organizations—the Mélida Anaya Montes Women's Movement (Movimiento de Mujeres Mélida Anaya Montes, or MAM),[1] Women for

Dignity and Life "Breaking the Silence" (Mujeres por la Dignidad y la Vida "Rompamos el Silencio," or the DIGNAS), and the Association of Mothers Seeking Child Support (Asociación de Madres Demandantes, or AMD)—as their relationships to and histories with the Left provide insight into answering the revolution question. I will conclude this chapter by outlining how the five necessary factors converged in El Salvador to bring about a revolutionary feminist movement.

A Quick Look Back at Women's Mobilization

Perhaps the most explicit example of the connections between revolution and feminism in El Salvador are the women's organizations that started during the war. The pattern of leftist-initiated and -controlled women's organizations is not new in El Salvador. In 1957 the Salvadoran Communist Party (Partido Comunista Salvadoreña) founded the Sorority of Salvadoran Women. Though they addressed issues of particular importance to women, including equal pay for equal work, protection of domestic workers, and nurseries for working mothers, their structure was entirely bound to the Communist Party and disconnected from any sort of explicit feminist ideology. Aside from this organization there was not much in the way of women's organizations until the early 1970s, the same period when the political-military organizations of the Left emerged. The wartime decade of women's organizing, though started in part by the different parties of the FMLN with the goal of incorporating more women into the struggle spiraled into something grander, more feminist focused, and certainly more autonomous than originally intended. According to Dilcia Maroquin of the DIGNAS, speaking at a group meeting in 1994, "[A]ll of the women's groups came into being for convenience sake because the men wanted them to, because they [the Left] could get resources; they were not formed by women because of their needs." That is, the FMLN used women mostly for their potential to recruit new women and obtain access to international funding that women were more likely to receive. This assessment was one repeated to me by virtually every feminist I have met in El Salvador since 1994.[2] Indeed, as a founding member of one of the largest wartime women's organization, the Association of Women of El Salvador (to be discussed below), explained during the war, "[M]any women are frightened of joining an overtly political organization but are prepared to organize with other women around issues which affect them immediately" (quoted in Thomson 1986, 95). What this suggests is that the members of the wartime women's organizations were perhaps the most obvious examples of gendered revolutionary bridges as they explicitly used gender to attract unincorporated women to the FMLN. Their potential was not overlooked by the leadership of the FMLN, as evidenced by the series of women's organizations it established during the war.

In 1975, again under the control of the Salvadoran Communist Party, the Association of Progressive Women of El Salvador (Asociación de Mujeres Progresivas de El Salvador, or AMPES) was founded; its focus was on women workers and trade unions. By 1979,[3] one of the largest of the wartime women's organizations was formed—the Association of Women of El Salvador (Asociación de Mujeres El Salvador, or AMES). It was founded by the Popular Forces of Liberation (Fuerzas Populares de Liberación, or FPL), the largest of the five organizations that made up the FMLN, which likely accounts for the respective size of its women's auxiliary. Initially their work focused on women in the informal sector, including market vendors, domestics, and urban slum dwellers. From 1979 through 1981 both AMES and AMPES were forced to be clandestine in their work. Both organizations eventually resurfaced in the early 1980s but later permanently disappeared, due to severe repression. Between 1980 and 1983 the other three parties of the FMLN also formed women's organizations: the Lil Milagro Ramírez Association of Women and Democracy, the Unitary Committee of Salvadoran Women (Comité Unitario de Mujeres), the Association of Salvadoran Women (Asociación de Mujeres Salvadoreñas), and the Organization of Salvadoran Women (Organización de Mujeres Salvadoreñas) (Hipsher 2001, 138). What is relevant here are not the particulars regarding alliances among the individual parties of the FMLN and their respective women's organizations, but rather what proved to be an across-the-board tactic on the part of the Left of using women to expand the revolutionary movement. Additionally, as a result of the various party alliances within the wartime women's movement, the postrevolutionary women's movement has inherited similar sectarian tendencies.

The second phase of women's wartime organizing began in 1985 and continued until 1989 (Stephen 1997a, 67–68). A general restructuring of the popular movement was occurring at this time, and it impacted the women's sector as well. In 1986, the National Coordinating Committee of Salvadoran Women (Coordinadora Nacional de Mujeres Salvadoreñas, or CONAMUS) was formed, pioneering work around domestic violence by opening the first battered women's shelter on International Women's Day, 8 March 1989. Isabel Vásquez, organizational director of the CONAMUS, worked with the group since its inception. According to Vásquez, who spoke at a group meeting in 1994, the CONAMUS was the first women's organization to identify as feminist, which "motivated other women and their organizations to the point of having such a broad-based women's movement here in El Salvador." Also in 1986, the Institute for Research, Training, and Development of Women (Instituto para la Investigación, Capacitación, y Desarrollo de la Mujer) was formed by women within the FMLN to support grassroots women's groups in communication, law, and education. It was also at this same time that the first indigenous organization for women in El Salvador was formed—the Association of Salvadoran Indigenous

Women (Asociación de Mujeres Indígenas Salvadoreñas). In 1989 the coalition efforts of women began with the founding of the first national coordinating committee of women's organizations, the Coordination of Women's Organizations (Coordinación de Organismos de Mujeres).

As the war drew to a close, more women's organizations that worked explicitly from a feminist standpoint began to proliferate. In 1990, the Center for Feminist Studies (Centro de Estudios Feministas) started with the goal of disseminating feminist materials and organizing techniques. The following year, the Center for Women's Studies "Norma Virginia Guirola de Herrera" (Centro de Estudios de la Mujer "Norma Virginia Guirola de Herrera") was founded in order to provide technical assistance to grassroots women's organizations. Also in 1991, the Christian Women's Initiative (Iniciativa de Mujeres Cristianas) and the Salvadoran University Women (Mujeres Universitarias de El Salvador), both with strong feminist agendas, were formed. Eventually the women were able to coalesce as twenty-four organizations working under the auspices of the Women's Coalition for Peace, Dignity, and Equality (Concertación de Mujeres por la Paz, la Dignidad y la Igualdad). This organization was intended to be a place for women who wanted to identify themselves as independent of their parties. It was at this same time that the first, currently defunct, self-proclaimed lesbian group emerged, the Half-Moon Salvadoran Lesbian Feminist Collective (Colectivo Lésbico Feminista Salvadoreña de la Media Luna). By the time the peace accords were signed in 1992, both the MAM and the DIGNAS—two of the three organizations I will focus upon in the remainder of this chapter—had formed.

Feminism in the Revolution's Aftermath

Lorena Peña Mendoza—FMLN delegate to the Central American Parliament; longtime activist and militant with the FMLN; cofounder and board member of the MAM—explained to me in a 1998 interview that, for her,

> the women's movement and particularly the feminist movement is one of the areas that has developed the most after the signing of the peace accords. We have proposals for everyday, immediate problems as well as for those of a structural character; not only in the cultural realm—because a lot of people say that gender is culture . . . but here women have political, economic, cultural, and social proposals. . . . In addition, I believe that we have managed to get to the root of things, which is people's everyday lives. You cannot talk about the people without talking about the individuals; you cannot think of people without thinking about the daily things, and feminism addresses this. This, for me, is really important. . . . I have a very good opinion of the women's movement and it has opened up many important and controversial issues.

Lorena notes that Salvadoran women seized the political opening provided by the 1992 peace accords and have since grown into a progressively more articulate and pluralistic movement. According to Irma Amaya, an ex-combatant with the FMLN, current FMLN deputy, and president of the MAM, the women's movement in El Salvador is the only way that women's demands will be prioritized. "I see the women's movement as women's political subjectivity that can facilitate, from a position of an organized force, women agitating for change," she commented in my 1998 interview with her. "Any social organization in this country will not make women the first point of interest. . . . No one else will put [women's interests] at the top if it is not us." The goals, specific objectives, relationships with the Left, and internal structures differ, and indeed, the relationships with one another are not always harmonious. But the common ground in the women's movement in El Salvador is the desire of women to identify and project themselves as political subjects worthy of priority. One of the first collaborative efforts of this movement, which demonstrated its preparedness to capitalize on the political space offered by the peace accords, was the broad-based electoral coalition, Women '94 (*Mujeres '94*).

The Mujeres '94 platform was organized around the idea of "informed choice." The objective of the coalition was to pressure all of the candidates during the 1994 "elections of the century" to adopt the platform if elected.[4] The platform was composed of fourteen points organized around five categories seen as central to the women's movement: land ownership, employment, health, violence against women, and communication (Saint-Germain 1997, 88).[5] The coalition effort was more of a symbolic success rather than one with concrete results; the publicity and pressure generated by the feminists resulted in a new attention, energy, and direction for the women's organizations in El Salvador, and feminists did not let this opportunity pass them by. Feminists have taken up a variety of issues, including irresponsible paternity, political representation, and protection of women workers. The organizations that make up the feminist movement are in agreement in their overarching vision of improving the quality of life and status of women in Salvadoran society but differ in their strategies and programs for accomplishing this goal. In the rest of this chapter I will offer a brief discussion of a sampling of three of the leading feminist organizations.

Women for Dignity and Life "Breaking the Silence"

During my visits to El Salvador in 1994 and 1998 I had the opportunity to speak with many FMLN ex-combatants who have since become leaders in the postrevolutionary feminist movement. There was a striking similarity in their reflections about the relationship between the leftist parties and women's organizations both during and after the war. The organization Women for

Dignity and Life (the DIGNAS) has an interesting history that foregrounds the complex interactions between struggles for the nation and gendered struggles. Vilma Vásquez—ex-combatant and cofounder of both the DIGNAS and the AMD—recalled, in my 1998 interview with her, the evolution of the DIGNAS:

> After the final offensive [1989] and then in the early nineties, there was a political crisis in what had been the forces making up the FMLN, about its identity and political framework. . . . We needed to create new political frameworks and that was why at [that] time they gave me the job [of organizing women]. Because I had been in a supporting party [of the FMLN], I was part of the National Resistance, so they gave me the order, put me in charge and said I had a great opportunity to work with women.
>
> So I started, and I did not know how to do it. I could not figure out the best way, but it was not just me. Several of us got together and they gave each woman different areas, women who had been working with the masses, in the [armed part of the FMLN], in religious movements. So they gave [us] the order and about ten of us got together, maybe fifteen women . . . ranging from campesinas [peasants] to urban women, in order to create this new framework.
>
> [W]e started to think about it, reflect on ways to work with women, and that was when we began to realize that we could not do it the same way as we had when we worked with the unions. Instead [we] had to question all of that; to ask ourselves what had happened with our political participation, how had it been seen, how far had we been able to go in terms of decision-making levels. So we started to question both our individual and collective political participation in 1990 and 1991 . . . and there started to be friction with the leaders . . . in the party . . . because they were always trying to tell us what to do and how to do it. . . .
>
> Then some women from Mexico City came, and they were here for eight days, we were in workshops with them. Workshops about sexuality, and work, and methodology [for organizing], and that inspired us to understand women's position of subordination. Because of that, we started to question the whole issue of motherhood, the issue of couples, political participation, how women could take on leading roles and how we had broken with what had been traditional women's roles . . . so our response was rebellion. And that was how we started with our participation in the DIGNAS . . . so, this whole questioning led to us breaking with the party in 1992.

Much is revealed through this glimpse into history. Male leadership witnessed a floundering FMLN and recognized the potential of women to mend the emerging splits. We also see that women of the Left realized that not only were their own experiences within the Left contradictory to the FMLN's discourse of egalitarianism, but that they had already been challenging gendered norms through their presence in the Left. These realizations multiplied as women congregated in consciousness-raising groups. Rather than attempting to repair the damage to the FMLN, as the party leaders had hoped, the women abandoned it, acknowledging that their political livelihood and potential had been and would continue to be squelched if they continued to stay with the party. The founding members of the DIGNAS became what might be considered feminist casualties of the Left.[6]

It was these types of experiences that led members of the DIGNAS to leave the party and establish themselves as an autonomous organization. Dilcia Marroquin, speaking at a small group meeting in 1994, explained their need for autonomy, noting, "In the past we were a lot more rigid: we said if you were going to be a feminist you could not be in a political party. But since then we've reflected on it and we've written this booklet that reflects the notion that, yes, women can be part of parties and work within the parties and we can respect that.[7] But I think that it is a lot more difficult because it is not easy to change your way of thinking from thinking about the party line to a feminist way of thinking." The members of the DIGNAS's need to distance themselves from the party extended beyond organizational structure to include methods of organizing. Morena Herrera, ex-combatant with the FMLN and cofounder of the DIGNAS, explained that the Left's sectarianism proved problematic from a feminist perspective. She describes the DIGNAS's relationship with the Left as follows:

> We did know that we did not want to repeat the ways and styles of political participation that we had been participating in and where we felt [our] demands, interests, and proposals, as women did not fit. On the other hand we had already started noticing that the situation of women was more common to all of us, with different expressions, and in that sense it was like a dimension that crosses over all of us independently from our political positions. Knowing what we didn't want [organizationally], we started to look for other models, and to build the DIGNAS. There was a process for the struggle for autonomy in relation to the party and that struggle consolidated us in regards to a group identity. At first our autonomy and identity were very defensive, very internalized. Through the process we started to realize that we all had different kinds of links with these parties . . . and we were able to decide that we wanted to be a feminist organization. This has also meant that some of the *compañeras* that participated in the initial meetings, that wanted to have a project or a women's organization that accompanied the popular struggle but that did

not raise feminist demands, well, they have withdrawn and others have come to participate. (Personal interview, 1998)

In other words, the members of the DIGNAS have struggled to be both pluralistic and feminist, and this has led to internal conflicts where they have had to acknowledge that though Salvadoran women have many common demands, politically they do not all embrace the same organizational strategies. Theoretically they do not want to privilege some voices while silencing others, but through the turnover rate it became somewhat inevitable. Related to this, in Lynn Stephen's case study of the DIGNAS, she suggests that in order to rectify splits between rural and urban women, as well as party-identified and autonomous women, the members of the DIGNAS have gone in four years from demanding full autonomy to creating an agenda that meets the needs of a range of women (1997, 82).

Feminism for the DIGNAS is a political movement that challenges relationships of power. Their conception of feminism is as influenced by the lived experiences of the women of the DIGNAS on the Left, and the contradictory power imbalances experienced within the organizations fighting for liberation, as it is the discursive debates generated in their initial and ongoing consciousness-raising sessions. Gloria Guzman, former director of the Women's Commission of the Archdiocese in El Salvador, ex-combatant, and current leader of the DIGNAS, describes feminism as "a political proposal, a political struggle for the eradication—well, the gradual decrease—of women's subordination. It is a proposal for a change in the relations of power between people, men over women, and the relations of power expressed in the different realms of life. We believe that it is a political struggle that will take us specifically to new kinds of relations, economic as well as relationships of power between men and women" (personal interview, 1998). To accomplish their goals the members of the DIGNAS initially began working on what they called productive projects, or programs that helped women in the economic realm. According to Aracely López, who spoke at a small group meeting in 1994, when the DIGNAS were first starting, among their objectives was "to work with projects that [were] productive. We also decided to have a department that focused on training, to be able to reproduce the training that we had received here with other women in different [parts of the country].[8] Another area was the development of proposals, and the other was internal organization." Eventually the DIGNAS expanded their focus a bit to national coalition politics, including domestic violence. They also incorporated women into productive projects with the hopes that a female space would lead to feminist consciousness-raising.[9] These projects, largely attempted to facilitate economic independence for women, proved ineffective in both the immediate goal of supporting women and the more long-term goal of empowering them sociopolitically. It was during this transition in strategies that the DIGNAS started the AMD, which now plays a leading role in feminist coalition politics, and in the advancement of rights of single mothers.

Association of Mothers Seeking Child Support

As the feminist movement evolved in El Salvador more organizations emerged in order to address the specific issues of women that were identified through their coalition platforms, most notably, irresponsible paternity. The AMD (also known as the Madres) was formed in 1995 by the DIGNAS in an effort to both promote an understanding of gender as socially constructed and thus amenable to reconstruction, as well as meet the needs of the escalating numbers of single mothers in postwar El Salvador. The primary goal of the Madres is to challenge what they identify as the most serious social repercussion of inequitable power relations between men and women—irresponsible paternity. When I interviewed her in 1998, Vilma Vásquez, a cofounder of both the DIGNAS and the Madres, explained to me how the Madres perceive such power imbalances and thus the need for and impetus to their organization:

> [Irresponsible paternity] is undignified for a child and also a great trauma for society as a whole, to come into this world being rejected and denied by your father. There is never any question about . . . who the mother of a child is . . . but a father chooses; a woman has no choice to opt whether she wants to be a mother or not, but a man has the privilege of saying whether or not he wants to be responsible, whether he will or will not be the child's father. So there is a very serious structural problem that has to do with privilege and power relations between men and women. It is a harmful power because for the woman it is a chain that does not allow her to develop and for men it is dehumanizing because they just stroll through life like children themselves, as if they were making dolls and not thinking about the human life. That is the essence and, deep down, it is ethics, too. . . . So we have long-term cultural, ideological, economic concerns about single mothers here. But in immediate terms this is somehow a way for men to take some responsibility. Maybe not emotionally, if they have already decided not to have a relationship with their kids, but at least maybe then in material terms, even if it is just economically. Like child support. . . . You cannot put a price on it, children are not worth two or three hundred pesos, but still, it is something.

In other words, the Madres recognize that, under the current sociocultural arrangements in El Salvador, where abortion is illegal and women are expected to be devoted mothers, motherhood is required, whereas fatherhood is optional. As a result, women's power over their life decisions, their bodies, and their economic well-being are all greatly impacted by the decisions and/or (ir)responsibility demonstrated by the biological fathers of their children. These deep power imbalances have led the Madres to reappropriate the revered Catholic icon of motherhood and finesse it toward the political goal of empowerment for women. Additionally, the Madres have acknowledged the individualistic approach toward women's labor and the need for the state to rectify the inherent structural power imbalances that result from such arrangements (Baires, Castañeda, and Murguialday 1993; Vásquez and Murguialday 1996).

What all of this means in practice is a two-pronged, interrelated approach of empowering women as mothers and political subjects to press the state for their due child support. The goal of empowering women, specifically single mothers, has been particularly important to the Madres. A thread that is central to the feminist movement in general is the desire to move away from the hierarchical organizing structures that plague the left. The notion of a vanguard (as discussed in chapter 1) suggests that an elite group, as we saw, of typically men is entitled to make the choices that will effect the masses. The vanguard is supposedly imbued with this decision-making power as it is believed to know what will serve the masses best. The feminist organizations, particularly the Madres, reject this structure. As Vilma Vasquéz explained to me, what she really strives for is for women "to feel and to see themselves as protagonists as far as their problems go; that was my motivation and my basic desire in Madres Demandantes as far as the creation of the group goes. Not to see them [the single mothers] as beneficiaries—no, there are no experts here, there are no people here to solve their problems for them. Each and every one of them has to improve their own lives as single mothers, particularly [those] from the working classes." Vasquéz is not suggesting that each woman is expected to work out her problems at an individual level; rather, the organization seeks to empower women to work through these issues rather than have the "leaders" solve their problems for them in a paternalistic fashion. As Vasquéz explained,

[Our organization] is helping women fight and be active leaders [who] creat[e] changes and transformations; that is the organization's main goal. That involves getting members sitting on committees, and on the board of directors and, well, working with different state civil servants, with the [the Legislative] Assembly, with judges, with institutions that deal with family issues. There is a sort of a mutual, reciprocal support, mainly within the organization, that is fundamental for Madres Demandantes. [It is] a place where women do not see themselves as alone but rather see that the problem is the same for us all, so we build solidarity [and] strengthen the ties among ourselves.

The sense of empowerment and ability to demonstrate the political leadership that the Madres has developed within its members has been used to help organize initiatives that have led to state-regulated child support. Such political self-confidence has encouraged the single mothers to press the state to make good on their laws. As a collective, the Madres have worked to pressure the Salvadoran congress, the Institution of Human Rights (Procuradora de los Derechos Humanos),[10] and the attorney general to ratify policies that mandate child support. As a result of the Madres's efforts in pressuring the attorney general, several decrees were introduced to and passed by the Legislative Assembly. Vasquéz explained,

> We . . . had an initiative that became a decree that required 30 percent of the severance pay of people who had been laid off in different state ministries [to be given to the single mothers as child support] . . . which was good because there were a lot of plaintiffs whose defendants worked in the public sector. We also got a decree on bonuses, because here they give bonuses to all the [state] workers at New Year's, so we won that, too, getting a decree for 30 percent of the bonus to be given to the mothers who had lawsuits against fathers; that was a year ago this December, so this year was the second time that happened.

Another major victory of the Madres was a bill called the Non-Arrears Bill, which decreed that all elected candidates must obtain a clearance that certified that they were not in default of their child support payments before assuming office (Ready 2001, 183). Through the coalition efforts of right and left wing women, initiated by the Madres, this bill was passed in 1996. As evidenced by the legislative successes of the Madres, they are in no way opposed to working within state structures to achieve their goals. That said, according to Vilma Vásquez, the real power of the feminist movement originates in the grassroots effort:

> Pressure is what determines that the ones that are [making the] demands get their specific demands met. In the Legislative Assembly there is a *machista* environment, very machista and the men there think of themselves as more machistas than other men because they have a lot of political power and they are in the structure that makes the decisions for the future and for the people of this country. So, the presence of these groups and having them be organized with the ability to mobilize [is important]. Of course there are those that have formed alliances and the women that have supported us in the Assembly who lobby men to get the votes so that the laws that we submit pass. It has to do with . . . getting organized, but no large victories are going to be won in the Assembly if the grassroots are not organized and there is no pressure from them.

The allies within the legislative assembly to whom Vasquéz refers are largely members of the MAM.

Mélida Anaya Montes Women's Movement

The work of the Madres could not have been accomplished without the organizational support of the Mélida Anaya Montes Women's Movement. The MAM was established on July 25, 1992 to confront sexism within the Left and respond to the material conditions of poor women in El Salvador. In my 1998 interview with her, Marina Ríos explained a bit about the development of the MAM, which, from her perspective, felt entirely natural:

> When the war ended, this was in 1992, . . . all of us women . . . were in the different areas of El Salvador, and even some compañeros like Leonel [Gonzalez[11]] and Irma Amaya and Lorena [Peña Mendoza] started to see that it was necessary to have a women's organization to work with the party's women. This was the initial idea. Very, very quickly I started working with women. I was in charge of the [department of] La Libertad and we had training going on. We had training in basic gender theory so this allowed us to hook up with a lot of women. So it was kind of easy to do. In addition, the war was over so we also had to have something that joined women together. We had a space, a place for us where we could go and talk about our history during the war and we talked about what we, as women, were going to do after the war.

Irma Amaya (to whom Marina refers) has been active with the MAM since its inception; in our interview, she described her impression of feminism and what makes a feminist:

> I have always said that I think there are three basic conditions you need in order to aspire to or feel yourself as part of the feminist movement. First, is to recognize your womanhood . . . and second is to recognize that because I am a woman, I am in a position in which I am discriminated against as compared to . . . men . . . and [that] I am at a disadvantage in terms of having the same opportunities, the same positions, and chances as men. . . . But the third thing is, I see that I am a woman and in an unfavorable position because of it, but I am willing to fight collectively with other women to make demands that are in my interest.

Though Irma was not speaking on behalf of the entire organization, her sentiment is reflected in its programs and ideology.

The relationship of the Mélidas (as the individual members are called) to the FMLN is different than that of the members of the DIGNAS. The Mélidas, though committed to maintaining a structure autonomous from the FMLN, have not broken all ties with the party, as the women of the DIGNAS have. Quite the contrary, Irma explained to me regarding her decision to leave the leadership of the MAM to pursue a position as an FMLN deputy in the legislative assembly. For Irma, and the Mélidas in general, this was not an abandonment of the MAM nor a prioritizing of the FMLN, but an attempt to secure a place within the state from which to serve as an advocate for the feminist movement:

> I left my organizational responsibilities as director of the MAM so that I personally could have the . . . experience of acting on this [as assistant deputy], being involved in parliamentary work. That is why I decided to step back from my job in the MAM, in order to spend my time on a different kind of job, but one that also politically benefits the organization, given that we are also interested to the degree possible in having women committed not just to the MAM but to the women's movement, to participate and hold parliamentary positions and be able to do this kind of job as service to the organization, the service of platforms, and the interests of women in El Salvador. I mean, it is not just that I want to be there [on the Legislative Assembly], it is also a personal commitment to trying to represent, from any position, to be on the assembly to facilitate information, to present initiatives, or to vote favorably on the [women's] movement's initiatives.

What this means is that the MAM has been very important to the women's/ feminist movement because of its explicit presence, limited though it remains, in the Legislative Assembly. For example, Lorena Peña Mendoza, FMLN congresswoman and leader of the Mélidas, was the one who introduced the Madres's Non-Arrears Bill to the legislative assembly (Ready 2001, 184). In other words, the MAM serves somewhat as the institutional anchor to the Salvadoran feminist movement. Despite the commitment of the Mélidas to working in part within the FMLN and its formal structures, the MAM remains an autonomous organization. From Lorena's perspective, regardless of the role the FMLN has played in enabling the feminist movement, it is precisely this autonomy that has guaranteed the strength of the feminist movement:

> Most of the women's movement's strength has come from the autonomous organizations, especially after the signing of the peace accords, because a space opened up. We have to recognize that the FMLN opened up a political space for the people . . . and women were there too . . . the FMLN included us. We as women have taken advantage of the spaces and we have had the ability to make proposals, etcetera. I see this as a result of our autonomy because we did not stay around waiting to see what the FMLN was going to do, no. We have set our own strategies, and that . . . has upset the FMLN a lot.

As Lorena explained above, the Mélidas established their own agenda independent of the wishes and approval of the FMLN. However, they never severed their individual or collective ties to the party. Rather, the Mélidas have very much maintained a strategy of double militancy, or simultaneous activism in leftist parties and feminist organizations. From Irma Amaya's perspective this strategy has proven beneficial to both the MAM and the FMLN:

> I think what we have is an opportunistic relationship between the women's movement and the FMLN. It is not a permanent, systematic relationship, I think it is a respectful, mutually beneficial relationship. . . . We did not allow the FMLN, through FMLN women members, to come here and set our course—no, none of that. Nor did we abuse the relationship, nor should we have an attitude about the workings of the FMLN, thinking they should accept everything we say. We think that both spaces are totally separate spaces and that both of them have their autonomy and that both spaces, well, they will both go in the directions that they see as beneficial to them. But we think we have something in common and that is why sometimes we pull closer together and sometimes we get pushed farther apart, but when we pull together it is because of the common ground that we see in that party, that we see in the FMLN as a political body, too, as a political party, as a political subject, that can bring about changes, bring about real changes and we see the FMLN as a body that can incorporate proposals from the women's movement, so on any level we could say, we could sum it up by saying that we have a respectfully opportunistic relationship and that what we really have in common, the biggest thing, is that we all believe we have to change things and favor women.

What all of this suggests is that for the MAM, effective feminist changes result from working simultaneously outside and inside of leftist political parties by promoting feminist agendas to be brought back to the parties who will, ideally, be held accountable to their feminist members. The MAM's goal, however, is not to simply establish a feminist agenda upon which the FMLN will act; the FMLN has its own women's commission, which is a separate entity from the MAM. An entity, despite its similar objectives to the MAM, according to former director Lety Mendez, is partially limited in achieving its goals as being formally subsumed by the FMLN has meant being limited with respect to resources. As a result, the MAM remains committed to advancing its autonomous structure as it has proved far more effective than the FMLN's Women's Commission.

Drawing from their Marxist roots in the FPL, the Mélidas direct their energies to the "poorest sectors of society" (Ríos interview, 1998). In addition to working toward formal political representation of women in elected positions, they have also worked to pressure the state from the outside. They have proposed reforms to already existing laws to incorporate a gender perspective. They have worked on literacy campaigns for women, helping to transform formerly illiterate women into leaders. Despite their attention to state structures, Marina Ríos explained that they resent the paternalistic attitude of the state and reject, as do the Madres, the notion that the state is the expert and the poor women are passive recipients. The Mélidas have also directed their attention to the escalating problems of the exploitation of women's labor as a result of the proliferation of the *maquiladoras* (factories) in free trade zones. In short, for the Mélidas, notes Ríos, all issues with which poor women are faced are feminist issues.

REVOLUTIONARY FEMINISM: THE CASE OF EL SALVADOR

I picked up the term *revolutionary feminism* in my conversations with Salvadoran women. As Lety Méndez's quote opening this chapter explains, for her, feminism is not feminism if it is not also revolutionary. Two things distinguish a revolutionary feminist movement from other types of feminist movements. First, the leaders and majority of the grassroots members gain their political consciousness and organizational skills as a result of their experiences in a revolutionary process that preceded the emergence of feminism in their nation. As a result—and the second distinguishing feature—is the fact that such a movement is one that not only challenges sexism but also the larger political structures that may not explicitly be perceived as patriarchal in nature yet are from the perspective of feminists, and thus entirely bound to the oppression of women. In the case of El Salvador, the larger structure is class stratification. Because the majority of the leadership of the revolutionary feminist movement in El Salvador comes from the Left, which is heavily rooted in Marxism, many of the issues upon which feminists focus their energies are directly connected to women's economic exploitation and disenfranchisement. An obvious example is the prioritization by the Mélidas of issues pertaining to women *maquila* workers. A less explicit example comes from the Madres's attention to child support. If these single mothers were from more privileged social classes, economic resources like child support would be much less of a concern.

In other words, the revolutionary feminist movement in El Salvador is one that continues the Marxist struggle for equality among the social classes from a feminist perspective. In order to continue to answer the revolution question—What is the relationship between women's revolutionary experiences and feminism?—in the rest of this chapter I will discuss the emergence of revolutionary feminism in El Salvador.

As I discussed in the introduction of this book, five factors need be present for the emergence of feminism in the aftermath of a revolutionary struggle. First, during the revolutionary struggle the presence of women should have presented significant challenges to traditional notions of gender—that is, gender-bending will have occured. Second, and of a more logistical nature, women revolutionaries need to have acquired organizational skills as a result of their contributions to the revolutionary period. Combined, these two factors are able to flourish within a previously unavailable political space, the third necessary factor. The fourth factor is the sociopolitical impetus for such a movement, or the feeling on the part of the women that their revolution remains incomplete; in the case of El Salvador this feeling was experienced as an intense sense of betrayal. As a result, and the fifth necessary factor in the emergence of a revolutionary feminist movement, is the development of a collective feminist consciousness. I will discuss these each in turn.

The first factor that was in part responsible for the development of feminism in the aftermath of El Salvador's revolutionary movement was the implicit and explicit challenges to prescribed notions of gender or, more specifically, expectations of what constitutes feminine behavior. It is debatable how much male-female gendered relations actually changed through the wartime process. As we saw in chapter 1, women tended to be relegated to the support roles in the revolution. In the revolutionary model used by the FMLN the vanguard was the sector of the struggle perceived to be the most important, and indeed, the most visible to the masses. Men were the ones who typically held such positions reinforcing a traditional division of labor by suggesting that the work of men was indispensable whereas that of women was merely there for purposes of support. However, as we have seen, the mere presence of women in such a masculinist struggle—guerrilla warfare—certainly shook things up with respect to traditional expectations of feminine identities. Regardless of whether the men were prepared to bequeath their patriarchal privileges or not, the presence of women in the struggle certainly forced them to experience gendered relations is a new way. As María Morales explained when I interviewed her in 1993, "During the military actions, women for the most part took secondary roles—for example, taking care of the rearguard, communication, logistics, health; work that was very important, and put their lives in danger, but was not officiated. And when a woman would go to the front lines into battle that would be a very new kind of thing which had a great impact upon the populace as well as the men in the fighting force."

As we will see in the case of Chile, regardless of whether women's roles were entirely restricted by a traditional gendered division of labor, their presence in a radical political movement presents direct challenges to the expectations of women proscribed by femininity. Linda Lobao (1990) reminds us that the Latin American military is the epitome of patriarchy, a structure entirely closed to and physically exploitative of women. As we saw in chapter 1, in El

Salvador the armed guerrilla movement, while not entirely open to women, was certainly not entirely closed, either. Additionally, as we have seen, women revolutionaries played leading roles in the urban popular movement, demonstrating their capacity as leaders. Together, despite the restrictions placed on women's activities, their presence certainly challenged traditional notions of femininity. Indeed, as a result of women embracing their traditional feminine identities—mother, teacher, Christian, caretaker—and reconfiguring them to embody revolutionary praxis, expectations associated with femininity would, in many cases, be permanently transformed. Perhaps the fact that women activists manipulated gender was entirely the result of women's agency. Though this question is largely unanswerable, I would suspect some combination of conscious and unconscious manipulation of gender roles occurred. These women were certainly conscious of their revolutionary commitments and it makes sense that they would be conscious of their revolutionary strategies as well.

The fact that the Salvadoran revolution was not successful does not eliminate the political training, the second necessary condition for the emergence of revolutionary feminism, obtained by large numbers of women during the war. The organizational training that Salvadoran women acquired was in large part the result of two factors: the length of the war, and, limited as they were, the leadership positions that were held by women in the popular and armed movements. Because the war officially lasted twelve years, but in practice lasted closer to twenty, many of the current leaders of the feminist movement at the time of the signing of the peace accords had spent at least half of their lives active in politics. Even if a woman spent twenty years delivering messages from one guerrilla camp to another (a highly unlikely scenario, to be sure), she still would have spent the majority of her life submerged in political organizing, eventually making it second nature. Additionally, many women—especially in the popular movement, where we saw a significant presence of women—did play at least central if not leading roles in organizing demonstrations and other forms of protest. The skills that women picked up in their various capacities as revolutionaries have proved indispensable as they continue to organize, this time as feminists. In other words, as Lorena Peña Mendoza explained, the Salvadoran revolution contributed to women rethinking their conceptions of womanhood while also training them to organize. "I do not know a single feminist that did not participate in the leftist struggle," remarked Lorena. "I think it has been an unconscious contribution, but a contribution nevertheless. The leftist struggle here in El Salvador, without really meaning to, took a number of women out of traditional gender roles and put us in a position to confront different types of situations. It forced us to develop organizational skills, decision making skills, to develop our thinking process."

It was the availability of a political space—the third factor—that enabled women's experiences with gender-bending and logistical training to converge and lay the foundation for the Salvadoran revolutionary feminist movement. In El Salvador, the political opportunity provided to the women was the peace accords, which acted as a catalyst in two ways. First, once the war ended, so too did the urgency of the struggle to militarily defeat the enemy. The never-ending threat of repression with which the population was faced was a situation that prevented women from sitting down and reflecting on their lives in any capacity beyond the immediacy of the war. Second, the peace accords brought about relief from that crisis and provided women the time to really reflect upon and respond to their experiences. More concretely than the threat of physical violence subsiding and thus allowing women the time to focus upon themselves, the newly emerging democratic structure was one that feminists refused to let pass them by. As I discussed above, the 1994 "elections of the century" created a prime moment in which women could mobilize and demand that the new El Salvador, which they had helped build, address their needs. As such, they advanced the Mujeres '94 platform, which, despite its lack of practical results, proved to be an organizational milestone in advancing the feminist movement in the postrevolutionary structure.

Additionally, after the war ended the Left was in a process of restructuring itself and adapting to the new context of a democratic transition. The fractures and reformulations within the Left that resulted from the accords also contributed to the political space that women usurped after the war. As Lety Méndez explained to me in our 1998 interview,

> As a result of the peace treaties, we have seen how women have taken more spaces in the struggle. I don't mean that we have the same conditions [as men] but what [we are] seeing are more women struggling; that they have become conscious of their gender, and this is very important. Nevertheless, the [women's] movement has carried with it the situation that is going on within the parties on the Left. Many of the women's [organizations] came about as a result of the parties and the divisions, the mistrust, and all of that was going on in the parties and is still present today within the ex [guerrilla] organizations. It also took place with the [women's] movement even though there was a divorce between the party and the women's movement. I feel that inside the FMLN we have not fought as well coordinated as women on the outside, precisely because of the divorce that took place.

In other words, the sectarianism on the Left that in part reemerged as a result of the peace accords served as an impetus for women distancing themselves from these fractures and starting anew. As a result, the most notable example of this is in the case of the DIGNAS, where feminists began to organize autonomously from leftist parties. Mendez acknowledges that the women's movement has not been immune to these political divisions that have plagued the Left, but that it has also made a more concerted and successful effort at dealing with them than have the leftist parties.[12]

The fourth factor necessary to the emergence of feminism in a revolution's aftermath is the feeling on the part of women that their revolution remains incomplete. In the case of El Salvador this sense of dissatisfaction was the result of two things: first, women were confronted with practical gender needs—for example, child support—that remained unmet; and second, women often felt a painful sense of betrayal as a result of the various forms of sexism to which they were exposed during the struggle for their nation. As women were made to feel invisible and insignificant to the revolutionary process and reconstruction of peacetime society, the revolution for which they risked so much tended to feel less complete than before they started fighting. Through consciousness-raising groups and informal discussions with each other, women realized that frustrations with men on the Left were not individual or personalized attacks but systematic manifestations of sexism. Female ex-combatants repeatedly said that they knew they had contributed significantly to the struggle, even if their work had since been ignored by their male compañeros. Though it was not a common experience to all women ex-combatants, the feeling of betrayal—due in large part to the machismo to which the Left is not immune—was one of the most potent fuels to be poured upon the contemporary women's movement in El Salvador. Indeed, Aracely Lopez explained in my 1998 interview with her,

> A lot of men harassed women too much or they abused them on some level. . . . It was also a very hidden thing, and the women didn't really understand it either, and I did not understand how to get the message across or how to really question the attitudes. You know, little things that I see in this chauvinist system, because if you go back and analyze, for example, what we went through in the revolutionary movement compared to what women went through with other men who weren't revolutionaries, it really is not much different. . . . It is not true that a relationship of respect is found more often in people who are trying to transform, say, economic, political and social issues.

Experiences and sentiments such as this were repeated to me in virtually every conversation I had with women ex-guerrillas.[13] In short, the revolution did not resolve the practical needs of women, and at the same time it did subject them to emotional, psychological, and, at times, physical sexism, which implicitly dismissed their significance to and personal risks taken for the struggle.

In addition to the reflections of women upon their past experiences with the FMLN, their experiences within the transition to democracy have, in many cases, also been negative. Because women played more behind-the-scenes positions during the revolutionary struggle, their experiences were perceived as apolitical and nontransferable to the realm of formal politics. As we saw, the guerrilla combatants and strategists were seen as the true revolutionaries. Despite the fact that women of the popular movement were heavily entrenched in the brutalities of war where they were subjected to rape and torture for their political activities, their contributions were not considered as prestigious as those of combatants. Additionally, as we saw, there were few women in top leadership positions in the FMLN during the war. As a result, women have not been given the same opportunities to contribute to the reconstruction of El Salvador as have men.[14] Of course, there are exceptions: Lorena Peña Mendoza, Mária Marta Valladres, and María Ofelia Navarrete de Dubon are three who have remained active in leadership positions within the formal political structures of the FMLN. Not coincidentally, these three women were also seen as leaders during the war. But the mothers of the Committee of Mothers and Relatives of Political Prisoners, Disappeared, and Assassinated of El Salvador (Comité de Madres y Familiares de Presos, Desaparecidos y Asesinados de El Salvador) or teachers in the National Association of Salvadoran Educators (Asociación Nacional de Educadores Salvadoreños) were not, from the perspective of the Left, the logical candidates to formally build a democratic El Salvador. As a result of the Left's limited definitions of what constitutes a "revolutionary," the types of things that women did during the war are now seen as apolitical. These experiences of having their contributions devalued, their practical needs unmet, and limited access to the formal political structures, have been central to the development of the fifth factor necessary in the evolution of revolutionary feminism, a collective feminist consciousness.

Salvadoran women were experiencing these frustrations and disillusionment with the Left as women in other parts of the world, including Latin America, were enveloped in second-wave feminism. As revolutionaries, Salvadoran women were quite predisposed to rigorous political theorizing that made feminist theory a natural evolution for many women. As Vilma Vasquez has explained, the exchanges with Mexican feminists were quite central in exposing Salvadoran women to feminist theory. Morena Herrera, ex-guerrilla and cofounder of the DIGNAS, in an interview with Lynn Stephen explained her own travels to Mexico where she was exposed to feminist discussions and materials that she brought back to El Salvador. As a result of her experiences in Mexico she learned of the fifth Latin American and Caribbean feminist *encuentro* (as I discussed in the introduction), which was scheduled to be held in Argentina. She was able to attend and it was in Argentina that she "fell in love with feminism" (quoted in Stephen 1997, 106). Additionally, in 1993 the sixth Latin American and Caribbean feminist encuentro took place in El Salvador. Much to the chagrin of the Salvadoran government, hundreds of women activists and feminists from throughout the region converged on the tiny country where Salvadoran women were already in the throes of articulating and structuring their own feminist movement. The exchanges that Salvadoran women had with U.S. and European solidarity activists who were, in the great majority, women also contributed to the collective feminist consciousness. North Americans and Europeans traveled frequently to El Salvador and invited Salvadoran women to their own countries, fostering rich exchanges about issues of feminism (Hipsher 2001; Meyer 1994; Stephen 1997). Together, the experiences of Salvadoran women revolutionaries as gender benders while simultaneously being exposed to training as activists during the revolutionary period, in conjunction with the political opportunity, incomplete revolution, and a collective feminist consciousness in the postrevolutionary period, led to the emergence of revolutionary feminism in postwar El Salvador.

CONCLUSIONS: INSTITUTIONALIZED GRASSROOTS

All of the feminists we met above, and the many whose voices I was unable to weave into this narrative have connections, severed or intact, to the Left. Most joined the revolutionary movement in the 1970s and 1980s in hopes of transforming their nation from a repressively classist society to one that respected the dignity of its citizens. Despite their immersion in a movement ideologically committed to egalitarianism, women revolutionaries were subjected to implicit and explicit forms of misogyny. Just as their responses to the injustices in their nation writ large were organized and militant, so too were their declarations against sexism within the Left. Committing themselves to an incomplete revolutionary process, fraught with all of its problematic gendered relations, has led the women revolutionaries to continue and expand their battle to the feminist front.

El Salvador's postwar period has provided us with a clear case of revolutionary feminism. I have suggested that feminism is strong in this case as it is both institutionally grounded and grassroots-based. That is, women's organizations are working with the few feminists and women's allies in the Legislative Assembly to advance their causes—most notably, responsible paternity. On the other hand, they have anything but abandoned the grassroots cause, as many of the feminist organizations are just recently emerging from autonomous reclusion where they stayed distant from the Left (not to mention the Right). In short, the feminist front in El Salvador, is clear in theory, practice, and praxis, and maintains a two-pronged strategy of working through the state and with grassroots popular organizations.

CHAPTER 3

The Tenure of Salvador Allende
through a Feminist Lens, 1970–1973

Surely this will be my last opportunity to address you. . . . My words are not spoken in bitterness. I shall pay with my life for the loyalty of the people. . . . The seed we have planted in the worthy consciousness of thousands upon thousands of Chileans cannot forever remain unharvested. . . . They have the might and they can enslave us, but they cannot halt the world's social progresses, not with crimes, nor with guns. History is ours, and the people of the world will determine it.

—Salvador Allende's last words to the Chilean people,
quoted in Lois Hect Oppenheim, *Politics in Chile*

SEPTEMBER ELEVENTH is a date no more easily forgotten by Chileans than North Americans. It was on 11 September 1973 that a period of vibrant democracy was violently ended by a bloody coup d'état against Chilean president Dr. Salvador Allende, the first ever democratically elected Marxist. For many, prior to September 1973, Chile was a model for both democracy and the Left in Latin America, and indeed around the world. Allende's presidency is a case of what I am calling a *partial revolution*.[1] I use the qualifier *partial* for three reasons: First, Allende's term was not even half of what a constitutionally guaranteed term is supposed to be; second, he was elected with only a slight margin,[2] which suggests that he didn't have overwhelming support from the populace; and third, as evidenced by the coup, he never was able to gain full control of the military. While in office, Allende's platform of nationalization of the economy and government subsidized social and cultural services was in the nascent stages. If it were to have truly emerged as the Popular Unity (Unidad Popular, or UP—the leftist coalition that Allende represented) government intended, Chilean society's basic class and ideological structures would have been transformed, which, according to Theda Skocpol, is the way to measure if a revolution is successful (1994, 240; I will discuss this more below). In this chapter I revisit the first part of the revolution question—What do women do for revolutions?—through the case of Chile. Through this discussion I will expand the focus of this important point in history from discussions that for the most part address the roles of right wing women in their infamous mobilization against Allende to address the roles of women in the Popular Unity coalition and the effects of this revolutionary project on gender roles in Chile.[3] I will begin this chapter with a brief background on the election of Salvador Allende and then provide a feminist interpretation of his presidential term. I will conclude this chapter by revisiting my concept of *gendered revolutionary bridges* as it relates to the Chilean case.

THE ROOTS OF CHILEAN DEMOCRACY

Given its competition, Chile has long been considered the model democracy in the region.[4] Despite this, Chilean political history is also marked by a requisite amount of turmoil. What differentiates Chile from other postindependence Latin American nations is the democratic infrastructure that always lay just slightly below the surface. Since the mid- to late nineteenth century, party alliances were largely based on social class positioning: the Liberal and Conservative Parties represented large landowners while the Radical Party, a group that splintered from the Liberals in 1861, was made up predominantly of middle-class Chileans and/or professionals from the lower tiers of the labor force. The Democratic Party was comprised largely of lower-middle-class workers. One of the earlier causes of social and political tensions in Chile was unregulated foreign investment by the British and North Americans. Though this foreign investment did bring some revenue to the country it was focused almost entirely on the copper and nitrate industries, both of which were highly isolated from the rest of the nation's economy, and further entrenched the political and economic power of the oligarchy. At the same time the mining industry also spawned the growth of an industrial working class and subsequent labor movement. Indeed, in 1901 the miners organized a strike that would last two months. Not long after, in 1907, more miners struck, only to be met by government troops who killed two thousand workers. It was also during this same period that women began to mobilize; Marjorie Agosín notes, "As early as 1913 . . . miners' wives organized the Bellen de Zaraga Center in the northern mining regions of Chile to protest employee exploitation and human rights violations. A variety of women's groups also emerged in the 1900s to work for women's education" (1996, 130).[5] In 1919, the Chilean Women's Party was established. It called for reform of legislation with respect to women as well as suffrage, civil rights for women, improvement on the conditions of children and women, protection for children and pregnant women, and "women's rights to be independent and autonomous in all political and religious groups" (Agosín 1996, 131). This party, however, was unsuccessful.

Capitalizing on women and their newly articulated demands, as well as the frustrations of the middle and lower classes, Arturo Alessandri was elected president in 1920. He promised to relieve general social strife, to enact constitutional reforms, and even to create laws to protect women as paid laborers. The Chilean congress, however, representing the elite sectors of society, prevented any real reforms from being implemented. Allesandri's attempt at social programs could have only been realized by taxing the oligarchy, an option that simply did not exist. The reform minded military staged a quasi-coup against the congress demonstrating its support for Allesandri and his agenda. Politically, the tactic worked; Allesandri successfully passed the constitution of 1925. His constitution restored the balance of power between the congress and the president, and allowed for the election of the president through a direct vote to serve a six-year term and be ineligible for immediate reelection. The constitution also called for the right to private property, a right that could be limited; progressive labor laws; voting rights for literate men over twenty-one; a small income tax; the establishment of a central bank; and a voter registry in order to reduce electoral fraud. Allesandri felt compromised, however, by the antidemocratic means by which the gains were accomplished and resigned.

The seven years after Allesandri stepped down were marked by a series of military governments. This political and social instability was further exacerbated by the onset of the Great Depression in 1929. It was not until 1932 that constitutional order would return to Chile with the democratic reelection of Alessandri, at which point his priority became economic recovery. As the government increased its involvement in the economy and the nation grew considerably dependent on foreign sources for development, Chilean workers became markedly disaffected. Alessandri attempted to quell opposition movements through considerably repressive tactics—the shutting down of newspapers, the exile of political critics, and the challenging of the congress's autonomy. Not surprisingly, his tactics inspired a collective response on the part of workers, peasants, and the urban middle class. Women also continued to form groups at this time, shortly after winning the right to vote in municipal elections (1931). Not long after this partial victory for women, three different women's organizations were to emerge in 1936, including Feminine Action, a group associated with the Chilean Women's Party, the Movement of Chilean Women (Movimiento de la Mujer Chilena), and the Movement for the Emancipation of Women (Movimiento Pro-Emancipación de la Mujer, or MEMCH). MEMCH drew its vision from the Left and was consequently more politicized than the other two organizations;[6] it would eventually become foundational to Chilean second-wave feminism, which will be discussed in chapter 4.

It was at this same time that, with the assistance of Salvador Allende, the Socialist Party was formed. Years later, when asked in an interview why he found it necessary to start a Socialist Party in 1933 when there was already a

Communist Party, Allende commented, "[W]hen we founded the Socialist Party, the Communist Party already existed, but we analyzed the situation in Chile, and we believed that there was a place for a Party which, while holding similar views in terms of philosophy and doctrine—a Marxist approach to the interpretation of history—would be a Party free of ties of an international nature" (Debray 1971, 62). As a result, in 1938 a coalition of Communist, Radical, and Socialist Party members united as the Popular Front (Frente Popular), with their presidential candidate, Pedro Aguirre Cerda, narrowly winning the elections. The leftist coalition continued to make and remake itself, with the participation of the Communist Party being one of the larger points of contention. As the parties continued to transition and regroup, the voting population also grew as women obtained full suffrage in 1949. During Radical Party member Gabriel González Videla's presidency, the Communist Party was declared illegal. This conveyed a forceful message to the Left, as up until that point Communists had been part of the executive cabinet. At the same time, inflation was escalating and workers' wages were frozen. In 1952, discontent among the populace intensified, ushering in the reelection of former dictator and self-proclaimed populist Carlos Ibáñez del Campo. He again turned to North American banks as well as the International Monetary Fund to stabilize the economy. Despite the repressive nature of his government, it was under Ibáñez del Campo that the Communist Party was once again legalized.

By the election year of 1958 the Left had restored its unity through the Popular Action Front (Frente Revolucionario de Acción Popular). Salvador Allende narrowly lost this election to conservative Jorge Alessandri, son of the former president. Alessandri's plan of recovery was to inject foreign capital into the economy. Throughout this period, the politics of Chile (as in the rest of Latin America) were greatly influenced by U.S. foreign policy. The 1959 triumph of the Cuban revolutionaries prompted the United States to keep close watch upon leftist movements in the region. Further compounding the U.S.'s general fear was the formation of the Movement for the Revolutionary Left (Movimiento de Izquierda Revolucionario, or MIR) which was born in the 1960s and patterned itself after Fidel Castro's Cuban guerrilla movement. The near triumph of Allende in the 1958 elections led the United States to support moderate candidate Eduardo Frei, a Christian Democrat, in the 1964 elections. Frei won with 56 percent of the vote. Economic plans for what he called the "Chileanization" of the copper industry failed to expand production or raise government revenues. As the economy staggered and Frei fulfilled few of his promises, social movements, including trade unions, moved increasingly to the Left, paving the way for the election of Allende. Threatened by this victory, the far right-wing group Fatherland and Liberty (Patria y Libertad) formed to try and prevent Allende from taking office. In the short term they were unsuccessful. In 1970 Allende, representing the UP coalition, was elected and approved by congress as president. The coalition won with only a very slight majority of the vote: Allende received 36 percent, right-wing candidate Jorge Alessandri 35 percent, and Christian Democrat Radomiro Tomic 28 percent. Though Allende did not target women as an electoral sector, their share of votes for him increased 13 percent over that of the 1958 elections, thus providing him his razor-thin margin of victory (Keen and Haynes 2000, 347). Because Allende did not gain sufficient majority to take office, the election went to the congress, which approved him as president.

Allende's platform was based on the construction of a Chilean path to socialism. From his perspective as a Marxist, he believed that capitalism, with its inherently exploitative structure against workers and peasants, was responsible for the impoverished state of the third world. As such, Allende's revolutionary experiment was not a movement against the Christian Democrats per se. Allende would have challenged a right-wing, procapitalist candidate in the polls with no more or less vigor than he did the Christian Democrats. In other words, Allende's revolution was not about changing the actual political infrastructure in Chile because it was, after all, that very infrastructure that allowed him to democratically emerge as president and implement his socialist agenda. Rather, he was concerned with the transformation of the class and ideological structures in Chile.

The UP coalition's immediate goals were to better the standard of living of the working class, and to activate the economy. Toward that end, the coalition worked to nationalize industry and implement land reform. Unfortunately, Allende's project was plagued with opposition from his own government's fiscal arm, the Chilean media, much of the military, the United States, and from splits within the Left. He worked unsuccessfully to achieve a balance between structural reform and the special interests of the middle class. He was also unable to solve the agricultural crisis. By the spring of 1973 the balance of forces within the military had shifted, and preparations for a coup were underway. On September 11, 1973, the morning after Allende rejected a proposal from the military to resign, the coup began. The army and air force (with considerable aid from the United States) attacked the presidential palace (Kornbluh 2003). Allende vowed not to leave the palace alive and committed suicide after broadcasting a final message to the Chilean people.

If the presidency of Salvador Allende ended so abruptly, and his agenda was not even wholly embraced by his own government or electorate, why do I call his election and tenure a partial revolution? According to Allende himself, "the people of Chile chose the road of revolution and we have not forgotten a fundamental principle of Marxism: the class struggle.... We sought to form a government in order to obtain the power to carry out the revolutionary transformation which Chile needs, to break the nation's economic, political, cultural and trade union dependency" (Debray 1971, 81). If a movement is characterized as revolutionary based on its goals of transforming hierarchical classist structures and ideologies, then Allende's Chile should most certainly be considered revolutionary. Though it is tempting to dismiss the UP coalition as nonrevolutionary as it emerged to power through nonviolent electoral means, this would be incorrect. For one, the Iranian revolution of 1979 was nonviolent, and its results have endured for nearly a quarter of a century. More pertinent to this study, however, is not what tactics revolutionaries employ to achieve power, but what it is they hope to do with that power when/if it is achieved. Working from Skocpol's definition, we know that a revolution is "[rapid], basic transformations of a country's state and class structures, and of its dominant ideology. Moreover, social revolutions are carried through, in part, by class-based upheavals from below" (1994, 240). This definition accurately characterizes the UP coalition's structure and agenda. Organizationally, the coalition was cross-class as it included a spectrum that spanned from laborers to the upper classes. And since Allende became president through a democratic election, it is fair to characterize that process as "from below," particularly because Allende's electoral support came disproportionately from the organized working class. With respect to agenda, transforming Chile's class structure was precisely Allende's goal. Toward that end Allende and the UP coalition also brought about basic transformations to the state by implementing laws and amendments to the constitution that partially restructured the state in such a way as to enable the construction of socialism.

The UP coalition was made up of six parties. Of the three largest parties, two were explicitly Marxist. At the other end of the spectrum was a small non-Marxist Christian-based group that had splintered from the Christian Democrats. The guiding Communist Party–inspired strategy of the coalition was to create "a broad alliance of all anti-imperialist forces" (Oppenheim 1999, 37). The stated program of the UP coalition was to begin the construction of socialism in Chile. (Even if Allende had been able to finish his entire term, the coalition didn't expect that the transition from capitalism to socialism would be complete.) Central to accomplishing this was the implementation of agrarian reform and expanding the nonagricultural portion of the state economy. Allende sought to encourage communal forms of agriculture rather than individual ownership of land and aggressively worked to socialize the economy. The copper industry, which was Chile's main industry, was the central focus of this plan. Eighty percent of all of Chile's foreign exchange came from copper exports, and the three largest U.S.-owned mines equaled half of all of Chile's export earnings. While Allende was president foreign companies were kicked out of Chile and the government took control of factories. These two measures (land reform and socializing the economy) were, from the perspective of the UP coalition, essential to building socialism in Chile.

The UP coalition also had a series of other goals that were individually more moderate and welfare-oriented than that of socializing the economy but collectively added to the revolutionary agenda. They sought to guarantee employment for all Chileans at a living wage, stabilization of the monetary system, access to health services for the poor, and the construction of day-care centers and low-income housing. Politically, the coalition hoped to create a "Popular Assembly," a one-house legislature that would be better able to represent the working class. It also strove for greater state control of private schools, a program to which the upper classes were particularly hostile. The ultimate goal of the UP coalition was to use the power of the state to reorient resources in favor of the poor (Oppenheim 1999, 40–42). Allende's policies were measurably revolutionary, as evidenced in part by the fact that they eroded the economic power formerly held by the upper classes under capitalism. Indeed, it was the partial success of the UP coalition's revolutionary agenda that caused the upper classes to support a military coup. What I will focus upon in the rest of this chapter is the relationship of women to the Chilean revolutionary movement, and vice versa. It is my contention that women had the potential to contribute significantly to the Chilean revolutionary movement, but for a variety of reasons similar to those we saw in El Salvador, they were prevented from reaching their full revolutionary potential.

ALLENDE'S ANSWER TO THE WOMAN QUESTION

In this section I will discuss the sociopolitical relationship between women and Allende by analyzing his answer to the woman question and leftist women's answer to the revolution question. Specifically, I will discuss the roles of women in the Allende government and the women-focused programs he supported. Allende's program for and placement of women was very much rooted in a patriarchal division of labor. The question I hope to answer here is, Can women-focused programs that are organized vis-à-vis sexist ideologies contribute to the political empowerment of women?

While in Santiago, Chile, in 1999 I interviewed ten mid- to high-level *Allendistas*—ministers, members of the press corps, party members active in leadership positions, and grassroots activists. Of these ten women, seven described themselves as being from the professional middle class or the petite bourgeoisie, and three self-identified as either *campesino* or working class.[7] Chilean author Marjorie Agosín observed that during Allende's tenure, political participation was reserved for upper-middle- and upper-class urban women who had educations that lower-strata women lacked (1996, 134). This concurs with Linda Lobao's and Jane Jaquette's arguments (discussed in the introduction and chapter 1) that middle- and upper-middle-class women often have more time to give to revolutionary struggles. In the case of Chile, I found this to be the case. Agosín further notes that these women often identified their initial political participation or consciousness as occurring during the 1960s while they were either high school or university students. The few working-class and peasant women with whom I spoke identified the influence of their parents' leftist political ideology in conjunction with experiences resulting from their social positioning as the initial spark for getting involved. For example, Carmen Lazo, a seventy-eight-year-old woman of humble origins who has been active with the Socialist Party and was a congressional deputy during Allende's presidency explained it this way:

> My father was a laborer; he was a mechanic and a welder. He always worked as a supervisor in the mines for U.S. companies in Chile. . . . Because my father was a supervisor we did not live in the tin houses that the rest of the laborers lived in; instead, we lived in what was called a chalet. . . . My mom had seven children and she was a housekeeper. . . . Because of my father's work we moved around to a number of places in the country. From an early age I realized the differences between the lives of the workers and the lives of the North Americans that owned the companies. My father got a job for the Andes Copper Mining, a company that was in Potrerillos. . . . I became a member of the Socialist Party when I was thirteen years old. The miners lived in tin houses and the bathrooms were in the streets. It was easy to know where people went to the bathroom because the smell was awful. They had public showers. Men and women had to shower together in public places. They had terrible living conditions. When I was very young I realized these differences. I was aware that Chile exported important minerals like copper and with the copper they also took other minerals because the copper went out without processing so other stuff went with it.[8] (Personal interview, 1999)

While in Chile in 1999 I also spoke with Mireya Baltra, who at sixty-seven years old remained a militant with the Communist Party. She had a long history of activism with Allende, and her positions included minister of labor and social security, secretary general of the Allendista Women's Unit (a group of women who supported the UP coalition), and a variety of others within parliamentary and labor-related circles. Mireya explained her process of politicization:

> Well, my first contact was when I was selling papers. Here they call people who sell newspapers *suplementeros*. . . . My parents also sold newspapers . . . and they had their own newsstand . . . Later I got married to a silversmith, when I was four or five months pregnant, and the truth is that my life became really difficult, and I ended up having to set up my own newsstand to sell papers and magazines. I did that for something like fifteen years, sell papers there at the newsstand, and that allowed me, looking back, to get some perspective, I think, to see a world full of need. And it gave me the time to read and then later I developed greater aspi-

rations. I then had the time to bring a typewriter to the newsstand and to start writing for some papers on certain topics or events or things that had an impact on me, and using my name. One of the things that had the biggest impact on me, and it is something that was an historic event here in Chile, is that the suplementeros' guild I belonged to, the trade union and the federation of suplementeros, held a strike against *El Mercurio* newspaper. Now, that paper is the doyen of the Chilean press; it has been around for more than one hundred years, and it is the newspaper that represents the interests of transnational consortia, big business, and fundamentally right-wing ideology, so it had an important role before the coup and during the coup and it still upholds its rightist stance—ultraright on some issues.

These stories stand in contrast to those of Carmen Gloria Aguayo, a woman of the upper class who was a member of the directorate of the Movement for United Popular Action (Movimiento de Acción Popular Unitaria, or MAPU), which was one of two splinter parties from the Christian Democrats that supported the UP coalition. Carmen Gloría served as the national director of the Social Development Agency throughout Allende's term and only retired from that position when she was asked to run for senator. In my 1999 interview with her she recalled her own process of getting involved with the Left:

> I was not particularly interested in politics. . . . I was doing social work [and] I was going to a poor community that was close to my house. We lived in . . . a nice neighborhood, but very close to our neighborhood there was what we then called a *población* [shantytown]. The residents had built those little houses made out of thin wood and cardboard. . . . I accompanied my mother to this community and I kept going. When I was eighteen or nineteen years old I went every Sunday to help these people. Then my boyfriend at that time told me, "This is not good, this is a drop in the sea, we have to make a revolution, we have to change the country, change the society, we have to end capitalism and all of this." [H]e was the one who changed my idea of helping a small group . . . and deep down, it was because of him that at that time I joined the Christian Democrats. I was in the Christian Democrats until . . . about 1969 when they divided [and the] MAPU [formed]. The MAPU emerged and left the Christian Democrats to support the Popular Unity. This is why Allende was so interested in having my help because I was bringing in other people that were not from the Left.

Soledad Parada, former member of the Communist Party and director for the Chilean Presidential Women's Secretariat, also came from a privileged background and came to leftist politics through what might be considered intellectual or cultural channels. As she explained when I interviewed her,

> My mother is still alive, my father is not. They were theater actors, founders of the Chilean University Theater. My father was also a professor, he was a sociologist. . . . At this point in time there was a lot of social upheaval. It was the sixties and Eduardo Frei was in office. I was a restless girl. I compare myself to fifteen year olds today and it seems like I was extremely mature and I knew what was going on in Chile and in other parts of the world. Not only because of my family but the environment I was in—I read the papers, I listened to the radio. There was a debate around different ideas in our country and it was possible for most Chileans to take a political position. I naturally took the Left because it seemed to be the side that took up the defense of education and the ideas of changing the society. Even though I came from a family that never had major economic problems I did know the great contradictions that existed in Chile and in some way I felt I had to be on the side of those who had the least. The Left was the best position to do this from.

Carmen Gloría and Soledad's backgrounds differed significantly from Carmen Lazo and Mireya's. Carmen Gloría came from a privileged family with professional parents and highly educated siblings. Both of her grandfathers were from the professional class, one a lawyer and the other a doctor; as she noted in our conversation, "they were not rich but had certain cultural capital" (personal interview, 1999). Soledad's parents were both theater actors, founders of the Chilean University Theater, and her father was a professor of sociology. She explained that "in my case the cultural aspect also had a great deal of influence. My parents gave me access to theater, poetry, and all these things that contributed to having a more progressive vision of society." On the other hand, Carmen Lazo and Mireya came to their consciousness through living and/or directly observing the circumstances in which their parent's socioeconomic background placed them. In a sense, they joined the Socialist Party and Communist Party, respectively, in part out of what they saw as personal necessity to better their own lives and the lives of people who lived like them; or, what may be considered to meet practical needs. Carmen Gloría, however, was exposed to something very alien and, to be sure, unacceptable to her (the living conditions of shantytown dwellers) through her own charity work. Coming from a comfortable background she had the time to help others, and it was through this process, in conjunction with her soon-to-be husband, that she initially had her consciousness raised regarding the need for structural change in Chile. Similarly, Soledad was exposed to an intellectual and cultural environment enabled by her social class that allowed her to analyze the contradictions from which she benefited. What is interesting is that Carmen Gloría, though still a member of the Party for Democracy (Partido por la Democracía), considers herself retired from politics, as does Soledad, who is no longer a member of the Communist Party. Carmen Lazo and Mireya, however, remain active party militants, suggesting further that for Carmen Gloria and Soledad politics was a choice rather than the necessity that it appears to be for Carmen Lazo and Mireya.

In the formal political sense, women of all classes were very underrepresented in the Allende government. They tended to hold positions in what Nikki Craske calls the "caring ministries" (1999, 61; this is further discussed below), in areas of communication where they worked with the press, and in labor union and finance related organizations. A handful of leftist women were elected as senators and deputies while Allende was president, but on the whole women were largely absent from the formal political structures. One gets a variety of answers regarding the impact that the Allende administration had upon the daily lives and overall social status of women. A few of the women I interviewed (albeit the minority, and generally the less feminist-identified) felt that Salvador Allende was highly attentive to women and their specific concerns. Carmen Lazo affectionately remembers, "One of Allende's concerns was women, because he knew that Chilean women had been discriminated against by Chilean *machismo*. At the same time women had kept and maintained the homes just like the one I grew up in. . . . Women were very important. I was good friends with Allende. I even helped him in the 1952 campaign, so we knew each other well. We traveled from north to south, . . . and this is why I can tell you that one of his big concerns was women."

Teresa Valdés, a college student at the time Allende was president, worked within the UP government in a variety of capacities. Her assessment of the impact that the UP coalition had upon the social position of women is similar to Carmen Lazo's. Teresa explained in our conversation in 1999,

> This whole thing with the UP nowadays depends on how you look at it. Looking at it from the perspective of the UP, and what they offered [women] meant that there was an extraordinary increase in women's participation. When you look at all the mothers' centers [discussed below], the groups that controlled the food supply and the prices for stuff, all of these things in the popular sectors of society, women participated a lot more than they had before. There are estimates that say that around one million women organized during this time. . . . What is interesting is not so much the government but the organizational transformations, because women at the time were concerned with what was going on in the country in an overall sense. There was no real gender consciousness or anything like that. But there was a lot of women's participation. And there were an

impressive number of women in leadership and women doing volunteer work.

That said, the majority of the women with whom I spoke, including Teresa, felt that Allende's programs were both lacking in quality and in their potential for presenting structural challenges to the patriarchal institutions of Chile. Mireya explained that

> there was a lot of discrimination but we [women] also are partly to blame because we went beyond the specificity of the sectors to try to construct a collective organization with significant democratic participation on the part of women. I would say it was a sectarian movement, because in the country at that time there were already clear lines drawn, totally opposing political trends that made it impossible for the government to resolve women's problems. I think that not enough was done, except for the laws . . . that Allende drew up: he signed a law for nursery schools for working mothers, and of course for housewives too, and that now exists as a state organism. We also brought up the need for what we called the visibility of women's work from the home, an issue that Gladys's candidature has also taken up because it was something that had been raised in the [Communist] Party a long time ago[9]—that is, the need for housewives to be able to retire; that is, anyone over sixty should be able to retire.

In other words, though Mireya believed that Allende was truly concerned about women and even passed laws that supported them, the basic structural presence of sexism was not addressed. The same sectarianism, which was at least in part responsible for destabilizing the Popular Unity coalition, thus making it more vulnerable to the coup, also prevented an organized approach to answering the woman question. Mireya also suggests that women-specific mobilization perhaps contributed to the divisions and was too ambitious to happen simultaneously with the UP coalition's socialist agenda. In a 1999 interview I asked Alicia Basso, former leader of the Communist Party and member of Allende's presidential advisory group in her capacity as a sociologist, if she felt satisfied with Allende's programs for women. She responded, "I don't think we stopped to think about it, to consider if we were satisfied or not. At the time, . . . we just didn't have the time. We would do things at the same time as we thought about them." For Alicia, it was not as if Allende and the UP government intentionally excluded women but rather that the party, including women members, already had their hands full. That said, what exactly did the UP coalition do for women? In the rest of this chapter I will look at Allende's advances and shortcomings with respect to women focused programs.

Los Centros de Madres

In the late 1960s, with the support of the Christian Democrats as well as Catholic activists, a number of *centros de madres* (mothers' centers) were established in Chile. In the 1970s, during Allende's government, these centers became highly politicized (Miller 1991, 181). The mothers' centers served a variety of political and practical purposes, and were in no way intended to be feminist in goal or structure. I spoke at length with Carmen Gloría about the mothers' centers. Hers was a particularly interesting perspective, since she had helped organize many of the first centers as a member of the Christian Democrats and later, under Allende, worked with them in her capacity as director of the Social Development Agency. The UP coalition, however, did not initially support the centers. This was in part the result of their being created by the Christian Democrats. As Carmen Gloría explained,

> When the Christian Democrat government ended and the Popular Unity won the election, there was a discussion about the mothers' centers. The Left did not see the mothers' centers in a favorable light because they had been an idea of the Christian Democrats. They said the centers didn't work and were paternalistic; they said that women-only organizations should not exist and that women should instead integrate themselves with men and work together in unions and neighborhood organizations.[10] We had a big discussion about them. I had learned from my experience that women got together after lunch, when the kids were at school and the husbands were not home. The unions met at 7:00 P.M., and women could not attend the meetings at that time because they were at home serving dinner; the unions knew women were not going to get involved. There were not any exclusive spaces for women. This was a long discussion and at the end they decided to keep going with the mothers' centers. [Former first lady] Mrs. Frei was the first to lead the organization that got women work, and then Mrs. Allende took over.

Carmen Gloría explained that the UP government's decision to continue with the mothers' centers proved to be the correct one, since "many women began the road to becoming leaders after participating in the centers, and because of this women participated a lot in the Popular Unity government." Indeed, Carmen Gloría felt that the centers were socially and politically important for the Chilean women who were able to participate in them. As she explained,

> It was a very important program for women who had never left their homes. You have to situate yourself thirty or forty years ago to understand this. . . . When these mothers' centers were formed, women went out of

their homes for the first time to meet with their neighbors. The meetings were held at someone's house and they would start with very small groups. . . . After that it would grow, and grow very fast. They really liked it. One of the women would bring the tea and another the sugar and they would drink tea and talk. At first they would get together and just talk and share things. They came to realize that the lady down the street was having the same problems, like when her husband was cheating. They would notice that they had similar problems, and cry together. There was a sort of sharing life together and they learned how to communicate better. From the outside we taught them how to organize themselves.

In practice, the mothers' centers provided training in traditionally feminine tasks such as knitting and sewing. Under the Christian Democrats the centers only existed in urban areas, but Allende also made sure that rural women had similar access to such services. This expansion to the rural areas was significant, as it allowed for the participation of campesinas as well. As Teresa Valdés explained,

> The other day I was listening to a peasant leader who was talking about what the mothers' centers meant for peasant women. This had nothing to do with a feminist vision, but for them these centers were a space to develop—a space to see the world, to leave the private space—and this had an amazing impact. So it is a process. In this sense, the Popular Unity helped and supported this process; it recognized all of these organizations. . . . At the time, organizations had influence, they were recognized. There was a desire to transfer, to allow for decisions to be made in a collective manner even if the decisions were only at the local level. I would say that this is the [UP's] biggest contribution even though it is not something specific to gender.

The issue of autonomy was particularly salient with respect to the mothers' centers since their origins were clearly rooted in the government. Despite this explicit relationship, Carmen Gloría noted that a certain type of autonomy did exist in the mothers' centers. When I asked if the centers were autonomous from men or from the political parties, she answered,

> I would say from both. But I would have to say, more from men. At first many women went to meetings without telling their husbands. This is why they liked the time when they met, because their husbands were not around. They would say that their husbands would get mad at them for going. Men would say that women got together to gossip and talk about other people behind their backs. Men would look down on these meetings, but women still attended. The political party question is trickier. Women still had political ideas, which meant that the president or some-

one in the center had leftist ideas or Christian Democrat ideas. It was not so much about autonomy. The party could not take over a center, but it could have an influence through the directorate of the center. For example, if someone was running for office they could get access to the centers.

While the mothers' centers reified femininity and patriarchal divisions of labor, they also provided outlets for the exchange of ideas, experiences, and even philosophies that were, in some cases, later transformed into the foundation for political leadership in organizations such as unions and neighborhood associations. As a result of spending time together, often for the first time, the women at the mothers' centers transformed traditionally feminine spaces into locales for what Norma Chinchilla (1992) calls "doing politics." As Carmen Gloría pointed out, women were often forced to sneak out of their homes to go to the mothers' centers. They confronted and challenged their husbands' fears of and dissatisfaction with such happenings, thus initiating the development of what Temma Kaplan calls a "feminine consciousness" (1982, 545).

WOMEN'S LABOR: PRIVATE, PUBLIC, AND POLITICAL

While in Chile I interviewed Soledad Parada, who at twenty-one was the director of the Women's Secretariat created by Salvador Allende. She worked with the secretariat from its inception in 1971 through the coup, at which point she was forced into exile until 1985. Upon returning to Chile her brother was brutally murdered in an infamous attack against three communists.[11] Soledad pointed out that the creation of the Women's Secretariat predated the United Nations Decade for Women (1975–1985). In other words, women's issues were so unfamiliar at the time that it was inevitable they would not receive their deserved attention.[12] She also explained that the lack of precedent for doing work that addressed the needs of women presented further obstacles to such projects. Indeed, "there was no history of work done in regards to women by the government so we had to invent it all,"[13] she said. Allende, Soledad explained, wanted to focus some of his programs on women so in 1971 he established the Women's Secretariat, which took on such issues as women's health care (especially prenatal care), day-care centers, public food programs, and public laundry facilities. She also noted that they tried to establish decent working conditions for women at wages that would serve to empower them:

> In relation to work, it was about improving the situation so that women could incorporate themselves into the labor market with the same conditions as men. It was [also at] that time that most development in the child-care centers and in the preschools occurred. Other measures were taken,

that in my view, were very interesting. It was an isolated attempt [perhaps] . . . but it was oriented to improve the situation of the relation between the genders; that is, so that women did not have to be faced with domestic work. Two large programs were formed there . . . [and though] they were limited in their services, in my view they were important for the significance that they had. There was a food preparation program that . . . at very reasonable prices, people could go to eat. Food was given to women; they could buy prepared food at low prices and this was so they did not have to cook. . . . The other program that never went, though—just a pilot initiative—was the installation of popular laundries. . . . In addition, we also had some recreational and cultural activities programs. This is something that we tried to do so that women could get some relief from domestic labor.[14]

Carmen Gloría's perspective on the Women's Secretariat was a bit different. She noted, "The Women's Secretariat [like the Social Development Agency] also depended on the government. I was a member of the MAPU and the Women's Secretariat was headed by Socialists [Communists], so this caused political problems. The Women's Secretariat was created so that Socialist [Communist] women could also have something. The women's Secretariat, toward the end, did some good things but in general it was a pretty closed group without much projection to the future." Carmen Gloría's analysis provides a specific example of what Mireya identified as a sectarianism that touched women's organizing and subsequently undermined the potential advances.

Another program of Allende's that is invariably seen as an advance for women was his famous milk programs. Allende, being a medical doctor, was quite attentive to the health of the Chilean people and their nation. The children of Chile were the starting point for achieving this goal. When I asked Carmen Lazo, former deputy for the Socialist Party, about his programs for women she enthusiastically offered, "I tell you that women were their [the UP coalition's] main concern and one of the measures that the popular government took . . . was that each Chilean child was guaranteed one half a liter of milk [per day] . . . . This was a revolutionary measure because in Chile there was not a culture of giving milk to children in schools." Though it is debatable whether the betterment of children's health, an invaluable program to be sure, should be specifically considered a women's rather than a family's specific advance, most discussions of the Allende period and women are as likely to be punctuated with a discussion of the milk programs as they are the March of the Empty Pots and Pans (to be discussed in the next section).

Related to this, Soledad also explained that it was during this period that women began to be treated like and thus see themselves as political subjects.

Women had access to education at this time, not just academically, but politically. Despite the highly traditional gendered component of Allende's programs, Soledad saw them as empowering to women:

> We made a school for leadership training within the Women's Secretariate; we addressed, among other things, issues related to women's health. The concept of gender did not yet exist but rather finding ways to encourage women to actively participate in health politics . . . that basically had to do with children and with women's rights. Although we did not plan it that way, it was at this time that birth control and family planning programs had recently started in the country; it was about looking for possibilities so that women could actively participate as subjects in these programs. In relation to the children I remember that it was about allowing women to actively participate in the campaigns to decrease infant mortality which at that time was still high; through the participation in the fight against diarrhea . . . at that moment a big problem, [to] contagious and lung diseases.

In addition to discussing the mothers' centers and milk programs, Mireya explained two other women-focused projects. She was a leader in the historically Communist Party–controlled Central Workers' Confederation (Central Unica de Trabajadores, or CUT). She explained that under the UP coalition the general consciousness around gender led the CUT to include a more women-specific program:

> We also had a vision as women and I think it is very important to talk about it in regards to our organizations . . . because there were women's departments in La Central Unica de Trabajadores—not *Central Unitaria* like it is called today; in the textile confederation there was a strong feminine force; in health, public services, and educators, there was a large number of women, as many as in service as in production. . . . Through our [women workers'] struggle we obtained preschools—through large social movements; we obtained retirement for women at fifty-five years old, something that the dictatorship raised to sixty years old; we obtained maternity leave for which women were not penalized; we also obtained the amplification of various laws, including the prolongation of pre- and postmaternity actions. All of this was done by the CUT; it was the most open coordination with Socialists, with Radicals, with people from the MAPU, and from the Christian Left.

Mireya was also secretary general of the Allendista Women's Unit. She described it to me as a "pretty powerful organization." The unit's purpose, she explained, "was to group together all the leftist Chilean women in favor of the popular government." Mireya explained that the aims of the committee were to support the government and its program: to [promote] women's participation in issues concerning health and housing problems. . . . Classes that addressed these issues took place at the mothers' centers. These classes were, I would say, political, but there were also literacy classes, that went out to the countryside, and a strong push for culture. With Allende, there were culture trains, so that every sort of artistic manifestation could reach even the most remote villages where they had never before had a ballet, an opera, a symphony. That was what I would call a prime moment in that at least, well, this is a sort of a personal testimony, because human beings, who of course are not born happy, and are not happy, but with this program they can grasp certain parts or types of happiness in a commitment to realizing a dream that, for many people, is impossible.

These services provided women (and men) with access to what had previously been reserved for the urban upper classes. Not only were women exposed to education, health care, and—inadvertently—what I will argue were the potential seeds of feminist consciousness, but they were also provided access to culture that prior to the UP coalition's existence was not available to them. Though this was largely the function of a socialist government and not a woman-conscious or feminist agenda, in many instances the results were the same. Additionally, just as the main purpose of the Allendista women's committee was to draw women into the UP coalition as opposed to empowering them as women, the process of political organizing and exposure in some cases served as the foundation to feminism in the post-Allende period.

A feminist analysis of Allende's answer to the woman question is not a straightforward one. His programs, while providing basic services of which women were in dire need, served to perpetuate patriarchal forms of control through the reification of traditional gender roles and sexist relationships. Indeed, among feminists Allende is infamous for his reiteration of woman as mother: "When I speak of women I always think of the wife/mother. When I speak of women I refer to their function within the nuclear family. Children are the prolongation of the woman who is essentially born to be a mother" (quoted in Chaney 1974, 269). These words could have just as easily come from a politician on the right. Right-wing women, however, were oblivious to the ideological similarities with respect to their positions as women across the political spectrum.[15] Indeed, right-wing women became some of Allende's most vocal critics. As Lois Oppenheim explains,

One of the most striking events took place in December [of 1971], when opposition women organized the first March of the Empty Pots and Pans. Well-to-do women, often accompanied by their maids, marched in downtown Santiago to protest the UP's economic policy, which, they complained, was creating a scarcity of food. Although they were far from without food, the government policy of increasing workers' salaries, coupled with its efforts to ensure that food reached grocery stores in popular neighborhoods, had, in fact, decreased the food supplied to the more well-to-do areas (1999, 64).

This march was the first in a series of mass mobilizations organized by women against the Allende government. Wearing their traditional roles of homemakers and mothers like battle fatigues, right-wing women took a leading role in catalyzing opposition to the Allende government.

Right-wing women, however, did not have the last word. Miriam Orteaga Araya, former member of the guerrilla organization MIR and current coordinator of the Ana Clara Center for the Training of Women (Ana Clara Centro de Capacitación para Mujeres), an organization focused on women as paid laborers, explained that, in her estimation, left-wing women were surprised and even confused by the March of the Empty Pots and Pans. "What definitely radicalized the participation of the women on the Left was the mobilization of the women of the Right; it was incredible," she noted. "The women of the right go to the streets to bang their pans, then the women of the Left are saying, 'What is happening with these women? What pans are they talking about, if we are the ones who are hungry?' So then the women got organized to go out and support the popular government." What this suggests is that despite the fact that the roles of and ideologies surrounding women during the Allende epoch were varied, femininity was a decisive factor both in the making of the policies and as the catalyst for opposing them.

This discussion brings the complicated relationships among democracy, revolution, and gender to the fore. What the above suggests is that a democratic revolution provides significant space for the incorporation of women. An electoral revolution gives revolutionaries the advantage of being able to focus all of their energies on the implementation of their agenda without the very time-consuming process of fighting a war and rebuilding the country in the aftermath. I would argue that there are two reasons that an electoral revolution is more compatible to the needs and incorporation of women than is an armed one. First, peaceful democratic structures are more inviting in the practical sense, as there is no risk of the brutal physical abuse like that which we saw in El Salvador. (Certainly this would make a democratic revolution more inviting to men as well.) For example, the most basic level of involvement in an electoral revolution is casting one's vote in support of the revolutionary candidate. In an armed movement, the equivalent show of support may be making food, or providing shelter, or sewing a uniform for the guerrillas. These latter types of activities, despite their seemingly benign nature, present significant risks to those performing them. Voting, however, is very quick and virtually risk free. If we assume that these revolutionary projects (electoral or armed) were likely the first political events or even public ventures from their homes in which many women participated, anything that would reduce the obstacles to their incorporation would have proved significant.

Second, an electoral revolution means that a healthy democratic governmental infrastructure already exists. If such a government is composed of institutions like the ministries of labor, education, health, the insertion of women's agendas could potentially only take one step rather than two. If and when an armed revolution is victorious, the ministries will not even exist, let alone include women focused projects. In the case of the Chilean revolution, the ministry of labor could have focused more on maternity leave and child care; the ministry of finance on small business credit for women; the ministry of education on policies directed toward young girls in primary school, and so on. We saw that the UP coalition did make limited efforts toward most of these and related programs. But establishing a Women's Secretariat to accomplish nearly all of this meant that women's issues were ghettoized and thus deprioritized, and that women like Soledad Parada, who worked there, were also forced to create an entirely new institution in addition to implementing a new agenda. This is not to suggest the Women's Secretariat was a mistake. Rather, I am suggesting that to assume it would be able to address all of women's practical needs was to very much underestimate and underutilize the democratic structures already in existence for the benefit of women. This also meant that the ability of women to contribute to the collective well-being of society, the implicit goal of socialism, was largely untapped, thus preventing the revolution in Chile to reach full fruition. Keeping all of this mind, how then might we assess the roles of women in the Chilean revolution as gendered revolutionary bridges?

CONCLUSIONS: CHILEAN WOMEN AS GENDERED REVOLUTIONARY BRIDGES

Through this brief discussion of Chilean history we have seen the political and ideological development of Allende's revolutionary Chile. We saw that Allende's programs for and by women were firmly rooted in traditional notions of femininity. What most of the above examples demonstrate is the utility of femininity as a revolutionary tool. In this concluding section I will argue that though women did play the role of gendered revolutionary bridges in Allende's Chile, they were significantly overlooked for their revolutionary importance.

As we have seen, Chile under Allende was a revolutionary experiment interrupted, and there was nothing clandestine nor violent about Allende's approach to politics; indeed, quite the opposite. Salvador Allende, a long time Marxist politician, believed in pure representative democracy.[16] In this context, then, there was presumably no need for women to act as gendered revolutionary bridges as they did in the case of wartime El Salvador (and as they did, we will see, in Cuba). Logistically speaking, there were no weapons for women to hide in their clothing; there was no need to deliver messages in covert ways; there was no need to shelter or disguise male leftists. However, looking a bit more closely at the Chilean revolutionary state, I would argue that there was a need for, and in fact some women did play the role of, gendered revolutionary bridges. Certainly clandestine struggles, as we saw in El Salvador, necessitate a more urgent and creative way of both disguising and framing opposition movements, and femininity was the perfect tool with which to accomplish just that. However, as the UP coalition was not trying to hide anything nor were they trying to recruit people in underground ways, the exploitation of femininity happened to a lesser degree than in El Salvador. That said, as is evidenced by the bloody coup, the UP coalition could have benefited significantly from greater popular support.

Allende's government, as we have seen, organized projects that were quite woman-friendly. Women benefited from his support of their children vis-à-vis his milk programs, day-care centers, and shopping programs, and his continued economic and political support of the Christian Democrat–initiated mothers' centers. For the most part Allende's programs offered state support for the traditional feminine roles of mother and wife with the goal of enabling their insertion into the labor market. From a socialist perspective, if class hierarchies are flattened, then all laborers will be on equal footing—women included. The socialist answer to the woman question, then, is to enable women to participate in the paid labor market so that they will be empowered in society and equal to men. The way that Allende attempted to facilitate this was through his support of the mothers' centers, shopping programs, and the like in order to free women's time and direct their energies toward paid labor. The end result was that Allende's revolutionary program was partially communicated through expanded ideas of maternity and matrimony. As a result, I am suggesting, women like Soledad Parada and Carmen Gloría Aguayo did act as gendered revolutionary bridges because their revolutionary tasks were very much centered on traditional notions of femininity, the woman's secretariat, the milk programs, mothers' centers, and so on—programs with implicitly revolutionary agendas. In this sense they served more as ideological bridges that worked to deliver socialist messages to housewives who had likely never thought about politics prior to the UP coalition's attention to their practical needs.

As I have discussed, the coalition was faced with ongoing challenges, both internal and external. Clearly, the more popular support there was, the higher the chances for success. If Allende and the predominantly male leadership were able to fully accept and support women as political subjects, it is arguable that women could have potentially repaired some of the damage the UP coalition both inherited and cultivated as a result of its radical program. For example, right-wing women played a fundamental role in mobilizing popular sectors against the UP coalition. As Miriam Orteaga Araya pointed out, however, from the perspective of leftist women, their mobilizations were not understood to be representative of all Chilean women. Similarly, Mireya Baltra noted that, in December 1971, "the massive demonstration of the fascist right [women] took to the streets with their marches. So we [the Allendista Women's Committee] talked to President Allende. . . . We could see . . . it was a confrontation that had to be stopped . . . so we discussed with him the need to let us [women] march the day the [right wing] women were going out, and President Allende persistently opposed us because he thought there might be some altercation. . . . We had a big argument, and obviously Allende's position was taken." In other words, leftist women were willing to take to the streets in support of Allende, but he prevented that from happening and perhaps closed the door to untapped alliances. Leftist women were volunteering to overpower the message of right-wing women and demonstrate to the public that in reality Allende's programs helped women and their families rather than hurt them. If the right-wing women's marches were exposed as not truly representative of Chilean women as they claimed, they may not have had as much power to catalyze an opposition movement against Allende. Leftist women had the political potential and desire to reduce the damage inflicted by right-wing women but were prevented from doing so by Allende and the UP coalition.

As we have seen, Allende's programs for women had a decidedly feminine exterior, virtually posing no threat to the patriarchal structures at either the micro or macro levels. As Allende and the UP coalition felt no need to expand their gendered programs beyond the nuclear family, the threat to right-wing women would be potentially softened if women on the Left also used their maternal and wifely demeanors to aggressively promote the coalition's programs. If this happened, left-wing women would have been able to demonstrate that, in the case of revolutionary Chile, socialism was in no way antithetical to motherhood and/or family. In short, were femininity strategically subverted, we may have seen an expanded support network for the UP coalition among both women and men.

When asked if she was satisfied with Allende's programs for women, Mireya, one of the few women of this period I interviewed who is still a militant leftist, put it this way:

> [I'm not] totally satisfied . . . there was not development at the theoretical level, those were our deficiencies (ours I mean the women) . . . [and] I take responsibility for that. There was not enough theoretical development in regards to solving the woman problem; it was reaction politics, political activism to support the government . . . to support its program. But we

were not discovering what it meant to be a woman in terms of social roles. That is, women in the sense of being more than reproductive beings, of having the freedom of choosing to be mothers, of having solved the debate over divorce, of having solved the abortion problem in a better way, of a thorough sex education. I am going to tell you in all sincerity [that] I think we had a traditional vision. . . . There was not a theoretical development that allowed us to analyze the feminine problematic that was inserted into this new kind of government that was doing all these great things.

We will never know what a long-term and stable revolutionary government in Chile would have meant for women, but from Alicia Basso's perspective she did feel satisfied: "I always say that I had the sensation that we tried to touch the sky with our hands. We had the feeling we were about to touch the sky but the storm came and we got all wet. But I want to say, I do not know if you understand the feeling that we had, but I do think we were satisfied."

CHAPTER 4

Dictatorship, Democracy, and Feminism in Post-Allende Chile, 1973–1999

Early on in the dictatorship we feminists were the ones that marched with our fists up in the air.

—Graciela Borquez, 1999

WHEN AUGUSTO PINOCHET violently seized control of Chile in 1973 he promptly turned to Chilean women to thank them for their help in orchestrating the coup d'état and saving Chile from the evils of communism. Apparently it did not occur to Pinochet that just as women were in part responsible for his rise to power, so too were they going to be leaders in the movement to dethrone him. Certainly it never occurred to Pinochet that his very personal and political style of controlling the nation would be an axis for women to unite to liberate their families, their nation, and—perhaps most strikingly—themselves as women. Pinochet embodied the patriarch in the country, which served as a catalyst to mobilize Chilean women en masse against an enemy that they were to eventually identify as saturating both their private and public lives.

In this chapter I will use the case of Chile to continue to answer the second part of the revolution question: What is the relationship between revolution and feminism? I will provide a brief overview of Pinochet's reign, with particular attention to the role of women in resisting his dictatorship. I will look at specific women's and feminist organizations and their strategies that were in large part responsible for removing him from power. I will then very briefly discuss the contemporary women's movement in Chile during the transition to democracy.[1] I will conclude this chapter by arguing that a revolutionary feminist movement was present in Pinochet's Chile and was largely the result of the experiences of women during the earlier partial revolution of the popular unity government.

On 11 September 1973 the political face of Chile and its citizens would be forever changed by a military coup d'état orchestrated by Army General

Augusto Pinochet. I asked all of the women I interviewed in 1999 how the dictatorship affected them personally. Alicia Basso, former leader of the Communist Party and member of Allende's presidential advisory group explained, "I changed; I am another person. The consequences are still felt; they are a permanent mark in time. . . . I am telling you, it is incredible. I think it is hard to describe. No one has ever asked me that question. I cannot sort out the feelings but I do think it is what we were saying: there was immense brutality that assaulted the very essence of life, of ideas, and of freedom."[2] As Viviana Díaz, then forty-six-year-old president of the Association of Relatives of the Detained and Disappeared (Agrupación de Familiares de Detenidos y Desaparecidos, or AFDD) explained,

> In our country, when the military coup took place on 11 September 1973, what happened was that all of those Chileans that were militants or sympathized with the popular government were transformed into enemies of the military regime and those enemies had to be destroyed. Destruction was carried out by executing them, detaining them, torturing them, and making them disappear. This method of forcefully disappearing people was aimed not only at eliminating the victim but also the family group that surrounded the person . . . the goal was to cause fear in the population. This is the reason why here on 11 September 1973 the dictatorship closed down the parliament, political parties were also closed down, the unions ended, and also the student organizations; everything, everything, everything.

Under the guise of a "state of war" and an around-the-clock curfew, the military launched a reign of terror against leftist activists, government officials, intellectuals (a particular thorn in Pinochet's side),[3] union leaders, and the poor, with mass arrests, beatings, torture, summary executions, and military sweeps in the *poblaciones* (shantytowns). The military took control of all forms of the media and used their power to broadcast calls demanding that specified individuals turn themselves in immediately to the new authorities. Santiago's two major soccer stadiums were converted into mass jails, torture and death chambers filled with prisoners, while the hospitals overflowed with the wounded and the morgues with bodies. The misery Pinochet imposed on Chileans was beyond extreme: more than six thousand people were buried in mass graves in the first year of the regime; at least seven thousand activists of the Popular Unity (Unidad Popular, or UP) coalition were herded into the national stadium; several dozen prominent Allendistas, including cabinet ministers, were sent to southern Chile's Dawson Island, which was transformed into a concentration camp; arrests, including the disappeared, were in the tens of thousands; by the middle of 1978 there were nearly thirty thousand Chileans in exile in Western Europe alone, and by the end of the decade the number was into the hundreds of thousands (Collier and Sater 1996, 360; Miller 1991, 2; Oppenheim 1999, 116; Spooner 1994, 54–56, and Wright and Oñate 1998, 12). The dictatorship disrupted the lives of women (and, of course, men) in profound ways. Many of the women I interviewed went into exile for varying amounts of time while some opted to stay in Chile. Either path—physically, socially, psychologically, and emotionally—destroyed the lives they had lived prior to the coup. Teresa Valdés, who had worked with the UP coalition and would eventually be a cofounder of one of the most signif-icant women's coalitions to organize against the dictatorship (to be discussed below), stayed in Chile. As she recalled in our 1999 interview,

> I did not want to go. I am very obstinate. It was unthinkable for me [to leave]; it was unthinkable, that is why I stayed. I stayed all those years here and that was the most brutal destruction, there are no words to describe what this meant for us. It was too horrible, it was so brutal, the destruc-tion of all of your relations, and the fear, and not being able to do any-thing, and knowing that you are exposing yourself and at the same time trying to do something. [It was] terrible; terrible. So they whipped us, they whipped us. Of course, we survived, we invented thousands of ways to survive.

The experiences that resulted in and from exile, though entirely different, were also traumatic. When I interviewed her in 1999, Carmen Lazo, long time Allendista and former congresswoman for the Socialist Party, explained,

> The military called for me, Maria Elena Carrera [Socialist Party senator during the UP administration], and Laura Allende [the first lady] to pre-sent ourselves at the Ministry of Defense. I was going to show up because I felt that since I did nothing wrong, I was just a congresswoman, nothing was going to happen to me. Of course, we did not know what a military dictatorship was like. It was a good thing my husband did not let me go. He said, "you do not show up anywhere!" This is the only reason why I did not go. After hiding like we were criminals for a number of days I got asylum at the Colombian embassy. Our house had been stolen by the cara-bineros [police]. They took the furniture. Upstairs we had a bookshelf filled with books and they took them. This was a small house and I have always read a lot and my husband does too. They also took boxes with pictures. A whole history was in there from the 1952 Allende campaign. They took all of this and destroyed it. I had a few pretty good paintings and those were taken too. We had to go around these small towns at night, hiding. We wore the same clothes for twenty days. We could not bathe or even wash our hands. We hid in the compañeros' houses until we got asylum in the Colombian embassy. We ended up in Colombia and after a year there

we went to Venezuela. We stayed in Venezuela for thirteen years. . . . When we came back, Pinochet had given our house to someone in the military, an officer.

Related to this, Alicia Basso emphasized the depth and permanency of the scars:

> Then came exile, and we were uprooted with all the consequences that that had, the losses. It is feelings of permanent and constant loss, loss of everything. Loss of friends, the loss of the personal and political project. These are very personal losses. I lost a daughter. I gave birth to a daughter while I was in exile and she died. What did I lose? The uprooting of my family and my parents. And then the returning to the country when you go though a whole process of readaptation. The country I came back to was a country under a dictatorship and I also suffered losses. I continued to lose people I loved. Personally, as a survivor, and many people of my generation are survivors, I believe that it has meant a profound change and it continues even today.

Indeed, it carries on today, in, at the very least, symbolic ways. From the window in Alicia and Soledad's office where I interviewed them together one can see the street sign declaring the victory of the coup, Avenida 11 de Septiembre (Avenue of 11 September).

Pinochet received support from disparate sectors including Christian Democrats (who later withdrew their support), the Catholic Church (which also eventually became critical of his tactics), and Chilean and North American technocrats trained at the University of Chicago School of Economics. Their program entailed cutting public spending, a devaluation of the peso, privatization of the economy, and a reduction in import duties. Paulina Weber, cofounder of the feminist collective Movement for the Emancipation of Women '83 (Movimiento Pro-Emancipación de la Mujer '83, or MEMCH '83, which will be discussed below), recalled in our 1999 interview the human cost of Pinochet's economic agenda:

> Everything was privatized during the dictatorship. Before that, Chile was a fairly advanced country. It had a good public health system that was free. Chile had a free educational system and public education had a long tradition here. The university was free. You had to pay an enrollment fee, but other than that it had no cost. People who otherwise would have not been able to pay had access to higher education; it was much more democratic in that sense. During the dictatorship even the cemeteries were privatized.

Foreign companies eventually controlled the economy, and Pinochet revamped the constitution in 1980 allowing him to appoint one-third of the new senate and himself as a senator for life.[4] In an attempt to appease the international community while prolonging his hold on power, Pinochet's constitution called for a plebiscite, scheduled for 1988, that he hoped would secure his power for a second term through 1997. Much to Pinochet's chagrin, the population mobilized en masse and derailed his agenda. On 5 October 1988 Chileans went to the polls and rejected Pinochet—55 percent voted against him and 44 percent for him. Among women voters, despite the fact that polls predicted the majority would vote for Pinochet, 52.5 percent voted against him (Baldez 2002, 174; Oppenheim 1999, 182). Begrudgingly, Pinochet stepped down and in December of 1989 the first elections to follow the dictatorship occurred. Patricio Aylwin, a Christian Democrat with solid support from the Left, including the Communists who were prevented from running, was victorious and in 1990 assumed a presidency plagued with insurmountable problems. Pinochet presided over the military, which created a dual government. The new administration's initial tasks included addressing Pinochet's constitution, as well as the economic and social policies he had set in place that were aimed at foreign investors and their local allies rather than the Chilean working and middle classes. In the rest of this chapter I will address the roles of women in ushering in the transition to democracy and how they transformed their movement into one of revolutionary feminism.

THE MOBILIZATION OF CHILEAN WOMEN

Much has been written documenting the significant role of women in the resistance against Pinochet with the simultaneous emergence of feminism.[5] I don't intend for this to be an exhaustive discussion of women's resistance and feminism in the Pinochet era,[6] but a sampling with which to provide some insight into the relationship between revolution and feminism in the case of Chile. Specifically, I will look at the Association of Relatives of the Detained and Disappeared (Agrupación de Familiares de Detenido y Desaparecido, or AFDD), the Movement for the Emancipation of Women '83 (Movimiento Pro Emancipación de la Mujer '83, or MEMCH '83), and Women for Life (Mujeres por la Vida).

Women as Human Rights Activists

Among activists, unanimity in ideology, strategy, and interpretation is uncommon. Additionally, history as recalled through oral testimony also tends to produce varied narratives. However, while in Chile I posed the same question to every one of the twenty-three women I interviewed: What role did women play in the resistance movement against Pinochet? All of the women were in agreement about one thing: women were the first to take to the streets to oppose the Pinochet dictatorship. As Paulina Weber explained,

Women were the first to organize in Chile and they organized at first around [human rights violations]. They got organized out of necessity. A huge political persecution started taking place and husbands, sons, family men, started being jailed. Women [were] also, but at the beginning it was the men that were massively taken to the stadiums, to the jailing places and women started feeling terrorized from going to visit them in the jails. This generated the first human rights groups whose membership was fundamentally women; they were relatives of the victims of repression that got together in thousands of little groups like the women who would accompany each other to the visits to the jails. Through this, the embryo of the first [anti-Pinochet] organization emerged in Chile.

As Jo Fisher notes, it was the "public invisibility" of women in the era of Allende and the UP coalition that gave them the political space and opportunity to initiate the networks of resistance that would prove pivotal in bringing down Pinochet (1993, 25). In other words, as we saw in chapter 3, the main contributions of women during the Allende presidency were their activities in the mothers' centers and neighborhood organizations. Even if the mothers' centers were more public than their own homes, the women remained largely behind the scenes and were thus perceived to be apolitical. It was this political invisibility that meant that women were more easily able to enter the public realm of politics, very much taking the military by surprise. By July 1975 the AFDD was established. Like their counterparts in Argentina and Central America, these women often met repeatedly in line at police stations, detention centers, or government offices, trying desperately and determinedly to ascertain the whereabouts of their disappeared husbands, fathers, brothers, and/or sons.[7] There were female political prisoners as well, but the majority were men.[8] Many of the women in the AFDD were of humble origins. For example, their president was only able to attend the university as a result of Salvador Allende's policy of socialized education; indeed, the coup prematurely ended her postsecondary schooling. Some of these women had their practical needs met by the UP government and watched as their lives were turned upside down, their families torn apart, and their country's long history of democracy violently destroyed.

While in Chile in 1999 I interviewed Viviana Díaz, president of the AFDD.[9] Viviana's father, an Allendista, was disappeared after the coup, and she has been involved with the AFDD ever since. She explained how the AFDD initially began taking to the streets:

> [We eventually] conquer[ed our] fear to go out in the streets. We started to use the pictures because we were told that the people we were looking for were fabricated family members, so we had to show people these were

the people who we were looking for, and tell us where they are, because if they have gone clandestine, well then locate them and tell us; here they are. They were never able to do this and that is how we started to go out in the street; we were the first organization that conquered the fear of going out in the street and having small, simple demonstrations; like we would sit on the park on the side of the *moneda* [presidential] palace. . . . That is where we started to go and sit and we would have small signs that said, "Where is my father?" "Where is my son?"

As a result of women taking serious risks they were able to mobilize other communities and foster solidarity in a climate that was less than inviting to public dissent. According to Viviana,

In May of 1978 as a response to the amnesty law, enacted in that April, we went on an indefinite hunger strike . . . at the church and in an international precinct. That hunger strike started to cause a great impact through the Christian communities and it was transmitted throughout the priests and the nuns and it would go to the grassroots communities and solidarity started emerging from the mothers' centers, the unemployed pockets. It was in this way that after being at ground zero we started again to form organizations.

As we saw in the case of El Salvador, though these efforts were enshrined in femininity and initially were somewhat safer for women, members of the AFDD were indeed mobilizing in direct opposition to a military dictatorship. In this context, "more safe" certainly did not imply risk free. Viviana explains:

While we were on the street we would always get beat up and detained. On one occasion I almost lost my sight because the fire truck chased us and it locked us into a street and it sprayed water at me from less than two meters away and for that reason this part of my face ended up all swollen. I was hospitalized at the central hospital and I spent one month with my eyes bandaged . . . I looked like a monster. There are pictures that I look at today and I think how horrible I looked. My face was all black and I would say "someday I will recover my face" because I was transformed. We suffered a lot of things.[10]

Similarly, two of the cofounders of Mujeres por la Vida noted their experience with recourse from the military government. Teresa Valdés casually explained that she had been arrested twelve times, and had been at the police station on countless occasions. Fanny Pollarolo, Socialist Party deputy and cofounder of the Mujeres, as they are known, used the same matter-of-fact tone to explain that she too had been jailed many times: "I was detained for short periods of time during the protests. I would be detained for five days, three days. On two occasions I was in jail awaiting trial but they were not for long periods of time—three, four months. On one occasion I was detained in the south" (personal interview, 1999). (During the dictatorship, the south of Chile was infamous for its brutal detention centers). All of the women I interviewed, these three included, spoke rather casually about their experiences with detention. Through this they conveyed, among other things, that despite the gravity of the risks with which they were faced, remaining quiescent about the repression was simply not an option. The AFDD played an important role in the anti-Pinochet movement through its ability to lessen the fears of those supportive of but uncomfortable with the idea of participating in the protests. As a result of all of this the women of the AFDD are typically identified as responsible for catalyzing the movement against Pinochet. And indeed, though their actions were entirely unmotivated by, disconnected from, and at times in opposition to feminism, they would eventually help to inspire feminists to take to the streets.

Feminists against Pinochet

The mid-1980s were seen as the most vibrant period of feminist mobilization in Chile. All of the women I interviewed identified 1983 as the specific year when a feminist movement forcefully appeared on the horizon. This is largely due to the fact that in 1983 the Movement for the Emancipation of Women '83 (MEMCH '83) emerged as a leading women's umbrella organization that framed its actions in explicitly feminist terms. The organizers of MEMCH '83 took its name from MEMCH, a women's organization of the 1930s that had demanded women's suffrage. The founders borrowed the name from their predecessors to emphasize that feminism was indigenous to Chile rather than a European import (Baldez 2002, 164). MEMCH '83 played a leading role in coordinating the activities of women's organizations. At the time that MEMCH '83 was formed the women's organizations were structured around three central tenets: the human rights sector, self-help organizations, and feminist groups. These sectors were represented by three separate federations: the Committee for the Defense of Women's Rights (Comité de Defensa de los Derechos de la Mujer, or CODEM), Women of Chile (Mujeres de Chile), and the Movement of Shantytown Women (Movimiento de Mujeres Pobladores, or MOMUPO (Baldez 2002, 149). The first two were from left-wing parties, with the central focus being the end of the dictatorship. Though focused on women, both initially declined to identify as feminist organizations, though the CODEM eventually changed its position. The MOMUPO worked with pobladoras from the northern part of Santiago and were initially concerned with devising economic survival strategies (Valdés and Weinstein 1993). All three emerged as grassroots organizations that worked to unite and coordinate the activities of smaller neighborhood groups

(Chuchryk 1994; Frohmann and Valdés 1995). The focus on neighborhood organizations was more politically significant than might be assumed. Because the dictatorship forced political parties underground, political activities moved from the national/formal sphere to the very local, community level. Here the presence of women was particularly noticeable as their assigned roles as nurturers positioned them to collectively organize soup kitchens and the like (Mattear 1997, 86). The absence of male-controlled political parties meant that this new and highly untraditional locale for doing politics was women-centered and -dominated.

Paulina Weber, an activist who worked with MEMCH '83 from abroad, joined immediately upon return from exile in Germany, and became codirector of MEMCH's later incarnation, the Casa de La Mujer del MEMCH. Paulina explained, "When MEMCH ['83] was founded, over forty organizations and people [were involved] and it was then that a group of Chilean women in exile joined MEMCH. We were like MEMCH in exile. From Germany and other countries they also joined MEMCH. We started to do fundraising to support this organization that we wanted to see succeed." Paulina explained that MEMCH '83 was based on three principles: "the struggle for democracy, protection of women's rights, and solidarity." MEMCH '83 also served as the coalition for the women's organizations who stood in opposition to the Pinochet regime. In 1985, MEMCH '83 composed a document they called the "Principles and Revindications that Constitute the Chilean Women's Platform." They called for the restoration of democracy, and asked that women's demands be taken up by political parties as issues of national importance. The document explicitly linked women's subordination to social, economic, and political conditions, and suggested that women's participation was fundamental to the democratization process. The platform was divided into ten sections, touching on all aspects of women's lives: legal, political, labor, health, education, housing, family life, sexuality, international peace, and social problems like prostitution (Gaviola, Largo, and Palestro 1994, 238–43). The text of the document provides great detail, reflecting the complexity of feminism for Chilean women during this highly politicized time. Indeed, Paulina's definition of feminism very much echoes this holistic/pluralistic approach; she sees it as "an ideology that includes the cultural, [and] the political, absolutely. [It is] a proposal for social change that goes through changing the roles, rethinking everything; what is the role of women, and what is the role of men in society, and in the family, in the culture, inside of everything. It is a lot more profound than [simply] try[ing] to make some improvements for women in society."

It was not just feminist discourse that reflected the creative spirit of the movement's leaders but their actions as well. Paulina, as did nearly all of women I interviewed, recalled with pride the creativity and symbolism with which the demonstrations were imbued. International Women's Day (8

March) is a very significant day to feminists in Latin America. Indeed, it tends to be the benchmark by which to measure the presence or absence of feminism.[11] As with all events that feminists organized at this time, femininity was used as an analytic tool to identify the problem (the dictatorship as patriarchy) and to demonstrate against it. Paulina explained,

> March eighth had its fights, at that time it was not with the carabineros but with the military, with tanks. They would go out on the streets with camouflaged outfits and painted faces, very threatening, with heavy bullets, with the machine guns, and we women would also go out on the street. We would participate in the protests and we did a lot of things. MEMCH ['83] was a very powerful group during that time; it was the first to organize these things. During the time of the dictatorship women … did incredible things; we effectively used the patriarchal concept, this *machista* concept about women, we used it as a way to destabilize the dictatorship. We would yell at the military during the protests, [that] … they were not men enough: "How could you hit a woman?" These are the strong men of Chile.

The demonstrations that the women organized were often only a few minutes long. Despite this objective restriction, the women used other tools at their disposal, those with which the military was ill-equipped to handle. As Paulina suggests above, feminists appropriated the ideology that women and mothers enjoy a sacred position in society. They did this to imply that men who physically and psychologically violated that status of women were by extension disrupting their own sense of masculinity, as its social power was fully contingent on the position of women. The moral superiority of women gave further credibility to the statements and demands of the women. We saw this similar pattern in El Salvador with the Committee of the Mothers of the Disappeared (Comité de Madres y Familiares de Presos, Desaparecidos y Asesinados de El Salvador) and we will see it again in the case of Cuba. Furthermore, the women conveyed a moral imperative that others speak out against the dictatorship. As Paulina explained, "What we accomplished with these things [demonstrations] was to shed the fear . . . since there was this patriarchal notion . . . that if women dared to do it [protest] others had to do something. . . . There was a sort of demonstration effect that we would go out on the streets and then fairly quickly the students would organize a mobilization, the workers, that was kind of what happened." In other words, women's presence in the anti-Pinochet movement relayed a message to other sectors that it was time to mobilize as well. Paulina explained that as a result of these demonstrations, "MEMCH ['83], from that time to the present, has served as a bridge between feminists and the poorest women," as the poorer women tended to hold their primary alliances to leftist parties. Thus, MEMCH '83 played the very central role of navigating between the Left and the feminists as these two political sectors tended to clash rather than reinforce one another:

> There was a contradiction during this time . . . between being a party activist and being a feminist. If you were a party member there was . . . a false contradiction, because it was assumed that you could not be a feminist and a party activist; feminism was not [considered] political. Feminism was [seen as] a way to divert people's attention to things that were not important. [On the other hand] from the feminists there was a harsh critique of women who were political because they would say that they were being objectified by the political parties. . . . Most of us that were in MEMCH ['83] came from politics; some of us were militants and others had stopped, but in the MEMCH ['83] you started to see . . . an integration of the two concepts of political parties and feminism.

This imposed tension led women to articulate their position in this (and other) struggle(s) as *doble militantes* (double militants), as active in both leftist party politics and grassroots feminist organizations. Perhaps the most influential analysis of the relationship between the Left and feminism was offered by Julieta Kirkwood (1986), who is seen as the leader of feminist theory in Chile.

Another women's organization central to the movement against Pinochet was Women for Life (Mujeres por la Vida, or the Mujeres)—a pluralistic coalition of women's and feminist organizations that spanned the political spectrum from the Movement for the Revolutionary Left (Movimiento de Izquierda Revolucionario, or MIR) to the Christian Democrats. It was established in December 1983, six months after the birth of the MEMCH '83. As cofounder Teresa Valdés recalled, "Without the MEMCH ['83] it would not have been possible to do anything because the MEMCH ['83] was, at that time, the coordinator of a number of organizations. It was [the group's] voice that allowed for making this kind of gathering. . . . What we did in Santiago was used as a model and it was copied in [other] regions . . . but [we had] nothing resembling [formal] structures, never." The gathering that Teresa spoke of was a huge meeting of ten thousand women from which the Mujeres emerged. Paulina Weber described it as the first public act of women against the Pinochet regime. "There was a memorable event in 1983," she recalled. "For the first time a women's public act filled a huge theater—the Caupolicán Theater, where the circus performs—and there were thousands and thousands of women. This was the first women's large public event, and this gathering was for life, to protect life, women in the defense of life, which was terribly threatened by the dictatorship. All of the people that participated in organizing this event made up the group Mujeres por la Vida."

While in Chile in 1999 I interviewed (separately) the three cofounders of the Mujeres, Teresa Valdés, Fanny Pollarolo, and Graciela (Chela) Borquez. Teresa is a longtime member of the Movement for United Popular Action (Movimiento de Acción Popular Unitaria, or MAPU); Fanny, originally with the Communist Party, is now an elected deputy for the Socialist Party, and Chela is a leader in the Christian Democrat Party. On the one end were the Christian Democrats, who were vehemently anti-Allende, and in some cases, at least initially, were in favor of the coup. On the other extreme was the MIR who, even prior to the coup, felt that armed struggle was the only way to guarantee an egalitarian society. That is, for the members of the MIR the strategies of the UP coalition were not militant enough. The significance of this political pluralism embodied by the Mujeres cannot be overstated. An organizational tactic such as this very much implied that the way women do politics is quite distinct from the practices of men. That is, while men were still fighting with each other along partisan lines, the women were overcoming such sectarianism to collectively organize for a common goal. The logic here was that in the male dominated parties internal struggles for power trumped the main goal of ousting the dictatorship. The women, on the other hand, did not lose sight of their goal of returning democracy to their country. If the internal battles did exist for women the coalition would never have formed in the first place. The women of the MIR and the Christian Democrats were as opposite on the feminist political spectrum as was possible, but the women party members, while not dropping their party affiliations, put them on the back burner so as not to sidetrack the movement from its most urgent goals. Lisa Baldez argues that the strategy of the Mujeres was quite deliberate. That is, it was not simply that women do politics in a less partisan manner but that the Mujeres wanted to project an image of women as nonpartisan (and therefore apolitical). According to Baldez, they did this in order to mobilize even more people (2002, 154).

The members of the Mujeres por la Vida did not surrender their longtime allegiances to their parties, but they did emphasize their points of unity as opposed to disjuncture. As Chela explained,

> The truth of the matter is that we got a lot of things started and men copied what we were doing. For example, for the first Caupolicán [event] I was telling you we did more of an artistic event and it was hard to come to an agreement of what we were doing. Some said that one woman from each party should speak. At the time the Socialist Party was divided in many smaller parties, it was not a joint Socialist Party. It was about ten or twelve different parties. There was the MAPU, the Christian Left, etcetera. So I told them, "You are crazy! If we are going to the theater to listen to speeches we are never going to finish. We are all, for the first time, doing something together, we are one." So we came to an agreement that only one should speak from each side. Then we came to the conclusion that we were acting together at this point but there were things we did not agree on. We decided to make a list of the things that separated us. It was

horrible. There were thousands of things that separated us. So we agreed that what brought us together was that we were against the dictatorship and that was it. So, this was what we needed to talk about. Then we thought, 'Why should one person speak?' We started to think and we decided to create an artistic script instead of all the speeches. Instead of speeches we had songs. . . . What resulted from all this was an artistic performance that had the [antidictatorship] message in the performance.

Pluralism and unity were not only evident in the style in which the organizers articulated their message, but also how they displayed it visually. The epitome of political sectarianism is a party's flag. Teresa explained how the organizers mediated that inevitable conflict:

There would be Christian Democrats and even [members of the] MIR—something so absolutely incredible that in the Caupolicán [theater] it was projected through an area that had all of the [party's] flags including the MIR's . . . because this [was] a space of political negotiation. . . . So Mujeres por la Vida would put together the political and the social; the women were there as individuals and at the same time they were members of the party. . . . It was really a small group, because we were not more than fifteen that had the ability to go into larger sectors.

The significance here is twofold. First, the presence of the flags reflects the stance of Mujeres that it was not necessary to abandon one's political party to join with other women in denouncing the dictatorship. Second, having a centralized location for the flags guaranteed that no single party was projected as more or less important than the others.

Related to this, Teresa explained that the variety of political trajectories embodied by Mujeres served to enrich their approach to organizing rather than homogenize it. She noted, "Mujeres por la Vida is a strange mixture that involves politics, human rights, and feminism. . . . We moved from the beginning of having a clear number of trajectories, different positions, to something more articulated, more common and shared, in the political vision but also in the human rights vision and the feminist vision. It was not homogenous but we had clear, common perceptions about certain subjects and for this reason our options were always unitary; I mean, let us do all that we can do together." Teresa further emphasized the pluralism within Mujeres when she recalled the political span of party members who made up the organization. She did not suggest that the coalition was smooth, yet it did endure, to a certain degree, even through the contemporary period.[12]

The Plebiscite

The end goal of women's mobilization during the dictatorship was, as we have seen, the ousting of Pinochet and the return of democracy. From the perspective of the feminists, democracy includes and represents women. The first step in returning democracy to Chile was defeating Pinochet in the plebiscite. The plebiscite was established by Pinochet in his 1980 constitution with the expectation that he would eventually be elected as president. This tactic, as we know, backfired. Though the task of defeating Pinochet was an onerous one, the opposition successfully waged it, with women again playing a leading role. The first campaign of those at the center and the Left was to get people to register to vote. The second was to create legal parties, two tasks in which women were quite active. Despite the fact that Pinochet had created disincentives for the poor to register to vote, by the end of the first year 3,300,000 people had registered—about half of the eligible voters. Members that had been in the UP coalition formed a new party, the Party for Democracy (Partido por la Democracía, or PPD), headed by Socialist Party member Ricardo Lagos.[13] By early 1988 the various committees who organized the antiplebiscite campaign (known as the "No campaign") formed a coalition called the *Concertación por el No* (Oppenheim 1999, 180–82). They carried out a well-organized campaign and received international support. Six million Chileans went to the polls on 5 October 1988, with the significant majority declaring their opposition to Pinochet.

Women not only participated in the No campaign in 1988, but also worked to carry their agenda and demands to the national political arena. In July of 1988, twenty-two feminist groups and eleven well-known individuals took out a full-page paid advertisement in *La Epoca*, a major daily newspaper in Santiago. In it they called upon all Chilean women to participate in the rebuilding of democracy based on equality between women and men (Chuchryk 1994, 84–85). The four basic demands outlined in the ad were: the immediate ratification of the United Nations Convention on the Elimination of all forms of Discrimination against Women, the creation of a national government office with ministerial rank that deals with women's issues, the elimination of the reproduction of sexism and inequality in the educational system, and a requirement that 30 percent of all government decision making positions be held by women. For feminists, publicizing the No campaign was inseparable from also saying no to sexism and patriarchal authoritarianism as embodied in micro- and macrostructures in Chilean society; the Mujeres were integral to the campaign. "We had to do something so that people knew that they had to vote no," Chela explained in our inteview. "So we started to throw out ideas until we got one that became known worldwide, and then many copied us, it was good: black silhouetted images of a person that said: 'So that you do not forget me,' [or] 'Have you forgotten me?' And we wrote the name of a persecuted person. We made one or two thousand . . . we filled downtown Santiago with the figures." The silhouettes lined the streets, urging Chileans to cast their no votes on behalf of the disappeared, who would not have the opportunity to do so. In addition to the black silhouettes, the image of clean hands was also important to the women's resistance campaign against the dictatorship. Paulina explained,

> We made resistance visible. . . . There was a terrible massacre during Corpus Christi. They simultaneously killed fifteen people in different places in Santiago during one night in Holy Week. We had a very quick response. We went out that day and we bought red dye. We found that the fountains in Santiago . . . recirculated the water. So, we wrote the names of all the people that had been murdered on pieces of paper and stood around the fountains. As each name was read we would put a bag of red dye in the water. We did things like this. . . . The carabineros showed up pretty quickly but because they had white gloves on they did not dare put their hands in the water because by then the water was red. They had to go find the maintenance people. The water in the fountains was red all day because they took a long time to do anything. This got into the papers. We managed in one way or another to call attention to what was going on in Chile . . . not just within Chile, but we also called attention outside of Chile.[14]

In short, women used their public visibility and respect earned as a result of actions such as these to encourage people to register to vote in order to declare their opposition to Pinochet. Through this, they helped to rebuild the political parties, but, as Teresa Valdés explained, once democracy was reinstated they were largely unacknowledged and uncompensated for their efforts:

> [W]omen rebuilt the political parties; . . . it was women that rebuilt them. It is the same story as always. In Brazil it was the same thing. When you read the stories of all these countries at times of repression it was women who put together and built the organizations. When repression ends the men come back from exile . . . [they] get off the plane, and end up with a position in the party's leadership. This does not matter because we are still here. Patriarchy is going to take a lot to change but we cannot say that we have not moved forward, we cannot complain, we have accomplished some things. Women's contributions are decisive.

FEMINISM AND THE TRANSITION TO DEMOCRACY

In this study of Chile I am primarily interested in the relationship between the revolutionary period of Salvador Allende and the immediate postrevolutionary period of Augusto Pinochet. Here I will comment only briefly about the women's movement in posttransition democratic Chile.[15] The generally accepted argument is that women's movements tend to demobilize during transitions to democracy (Craske 1999; Friedman 1998; Waylen 1994).[16] The case of Chile, however, complicates this pattern a bit: the women's movement has certainly lost the grassroots unity and energy that was so characteristic of it during the dictatorship, as confirmed by my discussion with leaders of contemporary feminist organizations, but it has, at the same time, refocused its attention, discourse, and strategy to adjust to this very different period (Franceschet 2003).

The No campaign was triumphant, in large part due to the efforts of Chilean women of all classes, sectors, and parties uniting against one common enemy, Pinochet, the ultimate patriarch. But were women's efforts even acknowledged, let alone, rewarded? Alicia Frohmann and Teresa Valdés suggest that the greatest achievement of women in the campaign for democracy is the fact that the Concertación's presidential candidate—Patricio Aylwin—made the women's demand for "[d]emocracy in the country and in the home" his own (1995). Paulina Weber noted, however, that women were largely absent from any of the real discussions regarding the new democracy: "Even though we had argued that we were being left out, out of that democracy, the same thing happened," she commented. "Evidently we were not at the negotiating table during the period of transition and all of the political decisions were made without women being present." In other words, the transition to democracy and its official male politicos did not adequately account for women and their contributions to this victory. What this suggests, according to Marjorie Agosín, is that the subordination of women is merely being prolonged through a reinstitution of democracy which does not reexamine patriarchy and its social structures that separate the public and private spheres thus excluding women from politics (1996, 84).

Nearly all of the women I interviewed in 1999 maintained that there was no women's movement in contemporary Chile, but rather a cross-section of different organizations. For example, Eugenia Hola, a sixty-two-year-old researcher with the Women's Studies Circle (Círculo de Estudios de la Mujer) and with a long history with the Left and feminism said,

> Well, the first thing that I want to tell you is that a movement in that sense does not exist in a strict sense. No, women in a movement, it does not exist. What does exist is something that answers to what society is living today, that is to say, the fragmentation of civil society into small nuclei that operate in regards to their own interests and face conflict with other interests and as a product of that conflict they appear as active forces or as pressure groups in regards to certain issues. That is what is happening today with women. Now, the difference with other pressure groups is that women have had little expression of their demands to the state.

María Elena Acuña, a twenty-nine-year-old graduate student and member of the newest feminist collective Under Suspicion (Bajo Sospecha) described the women's movement from a different perspective, yet in a very similar manner:

Well, I believe that there is not a women's movement in Chile—that is my personal view. I believe that what we call the feminist movement falls into a very fragmented thing that is composed of a diversity of voices, a diversity of issues. It seems to me that there is little will within the official voices to admit that there are different voices, that the issue of equality is not for all of us about equal pay and it is not for all of us about equality in the quotas for the access of power. Instead, equality is something deeper that of course has to do with structural things, but is also an everyday process. So that the everyday version of equality is what is not being integrated and I believe that there is a sector that gives itself the voice of the women's movement and the voice of the feminist movement in Chile, that are those that I call official ones, the ones that are public ... here they are called the *historicas* [historical feminists]. . . . Honestly, they believe that on the 8 March celebration, when three thousand women show up to march, that that is the feminist movement.[17]

Though María Elena would certainly consider Chela to be an historica, Chela sees the contemporary women's movement much the same way—splintered and demoralized, like the majority of the opposition in this current political juncture. She commented that the women's movement was "not united; [it is] very absorbed by the political parties. We have to also start with the fact that in general social movements in Chile are very depressed ... people are demoralized, they have become disillusioned by the democracy that we have established with or without reason." According to Ann Matear (1997), the reasons for these divisions are multifaceted. They are in part due to the fact that women are a heterogeneous sector with disparate goals. She also notes that the class splits and mutual distrust between popular (working-class) feminists and middle-class feminists have been exacerbated as the common dictatorial enemy has been toppled and the need for unity less urgent.[18] Coti Silva, a sixty-two-year-old former leader of the MOMUPO and later director of the Santiago office of the Violence Prevention Program of the National Women's Service (Servicio Nacional de la Mujer, or SERNAM) offered this analysis when I interviewed her in 1999:

I believe that it was very nice to mutually discover each other during [the dictatorship] but I feel that it ended after we returned to democracy, each one went back to their places. I believe that necessity was what made us get together more, the truth is that we needed each other; the professional women, the intellectuals needed us, and we needed them. . . . I believe the chance for solidarity emerged; it was a necessary alliance. I know that it continues to be necessary and there are still some that do it that way, but it has been hard to reestablish, interests are different, other interests have emerged, but the women of the proletariat were again left alone.

Matear also suggests that women *as a sector* have no real leverage, as they have nothing to hold against the government if their demands are not met; this is in contrast to workers, for example, who can go on strike. All of this, Matear posits, has led to a highly institutional and even elitist women's movement (1997, 84–100).

This sense of powerlessness is ironic, since on 3 January 1991, in response to the demands of the women's movement as articulated before the election of Patricio Aylwin, SERNAM was created. Theoretically, SERNAM was an attempt to adopt a coherent and articulate approach toward policy making in order to address gender inequity, through employment, legislation, education, housing, and health care. The goal was to create long-term social change in both attitudes and behavior. SERNAM is comprised of approximately three hundred women that were active in the women's movement during the dictatorship. It has non-ministerial status (not what was originally demanded by the women's movement) and thus cannot implement its own policies but simply make recommendations. Because of this (and other factors) SERNAM, as of yet, has had only limited success. Additionally, its successes tend to be in the short rather than the long term. SERNAM has made some inroads into preventing violence against women, providing access to child care, affirmative action, and attention to female heads of household, but Chilean society remains irrefutably marked by gendered inequities, which a non-ministerial body is far too limited in challenging (Matear 1997, 93; Waylen 1996, 109–14). When I inteviewed her in 1999, Carmen Andrade, a forty-four-year-old member of the Socialist Party and coordinator of SERNAM's program for women as heads of households, described SERNAM and its limited power:

> SERNAM is an entity that emerged with [the transition to] democracy, expresses[ing] a response to the women's movement . . . [which] had stated that it was necessary to push for changes between men and women, that there is a need for an institution that takes care of this, that formulates policies, consults with the executive branch so that those policies happen, to formulate proposals for changes in laws. This is what it was created for. . . . It has concentrated on proposing legal reforms and concrete policies for . . . women in general. It is a small institution and I personally believe still has little weight in the state institutions and few resources. As a result, its actions are also restricted.

In all of my interviews, the issue of SERNAM was inevitably raised. For the *historicas* there was almost a love-hate relationship with SERNAM. That is, most women felt empowered and rewarded that their efforts in bringing down the dictatorship had been recognized by the state through this body, but most resented its nonministerial status and its unfeminist and class-blind analyses, as well as the fact that the heads of SERNAM had come from political parties rather than the grassroots feminist movement. In other words, the women with whom I spoke were frustrated by the unused potential of this hard earned resource.

On the other hand, as a result of interviews with feminists in Chile, Susan Franceschet argues that institutionalization is not in and of itself the problem. She suggests that SERNAM has provided an axis for the women's movement with respect to discourse and resources. She argues, that despite the fact that the women's movement in Chile is indeed fragmented and heterogeneous, and SERNAM is fraught with problems: "SERNAM's existence contributes to the strengthening of the movement in a number of ways." She continues: "a crucial resource that SERNAM provides the women's movement is a discourse of women's rights that organizations can employ to mobilize is members" (2003, 27–28). Franceschet concludes that though the women's movement is quite fractured and even restricted, it must be analyzed within the current neoliberal, posttransition context rather than the highly charged period that necessitated unity among women. Related to this, and something often left out of the discussion of feminism in posttransition Chile is the current status of democracy in Chile. Officially the transition to democracy is complete in Chile. That is, democracy has returned. However, if we compare contemporary democracy to that which preceded the dictatorship, it is arguable that democracy does not exist in Chile, or that if it does it exists with significant restrictions. If nothing else, the constitution that is the foundation of the current Chilean government was written by Pinochet. Needless to say, a constitution written by a dictator is anything but a document reflective of democracy. If Chilean democracy is not held to the same standards as that which preceded it, then why should feminism? In other words, if the current political structure is considered to be democratic, then the current women's movements should also be considered feminist. Or—and perhaps more accurately—if feminism only exists in Chile in a limited sense, then so too does democracy. What, then, does all of this imply for revolutionary feminism in the period immediately following the demise of the UP coalition?

REVOLUTIONARY FEMINISM: THE CASE OF CHILE

As the previous section suggests, a vibrant and unified feminist movement is absent in post-Pinochet Chile. That said, the period upon which this study focuses is the one immediately following the revolutionary period of Salvador Allende's government. In the postrevolutionary period of the Pinochet dictatorship, revolutionary feminism was indeed present.[19] As we may recall, a revolutionary feminist movement is one in which at least the leaders, if not the grassroots members, gained their political consciousness as a result of their experiences in a revolutionary process that preceded the emergence of feminism in their nation. The revolutionary feminist agenda is one that seeks to challenge sexism in addition to the larger political structures entirely bound to the oppression of women. In the case of Chile, that larger structure was the dictatorship inseparably linked to—and representative of—patriarchy. Though the structure of the Allende government was also patriarchal, significant differences exist from the patriarchy engendered by Pinochet. First of all, in the case of Pinochet's Chile, patriarchy was engendered through violence as well as ideology. Because of this it was much more explicit and identifiable. Additionally, Pinochet as patriarch was entirely inseparable from the lack of democracy in Chile. And as we saw, the feminists extended that logic to the lack of democracy in their own homes and personal lives. Under Allende, women's voices and roles, though very much situated in a patriarchal division of labor, were not violently nor always consciously silenced. The patriarchy embodied by Pinochet did however inspire women to reflect back on their experiences in the leftist parties during the tenure of Salvador Allende. In other words, despite the fact that the patriarchal framework from which the UP coalition functioned was significantly more benign than Pinochet's, it did eventually come under feminist scrutiny. This process of reflection was in part responsible to the emergence of revolutionary feminism in post-Allende Chile. In this section I will explain how women's experiences in the Allende government contributed to the revolutionary feminist movement in its immediate aftermath. As Teresa Valdés noted when explaining to me the roles of women in the movement against Pinochet, "You cannot understand what happened during the dictatorship if you do not understand what happened during this period [of Allende's presidency]."

As I demonstrated in the case of El Salvador, there is strong potential for the development of a feminist movement in the aftermath of a revolutionary struggle given the convergence of five factors: (1) gender-bending and (2) logistical training during the revolutionary period; (3) a political opportunity; (4) a feeling on the part of women that their revolution remains incomplete, and (5) a collective feminist consciousness in the postrevolutionary period. I will take up each of these in turn. In the case of Chile, what we have seen so far is that during the revolutionary period of Allende's UP government, women were quite involved politically and socially. That said, the question of gender-bending in Allende's Chile is a bit tricky. On the surface we could assume that rather than challenging socially prescribed notions of femininity (and masculinity), the Allende government was wholly responsible for reinforcing them. Indeed, as I discussed in chapter 3, women tended to be relegated to the "caring ministries" (Craske 1999, 61), as we saw with Carmen Gloría Aguayo as the national director of the Social Development Agency and Soledad Parada as the director for the Presidential Women's Secretariate. Additionally, women were quite active in the mothers' centers, teaching and

learning the prototypical feminine skills of knitting and the like. It is my contention, however, that women's participation in these tasks—even when organized entirely around a patriarchal gendered division of labor—were still acts
and processes that challenged traditionally proscribed gender roles, and were
thus examples of gender-bending.

Jane Jaquette (1973) and Linda Lobao (1990) argue that even when
women played the support roles of cooks and seamstresses within guerrilla
movements they were challenging the uncompromising view of the Latin
American military as the ultimate form of patriarchy. Women's experiences
here are similar: the formal, democratic political structure that served as the
backdrop to Allende's Chile was nowhere near as rigidly patriarchal as the
Latin American military, but it was certainly masculinist nonetheless. Because
of this, I argue that women's presence in the UP government's revolutionary
project did in fact lead to significant conflicts to stereotypical ideas of femininity. As was discussed in the last chapter, women felt very empowered by the
UP government. They participated en masse at the mothers' centers, in the
neighborhood associations, within unions (though to a lesser degree), and
even in some elected and appointed political positions. All of the women I
spoke with suggested that women felt empowered not as a result of a feminist
agenda, but from the opportunities that were presented to them as a result of
a socialist government. Women were often able to be educated and work outside of their homes for the first time; they felt entitled to receive support with
their domestic duties, entitled to keep their children healthy as a result of the
milk campaigns. In many cases they defied the will of their husbands by leav-
ing their houses, often for the first time, to spend time with each other. In
other words, as a result of the policies of the UP government and women's
experiences within it, they came to see themselves as political and social subjects. This empowerment very much collided with the prescriptions of femininity as docility to which women were expected to subscribe prior to the
revolutionary movement in Chile.

Temma Kaplan has drawn similar conclusions from her research on
women's mobilization in Barcelona in the early twentieth century. She maintains that women obtain their sense of female consciousness as a result of their
"obligations to preserve life," particularly when the actions necessary for
accomplishing this end are performed collectively—in, for example, a group
kitchen or laundry facility (1982, 546). As we know, the mothers' centers
served precisely this function. In Kaplan's research she found that these types
of activity, especially as a result of the close "physical proximity" in which they
place women, "contributes to the power of the female community" (547). For
Kaplan, "whether they act to serve the left or the right, women's disruptive
behavior in the public arena appears incompatible with the stereotypes of
women as docile victims. The common social thread is their consistent defense

of their right to feed and protect their communities with the support of the government or without it" (565). This is precisely what we saw happen in Allende's Chile. Initially the activities of the women in the mothers' centers and neighborhood organizations were largely hidden or unnoticed by the public. However, as the economic crisis worsened, the women of the mothers' centers and neighborhood organizations took on the increasingly public roles of keeping their communities and families fed while demonstrating support for the UP government. As the political situation in Chile became increasingly more polemic, even the supposedly apolitical activities of these women held new meaning. And as Kaplan notes, such collective and public activities cause ruptures with common notions of femininity, or, gender-bending.

Second, in addition to challenging socially accepted roles of femininity, women active in revolutionary struggles need to have received organizational training to be applied to the potential revolutionary feminist movement. As a result of women's experiences within the revolutionary project in Allende's Chile, they were indeed exposed to such training. As Paulina Weber explained, "[T]he women who had been involved in defending the Allende government, these were leftist women, women that were politically involved; they started to get organized [against Pinochet]." Echoing this, Soledad Parada and Alicia Basso (whom in 1999 I interviewed together) gave their responses to the question of what the role of women was in the anti-Pinochet movement:

BASSO: It was a very active role. Paradoxically, after all that happened during the Popular Unity government [the anti-Allende protests by right-wing women] I believe that Chilean women, especially in the poor and working class, participated in a big way.
PARADA: They were the first ones to go out and show their faces.
BASSO: They showed their faces first in the defense of human rights. I believe they have played an impressive role.

What all three interviewees are suggesting is that these women were empowered by and committed to Allende, making them that much more opposed to the dictatorship. Related to this, they learned how to organize and make their demands known within the Allende government, which enabled them to immediately transfer their energies to a new social movement. As I have discussed above, the first women to mobilize against Allende, those to whom these three women are referring, were not in any way framing their struggle as feminist. However, as time passed and various other factors were in place, a revolutionary feminist movement would eventually emerge.

The third factor that needs to be present to facilitate the emergence of a revolutionary feminist movement is a political opportunity in the aftermath of the revolutionary struggle. In the wake of Allende's government the tragic political opportunity was, ironically, the dictatorship. Male activists were disappeared, detained, killed, and exiled. This was compounded by the fact that the political parties that were led predominantly by men, and then forced underground, shut men out of politics as they knew it. The task, then, of protesting this situation both logistically and politically fell to women. Logistically it became the job of women to keep the resistance alive as their male partners were—literally—gone. Politically it fell to women, because they were able to more safely penetrate the hostile climate created by Pinochet. As Paulina Weber noted,

> Because the parties could not appear publicly, we [women's women's organizations] had a lot of press conferences denouncing grave human rights violations, etcetera . . . because there was no one else who could do it. We assumed a lot of the jobs of the political parties during the dictatorship because it was the only way that some things could come out publicly [and] there was a lot of recognition [for this]. At that time, we were in the political scene and we were absolutely visible as a movement, and I would say that during that time we were essential; there were a lot of things that would not [have] work[ed] if the women were not present.

Again, the women who filled this vacuum were not initially organizing as feminists, but they did carve out a public space that resulted, in part, from the absence of men, which was eventually filled with feminist demands as well.

Next, women who have participated in revolutionary movements need be left with the feeling that their revolution remains incomplete; this is often experienced as a sense of betrayal, as we saw in the case of El Salvador, that is in part responsible for facilitating a feminist consciousness. In the case of Chile, Allendistas were definitely left with an incomplete revolution and unfulfilled agenda. This process was somewhat circuitous; it was not so much that Allendistas had advanced a women's platform and that it was rejected but that, after time away from the leftist political parties, women started to reflect on their positions in the parties. That is, leftist women were prevented from reaching positions of leadership; leftist women were confronted with sexism from their own spouses. As Ximena González, a journalist who worked in the Presidential Communications office under Allende explained, "These men [of the Left] all agreed with the [UP] government plan [of equality], but in the home they had a hard time dealing with the fact that their wives were actively involved in politics and were not home. This was an intense and difficult discussion that took place in the parties. I know about it from inside the Socialist Party. There were some intense fights between husbands and wives and in the families when women demanded that men be held accountable" (personal interview, 1999). She went on to explain how women's issues were pushed to the back burner in an attempt at facilitating unity, noting, "These [abortion and divorce] are issues that have always been latent. It was premeditated that these topics were not in the political discourse. Allende had enough problems without even getting himself into these polemic issues. At the time the ability to calmly debate things like these did not exist." As a result, one of the central feminist analyses from which the women were eventually to organize included a critique of sexism against women in both the political parties and within the home. The motto "democracy in the country and in the home" spoke to patriarchy in both macro- and microstructures of society, leftist parties included.

And finally, a revolutionary feminist movement will not emerge in a postrevolutionary period if there is no collective feminist consciousness. In post-Allende Chile, a very strong feminist consciousness was present. Because nearly all of the women that joined the feminist movement begun thinking critically about politics as a result of their experiences on the Left, once the dictatorship began political theorizing was certainly not new. In the late 1970s women who had leadership experiences in the leftist parties began to gather informally in what they would later identify as consciousness-raising groups (Baldez 2002, 135–36). Initially women gathered to reflect upon their experiences under the dictatorship, but as a result of their political savvy the discussion eventually became explicitly feminist. While these conversations were happening in Chile, Chilean women who had been exiled were also coming into contact with feminists. It was at this time that second-wave feminism was emerging onto the global scene. While the Chilean women were abroad they were no longer in the throes of a revolutionary political program that was in a permanent state of crisis, as was the Popular Unity. This meant that women finally had the time to consider issues more directly related to their own experiences as women. While in exile they had the space and time to think, read, and talk about such issues. Chilean women were not only exposed to Western feminists, but to their feminist neighbors in Latin America as well. As Chela Borquez explained,

> It helped me a lot to be out of the country so I could talk to women. While we were fighting the dictatorship the world was experiencing the [UN] Decade for Women. Women elsewhere were making advances more than we were. The visits to other countries and the conversations with other women allowed us to see what was happening. For example, Nicaraguan women [after the victory of the Sandinista revolution] would tell us that they had made advances like having the Ministry of Women. But they would tell us not to make the same mistakes that they made—of creating the Ministry of Women—because we were going to always be segregated.

In other words, Chilean women were also exposed to the feminist praxis and experiences of women living through political trajectories very similar to their own. Upon their return, the feminist study circles and consciousness-raising groups greeted the Chilean women. Together, the experiences of Allendistas as gender benders while simultaneously being exposed to training as activists during the revolutionary period, in conjunction with the political opportunity, unmet needs, and a collective feminist consciousness in the post-revolutionary period led to the emergence of revolutionary feminism in the post-Allende period.

CONCLUSIONS: QUESTIONS FROM A POLITICAL PENDULUM

As we have seen thus far, Chile is an interesting case for the study of both revolutionary movements and feminism. In this chapter we have seen a variety of trends. Through the dictatorship of Augusto Piniochet, women were the first to protest , both out of necessity and political space. Men and women realized the potential of women mobilizing against the dictatorship, and thus women poured out en masse to become the vanguard of a movement that would eventually bring down Pinochet. After women had been organizing for nearly ten years, feminist groups began to form, also with an antidictatorial motto, but this time calling for "democracy in the country and in the home." In other words, Pinochet and his dictatorship provided women a strategic axis with which to articulate a struggle for feminism and democracy at all levels of society. Thus, the strongest feminist movement in Chilean history emerged in the mid-1980s, during the dictatorship. We have seen that the experiences of women as a result of Allende's partial revolution were also foundational in the emergence of feminism in the wake of his presidency. Though the empowerment of women under Allende was entirely bound to traditional divisions of labor, the connection between the revolutionary projects (socialism to feminism) was, as we have seen, quite significant. We also saw that women at the extreme left and into the center were able to coalesce under one common goal—fighting the dictatorship. One must then ask, If women were able to bridge such tremendous political gaps during this particular crisis, why not during the political crisis that eventually led to the coup against Allende? Might the coup have been averted if women were incorporated as the proactive political subjects that they clearly were rather than the Marxist afterthoughts in the Popular Unity coalition? Unfortunately, these are questions to which we will never truly know the answers.

CHAPTER 5

The Cuban Insurrection through
a Feminist Lens, 1952–1959

The insurrectional woman does not defend the project as the
vanguard sector of the women's sector, but instead as part of
this revolution that defends work, the right to work, the right
for schooling. In other words, she defends a particular way of
thinking; she defends certain laws that favor everyone, but does
not propose this as part of the feminist movement
—Gladys Marel García-Pérez, 1999

IN THE 1950s women in the United States religiously watched
Ozzie and Harriet, later emulating the well-kept mother, apron tied neatly around
her skirt as she happily tended to her home, her children, and her husband. At the
same time, just ninety miles off the Atlantic coast of the United States, Cuban
women also donned skirts, tended to homes, and served as wives. However, in
Cuba the skirts were sometimes used to transport weapons,[1] the houses to hide
guerrillas, and the matrimonial status to camouflage male militants.

An opposition movement capable of forcing a militaristic dictator from
power employs a variety of creative tactics. As I have discussed throughout this
book, femininity is one such tactic for its ability to cloak women's subversive
political activities. The role of women in the Cuban Revolution, albeit in a
limited fashion, further demonstrates the utility of the seemingly benign feminine archetype in the advancement of a revolutionary agenda. In this chapter
I will focus on the roles of women in the Cuban insurrectionist movement to
continue to answer the first part of the revolution question: What do women
do for revolutionary movements? I will begin by providing background to the
Cuban insurrection and I will then address the types of roles that women
played in that movement. I will conclude this chapter by revisiting my concept
of gendered revolutionary bridges.

FROM BATISTA TO CASTRO

Revolutionary nationalism has a long history in Cuba.[2] The heart, mind,
and soul of Cuba's history of resistance is embodied by José Martí, leader of

the movement for independence from Spain. Martí lost his life to the Spanish military nearly thirty years prior to independence, elevating him to an unprecedented martyr status. As a philosopher, journalist, and intellectual, he left behind collections of writings that were eventually to inspire young revolutionaries in their struggle to oust the dictator Fulgencio Batista. Batista emerged as a major player in Cuban politics in 1933 when he led a junta that was responsible for ousting one of Cuba's many corrupt and militaristic leaders, Geraldo Machado y Morales. Ramón Grau San Martín, a long time opponent of Machado, was appointed president by Batista's junta. In conjunction with a radical student organization and Batista, Grau ruled the country until 1934. In his attempt to bring about protective labor laws, land reform, and grant women the right to vote, Grau alienated the Right but was not radical enough for the Left. By 1934 he abandoned his position and went into exile.

Over the next decade Batista dominated Cuban politics through puppet presidencies and eventually his own elected position from 1940 to 1944. Bastista drew most of his support from the masses as he initiated partial land reform and opened politics up to the Communist Party and labor unions. By 1939 Batista, who had been ruling as a result of a coup, decided to share some of his power and permitted an elected constitutional assembly to draft the 1940 constitution. The constitution was a progressive document that included legal protections for laborers and women and limited acquisition of private property. Through these 1940 elections Batista finally became president through democratic means. At the same time, Cuba's sugar market, which was its main industry, was booming. As a result, Cuban elites reaped significant profits. The money, however, ended up contributing to corruption rather than implementing the social programs Batista had originally promised. Grau returned from exile and was elected president, providing a new inspiration for democracy and hope to the Cuban people. Like most of his predecessors, Grau failed to make good on his promises but rather inspired nearly fifty percent of the work force to become unionized.

In 1947 the charismatic leader Eddie Chíbas led a campaign to challenge government corruption. Despite the popularity of Chíbas, Carlos Prío Socarrás, a Batista front man, used his control over the electoral processes to win the election. Benjamin Keen and Keith Haynes have referred to Prío as "another in a long line of Cuban country club presidents" (2000, 438). In order to declare his opposition to the corruption and repression of the Prío regime, Eddie Chíbas committed suicide during a nationwide radio broadcast in an attempt to inspire a popular uprising. Instead, the political instability that ensued paved the way for Batista to once again take power, and on the morning of 10 March 1952 he led a victorious coup. He immediately implemented violent and repressive attacks against labor, collective organizing, and democracy. Despite this, within a week the U.S. government officially recognized

Batista's regime. Within twenty-four hours of the coup a student initiated resistance movement that drew its intellectual and spiritual inspiration from Jose Martí began a militant campaign against the dictator that would not end until 1 January 1959, when Batista was forced into exile.

The students were one of the first sectors in society to organize against Batista. Angela Elvira Díaz Vallina (whom I interviewed in 1999, and whom we will meet more fully below) was a student leader of the Federation of University Students (Federación de Estudiantes Universitarios, or FEU) throughout the anti-Batista movement. She explained the first action against Batista:

> Student leaders, upon hearing about the coup, within a few hours went to the presidential palace, where then president Carlos Prío Socarrás was, and asked for weapons to confront the dictatorship that they saw coming upon us. This was during the early hours of 10 March 1952. They did not have the support of any other organization. The students did not get the weapons but they still confronted the despot: they called the people to sign a pledge to fight until the 1940 constitution was reestablished; they organized protests in the streets of Havana demanding the restitution of the republic's constitution. They went to all the country's provinces and they did the same action of gathering the people in the schools to sign a pledge of allegiance to the 1940 constitution. In all these acts, the students and the people were repressed by the police.

In a symbolic attempt at holding Batista accountable to his reformist past, the FEU held a mock burial of his 1940 constitution, which had been the document that governed the republic up until the coup. In my 1999 interview with her, Nimia Menocal, a former member of the rebel air force (whom we will also meet more fully below) described the action to me. "The 1940 burial of the constitution took place in all of the preuniversity technological schools in Havana and was organized because of Batista's coup," she explained. "They [the students] got a coffin with the constitution and in the morning we went out with the coffin and a black armbands that were symbolic of mourning, and marched to the university [of Havana], where the activity ended. This was on March 10, 1952." In addition to students, women also started to organize early on. In an interview with Judy Maloof, Aída Pelayo, a founder and general coordinator of the Martí Women's Civic Front explained,

> In 1952, shortly after Batista pulled off his bloody coup d'état, Carmen Castro and I decided that the time was right to launch an organized resistance, an all-women's group, to fight against the dictatorship. In order to pay homage to the great Cuban leader José Martí on the hundredth anniversary of his birth, we named our organization the Martí Women's Civic Front. We convoked an assembly of about forty women affiliated

with different political parties. . . . Some of the women had no political affiliation; the women who came together to establish the Front had varying degrees of political experience and militancy. We wanted to set an example of unity for other revolutionary groups that were splintered and divided at this time. . . .

Our platform was very simple: we demanded Batista's ouster and the establishment of a government responsive to our [the "people's"] needs . . . we wanted to follow the path outlined by Fidel Castro. . . . The organization grew to include thousands of women throughout the island, although those whose names were actually registered numbered somewhere between six and seven hundred (quoted in Maloof 1999, 57).

Similar to what we saw with the Mujeres por la Vida in Chile, these women consciously took a nonpartisan stance against the dictatorship in order to contribute to a newly emerging anti-Batista movement and provide examples to other sectors on how best to organize.

As the protests continued to spread across the island and include different sectors, a guerrilla movement also began. On 26 July 1953, 165 young Cubans followed Fidel Castro, student leader turned guerrilla, in perhaps the most significant military action during the struggle: the attack on the Moncada Barracks in Santiago de Cuba. Of the participants in the attack, only two were women: Haydée Santamaría and Melba Hernández. Though they wanted to, neither fought in combat, but instead tended to the wounded. María Antonia Figueroa, head of the finance committee of the rebel movement (who we will meet more fully below) explained that there was a third woman who was also going to participate, but that woman's mother had passed away on 24 July and the combatants were scheduled to leave on that day and the next; because of this, Castro did not want to bring her along (personal interview, 1999). The goal of the rebels was to capture and distribute arms and incite an insurrection. María Antonia, though not present at the attack, explained it this way:

The chosen date was July 26, Saint Ana's day and also the height of the carnival celebrations. . . . The day was crammed with festivities . . . and everybody just wanted to have some fun. By the time they [the guerrillas] came down [from the mountains] the only noise one could hear was from the fireworks. He [Fidel] attacked Cuba's second barracks at 5:15 A.M. In such an offensive, surprise was the essential element. They [the rebels] were dressed in military uniforms. But in any situation, there is always an element that cannot be controlled. The plan was perfect. There was a place where they thought the guns were waiting for them. They were going to be passed on to the people, so that everybody would join the offensive. However, they [the military] had removed all the guns, all dynamite, and every useful thing to be used in the combat, since several music bands from other parts of Cuba were going to be hosted in that same place. There were no guns in there. Also, just by mistake, someone [a rebel] shot his gun. All this caused confusion and the element of surprise was lost. It became a bloodbath. However, the largest number of casualties was registered among the army, rather than among those leading the attack. (Personal interview, 1999)

After the Moncada attack Castro was incarcerated for twenty-five months.[3] During this time the movement was held together largely by women, including Haydée Santamaría, Melba Hernández, Natalia Revuelta, and Castro's sister Lidia. Haydée and Melba were captured along with the men but were released from prison long before Castro. (Castro would eventually appoint Haydée and Melba to the National Directorate of his revolutionary organization.) Together these four women created alliances with other anti-Batista organizations including the Martí Women's Civic Front and the Association of United Cuban Women. One of the most important tasks that the women performed during this period was producing and distributing ten thousand copies of Castro's famous speech, "History Will Absolve Me," which further enhanced his reputation as a bold and articulate leader.

In 1955 Castro was released from jail and was exiled to Mexico, where he met Ernesto "Che" Guevara. Che, as he was affectionately known, would eventually become second in command of the rebel army, and act "like a father or an older brother" to the troops (Teté Puebla, quoted in Waters 2003, 36). On 2 December 1956, Che, Castro, his brother Raúl, and seventy-nine other people sailed back to Cuba on a boat they called the *Granma*. Their intention was to coordinate their arrival with an uprising in Santiago. Though the attack was marred by logistical complications Angela Elvira Díaz Vallina explained that as a result, the guerrilla war was started in the Eastern Mountains and Castro's guerrilla organization, the Revolutionary Movement of 26 July (Movimiento Revolucionario 26 de Julio, or MR-26-7) militantly introduced itself to the public (personal interview, 1999). Gladys Marel García-Pérez (whom we will also meet below) was a militant in the resistance movement and explained to me, in a 1999 interview, that "in this struggle the 26 July Movement became more and more consolidated. It was like an arrow that became much more powerful, because it knew how to structure the people with a sociopolitical base."

The MR-26-7 was the nexus of the anti-Batista struggle because it carried out the armed component of the battle and provided leadership to the movement writ large. In the end, it was only successful because it was part of a broader movement of students, labor, women, and other militants from all over the country. Nimia Menocal explained that "the movement was made up of people in the *llano* (flatlands), who were clandestine, and people in the hills, which was the sierra, and there it was organized in *columnas* (columns)." In an article by Neil Macaulay about the size and structure of the Cuban rebel army he explains that Dickey Chapelle, a distinguished female war correspondent who lived in Oriente province with the rebel army for a month, "designated the '*columnas*' as 'battalions,' probably because they approached the size of a United States army or marine battalion, [and were made up of] 'about 500 men and 20-odd officers'" (1978, 290). Macaulay suggests that by 1958 the rebel army was made up of nineteen battalions (290, chart).[4]

The MR-26-7 continued to step up actions while other urban-based groups bore the brunt of the increasing repression. The United States had been rapidly losing patience with Batista and his strong-arm policies, the last straw being in September of 1957 when oppositional navy officers rebelled against Batista at Cienfuegos only to be met by U.S.-supplied weaponry. This was in direct violation of U.S. policy, and led to the cessation of military aid to the Cuban government. As momentum escalated against Batista, he became increasingly uncompromising, and this fostered more animosity toward him among the populace. In July of the same year the opposition forces signed an agreement that recognized armed insurrection and a general strike as the primary means to combat the dictatorship. By refusing to relinquish power, Batista further alienated his former supporters while fueling the radical nationalism of Fidel Castro, the MR-26-7, and the expanding network of urban revolutionaries.

As revolutionary fervor continued to intensify, so too did women's desires to participate on the frontlines of combat. On 4 September 1958 the Mariana Grajales Women's Platoon was formed by Fidel Castro.[5] As Isabel Rielo, captain of the brigade, recalled it, "At that meeting [where Castro established the platoon] that took place high in the mountains (at the rebel radio station), the Commander-in-Chief Fidel Castro proposed that Cuban women, with their heroism and exemplary behavior, with the countless sacrifices in the struggle against tyranny, both in the armed struggle and underground, had earned the right to participate in a direct and organized fashion in the final combat against the dictator" (FMC archives, 1988).[6] It was as a result of this brigade that women officially became combatants. The group was made up of thirteen women. Despite their small size, their presence was significant nonetheless as they participated in about twenty important battles (Randall 1981a, 23). María Antonia Carrillo, an Afro-Cuban woman in her late fifties, joined the Mariana Grajales Platoon when she was nineteen years old. She recalled,

> I was one of the women who fought in the all-woman platoon called Mariana Grajales. It was a beautiful experience. We were all so united and so in love with the Revolution. There weren't any bad feelings of rivalry or jealousy among us. I had to learn how to use a weapon; I didn't think

I would be able to, but I did. The sense of revolutionary fervor that enveloped us was so strong that fighting back seemed like the only thing to do. . . . We fought in a number of battles near the end of the Revolution, during the last months of 1958 (quoted in Maloof 1999, 64–65).

Castro taught the women to shoot. Delsa Esther "Teté" Puebla, founding member and second in command of the platoon, explained that once they learned to shoot, "Fidel informed us, 'You are now going to be my personal security detail.' . . . He did this to demonstrate his confidence in women, in women's equality" (quoted in Waters 2003, 48). She went on to explain that "Fidel's idea was to create two women's units, but the war ended before that could happen" (51). As a result of the breadth and strength of the revolutionary movement, on New Year's Day 1959, Fulgenico Batista fled Cuba, surrendering the island to Fidel Castro and the MR-26-7.

FEMININITY AND THE STRUGGLE AGAINST BATISTA

Without the participation of women in the revolutionary movement, it is unlikely that Batista would have been forced to flee Cuba. In this section I will argue that despite the seemingly low presence of women in the resistance movement, the roles that they played were in and of themselves fundamental to the advancement and success of the revolutionary movement. Unfortunately, there is no way to really know how many women (or men for that matter) actually participated in the anti-Batista movement. I asked Gladys Marel García-Pérez, Cuban historian, author of numerous books and articles about the insurrection and the roles of women within it, and a former leader herself, if she knew of any numbers and she explained,

> I really cannot give you a reliable number. Nor can I give an estimated figure. Even though there is no quantified number what is important is the qualitative aspect. In other words, women participated in the same way as men did in the insurrectional project. [The woman] was a leader, combatant, and contributor in the political, civic, and military apparatuses of the MR-26-7 at the municipal, regional, provincial, and national levels all over the island. She was a soldier in the Mariana Grajales platoon, having as leader Lieutenant Isabel Rielo. She occupied positions in the Exile Section of the [Revolutionary] Directorate, one of the leaders being Haydée Santamaría, a heroine in the Moncada Barracks Assault (1953). In the 13 March DR [Revolutionary Directorate] there were women who excelled as leaders, clandestine fighters, and guerrillas who occupied leadership positions in different municipalities and diverse leadership positions in the organization. (Personal communication with the author, 2003)

Similarly, Nimia Menocal explained, "I cannot say, categorically, whether or not at that time there were few women, because back then we were already trying not to meet each other if it was not absolutely necessary." Similarly, historian Louis A. Pérez Jr. notes, "anonymity was essential to the success of the local resistance—to be identified was often tantamount to a death sentence. The historiographic implications of anonymity are, of course, immediately obvious" (1998, x). In the rest of this chapter I will speak more directly to the roles of women in the movement in an attempt to, if only slightly, contribute to filling this historical void. I will argue that in many cases, the types of tasks women performed for the revolution were in large part the result of their gender.

In addition to the aforementioned Haydée Santamaría and Melba Hernández, two other women revolutionaries have received their deserved credit for the roles they played in the Cuban revolution—Celia Sánchez and Vilma Espín. Celia Sánchez was the first woman to ever participate in combat and emerged as a top strategist during the struggle. In response to a false report that Celia had been captured, Che Guevara noted in his diary "Celia was our [the guerrillas] only known and safe contact . . . her detention would mean isolation for us" (quoted in Smith and Padula 1996, 28). In a similar vein, Teté Puebla recalls Celia as "[t]he soul of the Sierra Maestra, very capable, yet very sensitive to the needs of others. . . . She was loved by all. Those of us who were guerrilla fighters consider her the mother of the Rebel Army, because of her firmness and loyalty, because of the way she conducted herself during the war" (quoted in Waters 2003, 34). Vilma Espín was another leading strategist of the MR-26-7 who worked along side the top male leaders to advance the revolutionary movement. Similar to what we saw in El Salvador and Chile, the women who were able to emerge to top leadership positions were from the more privileged classes. For example, Haydée Santamaría was born to a middle-class family in Las Villas, Melba Hernández was a lawyer, Celia Sánchez was from a well-to-do family in Oriente, and Vilma Espín was an engineer whose father was the vice director of Bacardi Rum in Santiago de Cuba (Franqui 1968, 18; Smith and Padula 1996, 24). These four women had no financial worries, were highly educated, and were imbued with cultural capital from which the revolution benefited. The case of Melba Hernández is quite illustrative: as a lawyer she was able to provide legal assistance that proved crucial for the rebel movement. And Vilma Espín, fluent in English as a result of studying engineering at the Massachusetts Institute of Technology, translated for Fidel Castro when he was interviewed by a *New York Times* journalist in 1957 (Smith and Padula 1996, 23–27).

Through my interviews it became increasingly clear that though these four women did contribute significantly to the revolution, there were also countless others who participated in all sorts of ways but have never made it to the history books. I was able to interview just a handful myself and they recounted their experiences and those of countless other women in vivid detail. One such woman is Nimia Menocal. Nimia was born in 1931 and grew up in a working-class family. Her father was in one of the revolutionary organizations that successfully brought down the Machado dictatorship in 1933. For her fourteenth birthday he gave her a pistol and told her to "never take it out without a reason and never put it away with dishonor." At that time, Nimia was studying chemistry at the Havana School of Arts and Trades, where she was a student leader in the movement against the government of Grau San Martin. She worked in a variety of capacities during the anti-Batista movement, with students, and in finance, propaganda, sabotage; she eventually joined the Rebel air force. As part of the air force structure she worked "in the factory where they made materials used by the rebel air force. [I] did things like refill used bullets with gunpowder. The shells that were found in combat would be brought to the factory, and we would make . . . bombs, Molotov cocktails, and also deactivate bombs that fell without exploding so that we could use the TNT." It was her training in chemistry that proved useful in making these weapons for the MR-26-7. Nimia's sister was also a member of the MR-26-7, but has since passed away. The two of them carried out major actions together, including transnational weapons purchases and hijackings.

I also interviewed María Antonia Figueroa. María holds a Ph.D. in pedagogy and was born in Santiago de Cuba. At the time of our interview in 1999, she was eighty years old. Her mother worked as a teacher for forty-five years and her father, who died when she was eight years old, was a composer who directed the symphony orchestra. She was raised in a middle-class family with two older brothers, both of whom were also involved in the resistance movement. She grew up in what she called a very patriotic household. Though she had been a member of the Orthodox Party (the same party as Fidel Castro) for quite some time, it was not until the Moncada attack that she became very active in the revolutionary movement. She explained that after the Moncada attack rebels who were able to escape the police were hidden all over Santiago so she, her brother, and her sister-in-law successfully organized to rescue them. Shortly thereafter, she dressed up as a lawyer and was able to sneak into the courtroom where the trial for the organizers of the Moncada attack was being held. After the rebels all confessed to the attack and were sent to jail, María stayed in close contact with them, especially Melba Hernández and Haydée Santamaría. Upon Castro's release from prison he sought out María because he knew that she had helped to rescue some of the Moncada fighters and tended to those that ended up in prison. Not long after their meeting, Fidel appointed her treasurer of the MR-26-7.

Angela Elvira Díaz Vallina (known as Elvira) is another revolutionary woman I spoke to while in Cuba. Elvira was born in 1933 and currently holds two Ph.D.s, one in historical sciences and, one in pedagogy. She is a full professor at the University of Havana and has taught there for over thirty years. She explained that she got involved in the anti-Batista movement on the day of the coup when she was eighteen years old. She was finishing up her last year at the Escuela Normal de Maestros de la Habana and was, like María, a militant in the Orthodox Party. Just six months after the coup, she began college and immediately joined the student movement. In her first year at the University of Havana, 1952, she was elected as the department of anthropology's delegate to the FEU, and the following year she was elected as the federation's vice president. In January of 1956, upon the invitation of Melba Hernández, Elvira joined the MR-26-7. Elvira explained to me that her decision to join "had profound roots in the early 1950s. At that time I joined the Orthodox Party Youth in the city of Marianao. . . . My mother was militant in that party and we both went to meetings where the [party] leaders spoke, amongst them, Fidel. . . . He visited the homes of the party's activists in which my mother's home was included. Less than a year after joining the MR-26-7, she was secretly elected to be the president of the FEU. Elvira participated in various capacities in the FEU and the MR-26-7, including the creation of a women's subversive cell (to be discussed below) in the Civic Resistance that "was [part of] the MR-26-7 movement that joined together people that were enemies of the regime but were not willing to engage in violence." She organized countless demonstrations and performed acts of sabotage, and, as she explained, "I know what a Batista prison was. I was captured seven times and I suffered beating and all sorts of humiliations." By November of 1958 she and her compañeros (comrades) decided that she should leave Havana and go to the mountains to join the women's battalion. She was informed by her superiors that she would need to wait for special conditions in order to do the transfer. She never made it to the mountains because less than a month later she was invited to participate in an international student conference and ended up in Venezuela the day that the MR-26-7 triumphed.

Sonnia Moro, who was only twelve years old when Batista took power, had different experiences than the aforementioned women. She came from a middle-class family and had the opportunity to study things like ballet and music. Though she was only thirteen on 26 July 1953, the day of the Moncada attack, she remembers it vividly. Her father was a big fan of the radio, and because radios were often used for rebel communication, those who listened to them often raised suspicion. In my 1999 interview with her, Sonnia recalled, about people who listened to the radios, "Their houses were searched and they [the police] tried to search ours. Luckily some friends who held some sway in the government intervened and they did not actually carry out the search. But seeing my father up against those violent policemen, with their big weapons and their bravado, was almost like a sign that we had to fight against that order of things." When the news about Fidel returning from exile in Mexico started to circulate, Sonnia decided to join the revolution. She explained to me that at the end of 1956 her association was fairly cautious, but by the end of 1958 she was "practically a professional." At the time that she joined she was a student at a private high school; later she attended the Institute of Secondary Education while she also worked as a music teacher at a private conservatory. Her mother and sister collaborated with the movement as well. Her mother, however, asked Sonnia to stay in school as long as it remained open. Her father, on the other hand, never knew what his youngest daughter was up to until after the triumph of the revolution. She did what she has since called "the historically female jobs:" transporting weapons, accompanying men to lessen the danger of their transfers, trying to get money, administering first aid, and the like. She worked primarily with the student movement, and in March 1958 the MR-26-7 created the National Student Front, in which she worked coordinating the girls' activities. It wasn't until some time after the triumph of the revolution that Elvira Vallina and Sonnia realized that they had relatively close relations during the struggle—by the end, Elvira was actually Sonnia's superior in the structures established to coordinate women.

Marel García-Pérez is the final woman I was able to interview, and at that time (in 1999) she was sixty-two years old. Marel was born in the countryside and raised in extreme poverty, in a house that had a dirt floor. Her father, who came from a peasant background, was a sugar cane worker with a fifth grade education who had started working at the age of thirteen. Her mother was illiterate and was also from a peasant family. After the triumph of the revolution she was able to study at the university and earn a Ph.D. and has since published several articles and books in both English and Spanish, analyzing and explaining the anti-Batista movement, including the roles of women within it. It was at the age of fourteen that Marel joined the student movement in the city of Santa Clara, in the middle of the island.

Marel held a plethora of positions too numerous to list here. Some of the more prominent ones included membership in the high school Revolutionary Directorate, which was made up of representatives from different schools, and the Action and Sabotage Youth Brigade, which operated in the countryside. On 26 May 1957 she joined the urban clandestine groups. She, like Elvira, was familiar with the "justice system" under Batista, as she was put on trial for thirteen different charges, and though she was acquitted, she was sent to her hometown for house arrest. Not long after, she escaped and returned to the MR-26-7 in the province of Matanzas. It was there that she was appointed leader of the MR-26-7 for one of the five regions in that province. She held that position from September of 1957 until the summer of 1958. Under her command operated the regional leaders of the Action and Sabotage groups, the Civic Resistance Movement, the National Student Front, the National Labor Front, and the Women and Family Brigade, which she directly coordinated. In her capacity as regional coordinator, she served as the liaison with governing bodies and guerrilla groups in other provinces. She was eventually transferred to Havana to do clandestine work and in 1958, the national coordinator of the MR-26-7 appointed her coordinator of the grassroots revolutionary cells in Havana. In this capacity she was in charge of, among others, a women's brigade that served as a liaison to the MR-26-7. Under the direct command of Fidel Castro she worked with other national leaders of the clandestine movement, including the second-in-command of one of the guerrilla columnas.

We can see that the aforementioned women played important roles in the movement. In this section I will discuss in more detail some of the things that these women, and others like them, did in the anti-Batista movement. It is important to remember that the period in question is the 1950s when, as I noted in the introduction of this chapter, many women in the United States were aspiring to be the perfect housewife. Let us recall that women did all sort of things in this movement. As Elvira Vallina noted,

These revolutionary women executed tasks and guided other women combatants in the actions that needed to happen. Many, many were the tasks that the city guerrillas engaged in: we raised money for the struggle by selling MR-26-7 bonds; we distributed propaganda about the development of the insurrection, or we threw leaflets from tall buildings that called the people to combat on a specific date; we moved weapons and explosives in the big skirts that were fashionable at the time, or in our purses; we did surveillance on targets; we did sabotage against property; ... we participated in the organizing of two labor strikes. . . . [And] police terror characterized our daily lives.

Despite the fact that women played countless roles in the movement their tasks were very much influenced by an identifiable, gendered division of labor. They tended to find themselves in positions of support, cooking, sewing uniforms, and the like. Though the work that Sonnia Moro did very much fell into this framework, she explained to me that "when I think about it I realize that all of those things, even the little ones, put me in a lot of danger."

In the context of guerrilla war, those tasks, which are understood to be support to the movement, fall under the rubric *logistics*. To the layperson logistics conjures up an entirely different image than that implied by revolutionaries entrenched in guerrilla war. In the revolutionary context, logistical tasks include transporting and making weapons, delivering messages, operating rebel radio stations, hiding compañeros, providing medical assistance, and the like; all these are things that fell to women during the struggle against Batista.

Nimia Menocal described a somewhat typical encounter while performing the logistical task of purchasing weapons:

> They gave me the task of taking money to the United States and bringing back arms. I left for Miami with my six-year-old niece and 100,000 U.S. dollars. I got to the airport, and the day before something had happened at the airport, so it was full of guards. . . . Suddenly I heard over the microphone, "Nimia Menocal, please come to the information desk." My sister [who was there on another mission] was walking over toward me with her eyes open wide, and they kept repeating the announcement. And I was saying, "What do I do? Should I go or not go?" The main thing was the mission; it had to be carried out. That is what I thought, and I said to myself, "Well, I might be killed, but the money has to get out." So I took my niece, and I went to the bathroom. I took off the sash [with the money] and I put it on the girl and I left her at the door of the bathroom and I said, "If you see me leave with some men, this is what you have to do: you go outside, you get a car and you tell them to take you to the Ten Cent on Monte Street, and there is a compañera who lives just next door . . . and she will pay for the taxi. You tell her that I left with some men." I told her that and then I started walking toward where they called me. . . . There was a compañera walking toward me, but she did not know me so she gave me a password, I answered her, and she gave me an envelope. Since she did not know me she could not have found me at the airport. It was a packet for Haydée (Santamaría). And just as I was picking up the envelope for Haydée, they started announcing on the microphone, "Flight number . . . whatever . . . go to gate number 1." I did not even have time to take the sash off my niece. I went to get her and she was standing there at the bathroom, and I took her hand and she was the one who got the money in.

Knowing that the mission was a dangerous one, Nimia carried herself as a mother by taking her niece with her. Obviously a six-year-old girl was incapable of providing physical protection, nor would anyone expect her to. But her presence allowed Nimia to travel more safely through an airport that was crawling with police, even when her name was being announced on a loud speaker.

In addition to buying weapons, women were also central to transporting and detonating them in acts of sabotage. As Elvira Vallina noted above, women were able to transfer bombs because of their skirts and purses, but such acts put them in danger. Elvira explained, "Some of these bombs exploded inside the compañeras' purses because it was very warm. One of the young women [who was carrying the bombs] was captured when she was trying to set the bomb. . . . Fortunately they did not kill her and she was sent to the women's prison where she no longer was in danger of death." Ironically, Elvira was relieved that this woman who was under her command was sent to prison. The risks that women took in these sorts of actions were not just in being captured by the police but, as Nimia mentioned, in traveling with live bombs. Women also helped in the delivery of messages from one locale to another. Once again, a seemingly benign task of working as a courier was also quite dangerous. María Antonia Figueroa described two women, "peasants acting as Fidel's messengers, [who] were killed here [Havana]. They came from the sierra [mountains], but they got killed here and their bodies were never found. It is said that they [the military] used cement to throw their bodies to the ocean."

In addition to delivering weapons and messages, women also helped male guerrillas travel from one place to another. On the streets, women members of the MR-26-7 would escort male members, using their feminine roles as wives to diminish the chances of unnecessary attention from the police, which allowed male guerrillas to move about more freely than they could if they were to travel alone or with one another. In other words, there were times when women were actually the ones in the positions of protecting men, and not the other way around.

The gendered division of labor, even in the revolutionary context, impelled women to work toward meeting the more domestic needs of the guerrillas. For example, women offered their homes as safe houses and places of refuge to guerrillas on the run or in hiding. As Natalia "Naty" Revuelta, former member of the MR-26-7 and mother of Fidel Castro's (unacknowledged) daughter explained, "I had sent the key [to the house] to Fidel with a note telling him that if they needed a safe hiding place for themselves or their families, they could count on us. It would be a safe refuge because, although I had developed a political consciousness, our family didn't have any tradition of political participation, any ties to politicians or political parties" (quoted in Maloof, 1999, 45). Related to this, women also found themselves serving as the emotional caretakers of the revolution. As Marel García-Perez explained,

> Under my direction I had the front that gave social support to prisoners. It was made up of women that would go to the jails and take messages from the family. We would gather things like rice, beans, food in general, toys, medicines, and children's clothes from the better off women to take to the jail and for other families [of the prisoners]. The prisoners' families were not abandoned. At the time, all women were related to one another in some way so their field of action was oriented not only toward their families but also toward other women.

Such tasks were directly related to the physical and emotional survival of the guerrilla movement. Indeed, a military project as risky and taxing as guerrilla warfare can only be sustained if the members of the movement do not give up hope. On the surface, it appeared as if the women that Marel organized were simply doing "good deeds" by supporting the prisoners and their families with food and gifts. But in reality, the result of their actions was to feed the morale of the movement, and this contributed to its longevity and ultimate success.

The ability of women to contribute to the movement in ways distinct from men was not overlooked by its leadership. Elvira explained that when she started to organize with the MR-26-7 she worked in the area of special functions. She recalled that

> my first boss was an extraordinary woman, Haydée Santamaría. She joined the Civic Resistance with the goal of working to radicalize its' actions and [to accomplish] this goal she gives me the order of creating a women's subversive cell that took part in revolutionary actions.
>
> The fundamental principle of the secret cells was the compartmentalization of the information to guarantee the safety of the compañeros in case another compañero fell prisoner and in [the] case of unbearable torture [which might lead to the denunciation of] other revolutionaries. For this reason the insurrectional structure was radial; in other words, the cells were made up of a cell leader and nine direct subordinates. Each one of them created similar cells. This repeated itself successively.
>
> The feminine cell that I was ordered to create was identified with the letter U because its members were university students; later on some men and women from other sectors were incorporated. . . . I can remember some of the names of the loyal and efficient compañeras that formed the nucleus of the feminine cell. . . . I did not meet or know the members that were subordinate to them, but after the triumph of the revolution I did have the honor of meeting . . . Sonnia Moro.

It was this clandestine and anonymous structure that meant that often times women (and men) who participated in peaceful demonstrations, strikes, and other activities outside of the armed guerrilla struggle were potentially more connected to the MR-26-7 than they knew. Indeed, the student movements had explicit connections to the MR-26-7, of which new recruits were not always aware. Sonnia Moro recalled that "it turns out that one day, without realizing it, I ended up in a group of young people who were conspiring to defeat Batista's tyranny." In this case, Sonnia may have even be referring to her participation in the women's cell of the MR-26-7 that Elvira oversaw.

Like Elvira, Marel also organized women's brigades. She explained that when she was a regional coordinator in Mantanzas from 1957 to 1958,

> Under my direction (as coordinator) I always had . . . a group of women, or a women's brigade that operated under certain clandestine tasks with more ease than men. For example, we would put on these large stomachs

that made us look pregnant and pregnancy was a way to cover up and move equipment, and other activities. A woman could go into the prisons without raising too many suspicions. Women would enter the prisons as links to find information that leaders and other militants that fell prisoner could have or to try to reestablish a web of contacts with those that had ended up without contact from the organization.

It was this relative ease of which Marel speaks that also allowed women to have a significant presence in the streets in demonstrations against Batista's dictatorship. According to María Antonia Figueroa, demonstrations of mostly women began right after Batista's coup and continued through the victory. To María, the average protester looked like her own mother and her mother's friends. When asked why it was that more women than men participated in these demonstrations María explained, "Many women thought that their husbands and their sons would get killed and that it was more difficult for women to get killed. . . . My mother was an organizer of the mothers' demonstration; it was all women. That was in . . . 1958. It was a beautiful demonstration: they came out of a church and they exited as if they were coming out of mass. But they were not in mass and they all marched like that through all of the main streets; thousands of women in Santiago de Cuba. . . . The main sign said "we mothers demand an end to the assassination of our sons." The political strength of motherhood was something that Cuban women exploited twenty years before the Mothers of the Plaza de Mayo in Argentina did. Sadly, the need for these types of committees seemed to multiply rather than diminish as the twentieth century progressed. It was, as we saw in the cases of El Salvador and Chile as well, the presumption that mothers were apolitical that allowed women to move more safely in the streets while conveying a bold political and social statement. Elvira also emphasized the importance of women to public protests, but she reminded me that even though women were safer than men, that in no way made them immune to violent recourse. She explained her experiences in a demonstration that happened on 26 July 1957, on the fourth anniversary of the Moncada attack:

On this date I was supposed to deploy hundreds of women in the main streets of the capital. . . . At exactly 3:00 P.M. we were the protagonists in an assault of these streets. The assault consisted in joining together with other women to cover the streets from one sidewalk to the other and show a sign of massive organization, of unity, and decisive struggle. This [protest] was meant to deny the declarations made by the tyranny that Fidel's guerrillas had been defeated in the Sierra and the MR-26-7 has been disbanded in the cities. The hymns and slogans chanted by the combatants were quieted by police brutality that managed to break the protection ring that the movement's compañeros and compañeras had created with their cars. Many of the compañeras were beat with sticks, some were severely wounded, others had broken bones, or their dresses completely ripped up. A group, in which I was included, were imprisoned and villainously [abused] at the police station and then sent to the Mantilla Women's Prison in a Havana suburb.

It is noteworthy that Elvira identifies herself and the other women who took to the streets that day as "combatants." With respect to traditional guerrilla discourse, these protesters were not combatants, but from the perspective of one of the organizers, and perhaps because of her intimate familiarity with the violent response that she and her compañeras were faced, their experiences were very akin to those of combatants.

Despite the fact that, as we have seen, the contributions of women were varied, important, and risky, the women were still subjected to discrimination from their male compañeros. For Sonnia, perhaps because she was lower on the hierarchy than Marel or Elvira the discrimination she experienced was somewhat subtle: [W]e [women] wanted to participate more," she noted. "That is why I also [in addition to belonging to student organizations] collaborated with the comrades in the 26 July militias. And you see, they [the men] were organized, from captain all the way down to soldier, but we women did not have all those ranks. We were their *collaborators*." In other words, for Sonnia, in addition to being somewhat restricted in the roles she was able to play, it was also the revolutionary discourse which partially devalued women. As a leader, Marel experienced the discrimination in the responses of men to her status, which often exceeded their own:

> During the armed conflict revolutionary men protected women. At the beginning in the Action and Sabotage [groups] some men tried to have women be more protected. But there was no difference in regard to participation. How? If a man or a woman set a bomb, or did any other kind of sabotage it was done depending on her abilities. In regards to having women lead Action and Sabotage, there were different kinds of thinking. Some men did not want women to lead them. [In one region] I led ... all the Section Chiefs of the MR-26-7, [and they were] all men. ... They got used to it, but the same did not happen with all militants in the combat section of the MR-26-7.

In other words, most men were at least initially uncomfortable with having Marel as their superior; some grew accustomed to it, particularly because she clearly proved herself, while others never really accepted it. Nimia's experiences were somewhat similar to Marel's. That is, she was very qualified for the job of making weapons as she had experience in chemistry but it still took the pressure of Raúl Castro for men to allow her to participate with them. She explained, [When] Compañero Raúl Castro found out that I was an industrial chemist he sent me to the Air Force factory. [The] captain . . . who was in charge there did not want any women at the factory, but Raúl said, "Women in general, no, but this one, yes." So I was very well-received and there were never any problems. More than anything, I was a sister to them all; I was the only woman. It was a column of about twenty men." Personally, Nimia did not feel discriminated against, as she was provided entrance into this factory. And from our conversation it was clear that she was quite proud to have been affiliated with the rebel air force because Cuba was the only guerrilla movement to have airplanes. But it was only as a result of the pressure exerted by one of the very top members of the MR-26-7 that she was granted entrance into this terrain. What all of this suggests is that, despite the commitment, and risks taken by these and other women like them, in the end it was the men who held all of the real power. As Marel noted, "Men were the ones who really had power; it was not women, because it was a masculine project led fundamentally by men and not women. So we—I, for example, thought I was leading the project because I was leading a part of the structure. Within the project as a whole, in the end men held the power."

Men holding leadership positions is consistent with the gendered division of labor we have seen thus far. Some roles fell to women as their femininity enabled them to perform such tasks more effectively, like providing security for male guerrillas. Other tasks, however, went to women as a result of patriarchal notions regarding the roles of women, for example sewing and cooking. A similar argument can be made with respect to leadership; these roles fell to men not because masculinity enabled them but because patriarchal notions of masculinity imply that men are born leaders.

Conclusions: Cuban Women as Gendered Revolutionary Bridges

Through this brief discussion of Cuban history we have seen the evolution of the revolutionary movement and the roles of women in that successful struggle. We saw that women served in many capacities in the movement, from delivering messages to doing transnational weapons purchases. In the two examples that I discussed above, the seemingly safer of the two missions, delivering the messages, resulted in the couriers being thrown into the ocean with concrete attached to their ankles. In the case of the presumably more dangerous transaction of bringing $100,000 cash from Havana to Miami for the purpose of buying weapons, the woman who carried out that action lived to tell about it. The point here is that neither activity should be considered more or less important and certainly not more or less safe. Because guerrilla warfare is the quintessential interdependent project, all tasks are necessary for its success.

Similar to what we saw in El Salvador and Chile, the revolutionary roles that women took on were for the most part dictated by a patriarchal gendered division of labor, and/or the ability of women to move about more safely than men. As the cases of El Salvador and Chile both demonstrated, traditional notions of femininity both enabled women to participate in such masculine projects as revolutionary war and politics, but it also served to partially inhibit women from really climbing the revolutionary hierarchies. What most of the examples in the Cuban case further confirm is the utility of femininity as a revolutionary tool.

As I have attempted to demonstrate through the cases of El Salvador and Chile, women bridged physical space in revolutionary exchanges and partially closed the gap between the organized Left and unincorporated citizens. As we know, I call the women who perform such revolutionary tasks gendered revolutionary bridges. As I have suggested, these links were as explicit as transporting bombs in skirts, or the equally important though seemingly more benign provision of the physical space of safe houses where guerrillas were able to hide and take cover. In both of these examples women used their feminine identities to exist anonymously among the civilian population in order to expand the revolutionary movement. Additionally, I have argued that the presence of women in revolutionary movements has the potential to minimize the apprehensions of unincorporated but curious civilians and provide the revolutionary movement with moral authority. For example, a political demonstration of mothers and wives, though directly confronting the Batista dictatorship, is less violent and thus less foreign to civilians than guerrilla combatants in the mountains. As we saw in the case of the mothers of the disappeared in El Salvador and Chile, many of the women protesters unconsciously and consciously camouflaged their revolutionary zeal by choosing to mobilize as mothers and wives. They used their motherhood in an attempt to be physically protected from the military. In Cuba we saw the same thing. María Antonia Figueroa shared this story about her own mother's experiences in one such demonstration with me:

> They were in the front, my mother was in the front, I was behind protecting her just in case something happened [like] she fell or something, because she was an elder. The guards were coming from the front and one of them used his rifle to block my mother. He was very young, I will never forget that. . . . My mother told him . . . "son, you think that you have power because you have a weapon, but you do not have power. The rich who sent you to do this have the power. You could be my son. Are you not going to let me get through so that I can protest the assassination of our sons?" Then he said, "Go ahead ma'am." She told him, "You are one of the people and those who they have assassinated are like you, from the people."

In this case the women used the moral authority attached to motherhood to get the military to physically move out of their way. It is unlikely that male protestors would have been able to appeal to soldiers as their offspring as did María's mother. And it is equally unlikely that the soldiers would have felt compelled to step aside for a group of young men with no claims of morality. What the case of women revolutionaries in Cuba helps to further demonstrate is that as a result of femininity, women have a revolutionary capacity to secure, promote, and expand revolutionary movements in ways that would be impossible for men to imitate.

CHAPTER 6

The Women's Movement in

Postinsurrection Cuba, 1959–1999

Here you cannot talk about *feminism*. Women do not accept
that term, even when I talk to brilliant women, to cultured
women, when I tell them that I am a feminist they say that
they are not, for whatever reason they don't want to use that
term. . . . They think it's an overused and an exclusive term.

—Lizette Villa, 1999

ON NEW YEAR'S DAY 1959, Fidel Castro declared himself
leader of the new Cuba, finally free of the dictatorial rule of Fulgencio Batista.
Those who lent their sympathies and/or participated in the struggle against
Batista supported Castro as their new head of state. The wealthiest sectors of
society and the former supporters of Batista fled Cuba en masse. Between
1959 and 1963, 215,000 refugees left Cuba for the United States, most com-
monly to Miami, Florida, while thousands more went to Spain and Latin
America (Gonzalez 2000, 110). As a result of the socialized economy these
refugees had the most to lose as their salaries dropped and their large plots of
land and mansions were appropriated and redistributed by the state. Immediately after the revolutionary triumph the United States initiated its relentless
hostility; Dwight D. Eisenhower was president at the time and in 1960 declared an economic embargo against Cuba, forbidding all economic trade and
travel to the island. To this day the embargo persists, significantly harming the
Cuban economy and its people. Additionally, the United States prepared itself
for war against Cuba, supposedly as a preventative tactic. From that point on
Cuba has been on the defensive. The hostility and animosity between the two
countries has anything but desisted. If anything, it has become more intense.
Most Cubans who still live on the island feel as though the United States is
waging a (gunless) war against them.

As a result of this socialist structure women (as well as men, of course) saw
many significant gains. Indeed, in 1995 the United Nations Development Program released its *Human Development Report*, which recognized Cuba as the
leader in gender equality within the developing world. There are many reasons

the UN came to this conclusion: (1) in 1995, the average life expectancy of Cuban women reached 77.6 years, which is the highest in all of Latin America; (2) every woman has access to free education, which means that in 1995, 57.7 percent of university graduates, 62 percent of middle- and high-school-level technicians, and 42 percent of scientific researchers were women; and (3) prior to 1959, only 15 percent of the Cuban labor force was comprised of women, whereas by 1995 that number jumped to 42.3 percent. In Cuba, women are found in all professions, including the medical profession: 48 percent of Cuban medical doctors, 47 percent of hospital directors, and 61 percent of the general practitioners are women. Additionally, 54 percent of those employed in the service sector, 65 percent of all technicians, 85 percent of administrative employees, 43 percent of the scientists, and 70 percent of the technical workforce in the area of education are women. These gains are the result of several factors, not the least of which was the establishment of quality, government-subsidized day care centers. According to a 1989 statistic, 136,000 children were receiving day care in these facilities (Fleites-Lear 2000, 35–37; Vallina and Pagés 2000, 24).

It would seem then that in this atmosphere that is attentive to the practical needs of women, an atmosphere that women were in part responsible for creating, a movement like feminism would be welcome and even encouraged. However, as we will see, this could not be further from the truth. In this chapter I will explain what accounts for the absence of revolutionary feminism in an otherwise ideologically radical society. First, I will address the social and political status of women in post-1959 Cuba, paying specific attention to the Federation of Cuban Women (La Federación de Mujeres Cubanas, or FMC). I will then discuss the short-lived women's organization called the Association of Women Communications Workers (Asociación de Mujeres Comunicadoras, also known as *Colectivo Magín*), and follow that with a discussion of feminism and a women's movement in Cuba where I will explain why a revolutionary feminist movement has never emerged in Castro's Cuba.

CASTRO'S ANSWER TO THE WOMAN QUESTION

The Federation of Cuban Women

On 23 August 1960 the Federation of Cuban Women (FMC) was founded by Fidel Castro (Molyneux 2001b, 79). The creation of the FMC is heralded by some as one of the many successes in the gender realm for which the Castro government can take credit. In 1971, FMC president Vilma Espín (the revolutionary leader we met in chapter 5) in this oft-cited quote described the basic function of the FMC as "[the incorporation of] women into the construction of socialism, elevating the general political, cultural, and technical level of the nation. All of the FMC's activities are designed precisely to mobilize women, to organize them, and improve their condition" (quoted in

Smith and Padula 1996, 33). From Espín's assessment it is clear that the purpose of the FMC was not to address discrimination against women but to mobilize them in support of socialism and incorporate them into the state and the economy. While in Cuba in 1999 I spoke with Clotilde Proveyer, professor of women's studies at the University of Havana, about the FMC. During our conversation she explained and outlined some of its basic objectives, noting advances gained for and by women as a result of the larger socialist goals:

> In 1960 there was a meeting of all of the [women's] organizations and each one . . . incorporate[d] into what was the Federation of Cuban Women. . . . That is why it is called the . . . Federation and not union; a federation in which all women's organizations that existed at that point in time participate[d] and . . . integrate[d] themselves. . . . the fundamental objective [was] fighting for women's incorporation and . . . participation as equals in the construction of a new society.
>
> The federation's task from that moment on [was] to achieve access to education for women, to work, to social life, with equal rights . . . the federation played an essential role in the women's struggle to access space in society that they had previously not had. . . . [It was] essential [in] guaranteeing the transformation of Cuban women's lives at that point in time. For example, prostitutes were trained to give them a trade; a lot of educational activities were created to help peasant women to better themselves. . . .
>
> Of course when [women] incorporate . . . knowledge, . . . learning, . . . access to culture, that is what guarantees access to work. . . . In addition, you know that it is not possible to create transformation in a subordinated group if they cannot first grow as individuals. First she [must] become master of her destiny and in ignorance that is not possible; with ignorance you cannot achieve this.

Here Proveyer explains that educational, financial, and even cultural empowerment became both a means and an end to the goal of fostering women's support for the revolution.

The FMC participated in a number of government-organized programs in order to move toward this goal. The FMC helped in the educational campaigns. Thousands of new teachers were hired, and abandoned or reclaimed mansions,[1] along with former army barracks, were converted into educational centers. With the help of the FMC, thousands of volunteers became "people's teachers," and in 1960 the great literacy campaign was launched. Over 100,000 people volunteered for this campaign, more than half of whom were young women. On 22 December 1961 Castro declared Cuba a literate nation: 700,000 Cubans, more than half of whom were women, had learned to read and write (Smith and Padula 1996, 83–84).

In reviewing progress made for women in postinsurrection Cuba, one of the more noteworthy advances is that Cuban women are protected by a safe and accessible health care system, which takes their needs into account—something that is in stark contrast to the rest of Latin America and the Caribbean.[2] Perhaps the most striking difference with the rest of the region is the fact that in Cuba abortion is free and legal.[3]

In order for Cuban women to be truly liberated, the Communist Party argued, they needed to be integrated into the paid economy. However, some Cuban women have pointed out that economic freedom as conceptualized in the socialist model of their nation is not necessarily the path to women's emancipation. As one woman noted, "Socialism liberated women by putting them to work. Done deal. If you were salaried, you were liberated; if you worked productively, you had already broken your chains. In the socialism that we learned, everything was so easy, everything went in a straight line: society emancipated itself from capitalism and was now happy; everything was now functioning. Women emancipated themselves economically and were now free. The family subordinated you: work liberated you. What sheer foolishness, gentlemen!" (anonymous quote in López Vigil 1998, 39). As this anonymous feminist explained, and most of my interviewees corroborated, incorporation into the process of production, while necessary, does not guarantee progress in undoing the gendered division of labor in the private sphere. Indeed, women have jobs in nontraditional fields, but what this woman is suggesting is that these advances are the result of twentieth-century socialism, not feminism. Additionally, it was repeatedly pointed out to me that though women have a significant presence in the labor force they are largely excluded from managerial positions. A retired political analyst who wished to remain anonymous shared a similar observation and had mixed feelings about the successes of women in the paid labor force, noting that women "are a very large part of the workforce. Perhaps it is fifty/fifty or forty-five/fifty-five; it is a very equal number in the workforce. They . . . are professional women. Also in the sciences, in medicine, in research, they are very . . . present there. But . . . if they have to get a director it is almost always a man. You hear the same thing: 'She will get married, she will get pregnant, she will have children, and then she will not come to work.' It is the same old story" (personal interview, 1999). Most of my informants spoke of a glass ceiling and the fact that women managers rarely go beyond midlevel positions. It is important to note, however, that despite the fact that women are underrepresented in managerial positions they do make up significant portions of the labor force that were previously open almost exclusively to men.

The aforementioned programs and advances were initiated in the first few years of the Castro government and are in part the result of the existence of the FMC. As time has passed the FMC has evolved in tandem with Cuban society; the result has been a significant loss of support for the FMC.[4] The women with whom I spoke had varying opinions regarding the importance of the FMC. While in Cuba I was able to discuss some of these issues with Rita Perrera, who has a thirty-five year history with the FMC and works in the area of Foreign Affairs.[5] She noted that

> the Federation of Cuban Women has gained, in its own right; due to everything that it has done, due to this practice, and due to its discourse, it has be[come] . . . a very important point of reference for the government on women's issues. Anytime that there is going to be a program that is going to be implemented that will have an impact on or relates to women, the Federation of Cuban Women is always consulted. I think that it is an important role that we have to play. . . . I feel that it is the national mechanism [for women] in Cuba. . . . We do not have a ministry, we don't have a women's department, we do not have a government organization, or a government body that handles women's affairs. . . . The [FMC] . . . is the national mechanism [for women].
>
> Although it is a nongovernmental organization [NGO],[6] it has a certain official status. Within the UN [the FMC] has this role as a national mechanism. This is because . . . when the United Nations made a call to all governments in the Decade for Women [from] 1975 to 1985 to create national mechanisms, [at this time] the FMC already [had] sixteen years of experience. (Personal interview, 1999)

Perrera suggests that the FMC is a grassroots organization, independent of and respected by the government, as evidenced by the fact that it receives no government funds and is financed through membership dues. And yet, Perrera also maintained that the research that my colleagues and I were conducting in Cuba should have been supervised by the FMC. Certainly if the FMC was a grassroots organization and independent of the government it would not have been imbued with the power to oversee our research. Additionally, most of the women with whom I spoke conveyed that the FMC was anything but a grassroots organization. The most scathing critiques came only after the women requested that I turn off my tape recorder. There was near consensus among the women I spoke to in 1999 that the FMC is extremely top-down in structure and inextricably linked to the government. As one woman who wished to remain anonymous in our interview explained it, "In Cuba [those which have] the category of an NGO are the popular organizations. So the federation is an NGO, the CDRs[7] are NGOs, and [there are] the others that are working [as] NGOs but they are tied to the state. The United Nations Cuban Organization is an NGO, [and] it is a state organism, [and] the Federation is part of that." In other words, the connections to the state virtually nullify any NGO status, a matter I will discuss further below.

Nongovernmental or not, the FMC became the center of women's power within post-1959 Cuba. As a result, there were few women in positions with national power outside of the FMC. More than 130,000 women hold official positions in the organization. Rather than serve as a first step in the political training of women, the FMC tended to absorb women who might have otherwise pursued positions of leadership within the state and/or the Communist Party. The end result is a multilayered hierarchical structure parallel to that of the Cuban Communist Party.

Another frustration some women conveyed to me is the FMC's inadequacy in addressing what they consider to be the more pressing problems faced by women. The anonymous retired political analyst explained it this way:

> The purpose of the Federation of Cuban Women was allegedly to address the problems of women in revolutionary Cuba. They stopped after their main and only task ... to take women to the workforce, which is good in the sense that it gives women economic independence ... in a macho society, but it stopped there. ... It never addressed the problems of women living in a macho society, it has never addressed the problems of the impoverishment of women in a ... society where dollars are not the national currency [yet they dominate], and whose salaries are not paid in dollars.[8] It has not addressed the issue of dropping out by female students because of early pregnancies or simply lack of interest in pursuing their studies; it has not addressed the question of women who drop out of work because daycare centers are not functioning properly, and in general it does not address an issue that I think should become one of the central issues ... domestic violence. ... It is acknowledged that there are gender problems, but they are not [addressed].

There are many reasons that so many issues remain unaddressed by the FMC and the Communist Party. Perhaps the most ironic reason is that the Cuban government created a series of laws to support women.

Legalized Equality and Political Power

As a result of Castro's agenda to foster women's support for the revolution, in addition to establishing the FMC he also passed a series of laws that strove to guarantee gender equality in both the public and private spheres. The post-1959 laws regarding equality, labor, maternity leave, and the like are quite progressive. However, they have proved problematic. As a result of limited political will and the nature of some of the laws, they have not always been enforced and as a result have generally functioned as symbolic gestures that have gone no further than the original judicial process needed to ratify them. Additionally, the passage of the laws does nothing toward structurally confronting the historical roots and contemporary manifestations of sexism.

The Cuban constitution of 1976 mandates that "women enjoy the same rights as men" (Valdés and Gomariz 1995, 138). Then in 1992 it was modified to include the following:

> Every man or woman who is able to work is entitled to the opportunity to find useful employment; 2) the state protects the family, as well as motherhood, and marriage; 3) discrimination [of any kind] is forbidden and punishable by law; 4) all citizens . . . have access to (a) all state and public administration positions as well as employment . . . ; (b) all ranks of the Revolutionary Armed Forces . . . ; (c) equal pay for equal work; (d) men and women enjoy equal rights . . . ; (e) . . . free education; (f) . . . free health care; (g) . . . both men and women . . . can be elected. . . . The maternity law establishes the right to eighteen weeks of paid maternity leave, twelve of them to be enjoyed after the delivery, and an additional two more weeks in the case of multiple pregnancies or error concerning the delivery date. . . . (Vallina and Pagés 2000, 21)

With such a progressive constitution it would seem that the "woman question" has been answered. But from the perspective of my anonymous informant the laws are insufficient. She noted, "The constitution says that we are all equal in the eyes of the law; we are all equal and that we all have the same opportunities for jobs and opportunities for studies and all people should have the same rights. But apart from that, if you do not address gender problems as such, separately, it is very difficult to make an impact at a social level." In other words, addressing rights pertaining to women within the legal at the exclusion of the social realms has proved stifling to any real discussions about women's rights. As this woman notes, issues surrounding gender discrimination are so unfamiliar in Cuba that they are hard to identify, let alone discuss and address effectively.

As a result of the United Nations Decade for Women (1975–1985) the Castro government was pressured to rethink its approach to women's rights (Molyneux 2001b). One result was the passage of the Family Code, which was approved in 1975, stipulating that family relations should be based on love, respect, and shared responsibilities. When discussing the Family Code, a Cuban feminist told María López Vigil, "The code could be a thousand times better, but I think it helped create a good deal of awareness, in men and women too, of everyday machismo. It wasn't a law that forced anyone to wash dishes at home, but it did make many men aware of the idea that they have to wash the dishes. . . . And it taught a lot of women that washing dishes is a man's thing, too!" (quoted in López Vigil 1998, 30–31). Indeed, Sonnia Moro, whom we met in chapter 5, had this to say about the effectiveness of the Family Code: "My ex-husband always said that since we got married in 1962 and the Family Code did not come out until 1975, it could not be applied to him retroactively" (personal interview, 1999). A sentiment that I heard repeatedly while in Cuba was that the Family Code initiated discussions about sexism, but for the most part, this is where the challenge to the gendered division of labor ended. In a sense, there was even a backlash against women's rights as Cuban society perceived itself to be more evolved than other nations with respect to gender relations. The Cuban government falsely came to this conclusion due to the existence of an ineffectual law, thus surrendering a battle that as of yet is nowhere close to being over.

Some of the more revolutionary stalwarts with whom I spoke offered uncritical praise while the majority of the women found the code to be both the beginning and premature end of a necessary debate. There was high consensus however, that despite the actual existence of the Family Code, women still perform the majority (if not all) of the domestic duties, especially since the onset of the "special period" that began in September 1990 after the collapse of the Soviet Union. Since then the island has been on a strict rationing program that includes everything from gasoline to soap. Clotilde Proveyer believed that the code

> had its moment in which it was a very important legal instrument . . . even though it does not have the same character as other laws. I believe that it has contributed to expand[ing] people's perceptions of what the responsibilities are from a perspective of equity for all members of the family, and of course I now think that reality has been modifying things. Now . . . there is a need to change, to modify the code so that it reflects the times we are living in; there is no question about it, the code is not perfect. It has the same flaws that Cuban society may have . . . but undoubtedly it was a very important instrument for the Cuban family.

Again, we can see the praise for the initial idea, and the frustration toward the incomplete goal.

Though equality has been legally mandated, the one issue that women across the political spectrum agreed upon in Cuba was the lack of women in positions of power.[9] Sociologist and Communist Party member Mayra Espina explained power in this way:

> I believe that feminine organizing and the ways in which women have gotten involved in political activities and in the public life have been maintained within a framework of power that is masculine. This seems like a contradiction because the political changes that have taken place in the last four decades in Cuba are precisely what have allowed for Cuba to show so many achievements when it comes to women's social integration like in no other country or countries in . . . our development level. . . . It seems to me that this has happened within a framework of power that is masculine and I believe that that is where the limitation is. . . . In addition,

you notice that this is complicated because a part of that machista or masculine framework of power and the views of the male-female relationship is even flattering to women. That is to say, the positive side of the masculine model is a Cuban [man] that is the protector of the woman, gentle toward the woman, that feels responsible for the life of the woman, that does not allow her do anything that may supposedly hurt her. . . . I believe that the Cuban political climate has been at this level for a number of years; it is a view of women that excites her, that protects her, that cherishes her, but it continues to be maintained in this masculine vision. (Personal interview, 1999)

Mayra is suggesting that a gendered hegemonic culture functions in Cuba that both leads women to participate in the unequal distribution of power while enjoying it on perhaps a subconscious level. The results however are more than psychological: Between 1993 and 1994 there was only one woman minister of government, or 2.6 percent of the total. One of the (anonymous) women I spoke with in 1999 pointed out that health and education are two sectors that have disproportionately high numbers of women, yet there has never been female ministers for either sector. Similarly, in 1994 Cuba had no women governors in the provinces. For the same period of 1993–1994 the number of women in legislature was a bit higher: 134 women, or 22.8 percent of the total. And there were 1,809 women, or 13.5 percent of the total, on the municipal councils (Valdés and Gomariz 1995, 162–66). Overall, these numbers are anything but impressive; there are no women with executive powers in Cuba, and of these numbers the closest to that level of the hierarchy are the women ministers of which Cuba has little to boast. The highest level of female participation can be found in the legislative body, and even there only 22.8 percent of the positions are held by women. Another anonymous woman I corresponded with explained that there is only one female general in Cuba (and she is retired), two female politicians in the office of the Communist Party, and three female ministers, and that 30 percent of the deputies of the National Assembly are women (personal communication with the author 2003). Thus, equality may be stipulated by law but power sharing (both along gendered and party lines) is something that has yet to come to fruition in Cuba.

One way to measure the advances of women in Cuba regardless of progressive laws is to see how women fare in a period of crisis—in the case of Cuba, the special period. Because women are generally responsible for the well-being of the home and the family economy, they are forced into the position of making ends meet. As Belkys Vega, Cuban cinematographer and founding member of Colectivo Magín explained in our 1999 interview, this also had implications for women's struggles:

> This special period has weakened . . . the struggle of women's revitaliza-
> tion. . . . It [feminism] gets weakened because women are exhausted from
> trying to survive . . . other struggles become secondary, because the strug-
> gle is one for food, of "how do I feed my family?" "How do I keep my
> house?" "How do I manage to provide my children with shoes and cloth-
> ing?" And that takes a front stage role. . . . The work takes up so much time
> that all you want at the end of the day is to watch a soap opera to discon-
> nect, to evade things so you can sleep. Of course, that is if you have a place
> to stay.

Most women I interviewed, when speaking of the special period, made it clear
that this crisis was being managed by women. That is, though the Family Code
stipulates sharing the chores, when it came down to it, it was women who knew
how to make the minimal resources stretch seemingly beyond their limits.

The special period has interrupted the initial progress resulting from the
laws, which mandate equal distribution of chores, and equal access to government positions, and/or employment. The double or triple burden is very real
in Cuba. This was already the case prior to the special period, where women
were taking on the majority of the domestic work, working outside of the
home, and doing their political work.[10] Domestic work has become more time
consuming with the rationing of oil, soap, and other household commodities.
As a result, women have much less time to give to either politics and/or paid
labor. What this translates to is that women are unable to take on leadership
positions in politics or managerial positions at work. Another more pernicious
impact that the special period and the introduction of the U.S. dollar has had
upon Cubans is their mass entry into tourist-directed *jineterismo* (hustling). As
does everything, this effects women in ways distinct from men. A man might
sell counterfeit Cuban cigars or offer his services as a "tour guide," while
women are often put in the positions of selling their bodies. "A *jinetera* is a far
cry from the illiterate and homeless woman who worked Havana's red light
districts before the Revolution;" a woman may not have the typical transaction of sex-for-cash but instead "parlay her charm into restaurant meals, a
night at a disco, or possibly a pair of shoes for her child" (Fleites-Lear 2000,
48). Another effect of this crisis is "brain drain." Cubans are abandoning their
positions as scientists, professors, and medical doctors, professions where
women predominate, in exchange for working in the tourist industry. Driving
a cab or (in the case of women) prostituting oneself provides access to U.S.
dollars and thus "luxury" goods like soap. While in Cuba, I met a woman Ital-
ian diplomat who flew to Cuba on a plane where every single other passen-
ger was a man. These men may not be thinking of the desperate conditions
that have forced Cuban women into this "industry," but they are certainly personally enjoying the crisis. A sentiment I heard repeatedly in my interviews,

however, was that women were not so much becoming bitter toward the government as fatigued by their circumstances; the frustration one hears repeatedly is directed toward the U.S. government and the embargo for making a difficult situation nearly unbearable. As many Cubans will tell you, they feel as though there is a war without weapons being waged against them and in the case of the special period, once again we see women on the front lines using their femininity in creative ways to fight back.

FEMINIST CONSCIOUSNESS AND MOBILIZATION

Bearing the above critiques in mind, I will focus this next section on feminist political expression in Cuba. I will begin this discussion with an overview of the short-lived women's organization Colectivo Magín. I will then discuss the different meanings of feminism and feminist consciousness and conclude this section by looking at my model of revolutionary feminism as it relates to Cuba.

Colectivo Magín

Colectivo Magín, despite its short history, is an organization of utmost importance in tracing the evolution of a feminist consciousness in Cuba. The five original founders came together at a journalism conference in Latin America in 1993. They formed an organization called the Association of Women Communications Workers (Asociación de Mujeres Comunicadoras), and decided to nickname it Magín. In old Castilian, *magín* means "intelligence and inspiration, talent and imagination. Image. The image of woman" (López Vigil 1998, 40). One early member who chose to remain anonymous described the group's initial phase, explaining, "In creating Magín we decided to begin through the media, but starting from a very broad concept of 'media.' We didn't want only journalists, radio broadcasters, publicists. . . . We also began to bring in teachers. Who's a better multiplier of messages than them? And family doctors, who also multiply messages. And popular power representatives and academics and researchers. . . . The task we gave ourselves was to discover the concept of gender and apply it to the work that each one of us was already doing (quoted in López Vigil 1998, 41). The collective, though directly focused on gender and images of women, did not call itself feminist. Rather, the members of Magín understood themselves to be a group of professional women who wanted to change the image of women in the media. Some of the members considered themselves feminists at the time they joined, while others became feminists as a result of their work with Magín. Regardless of their individual relationships to feminism, the organization did not identify itself as feminist.

By July of 1994 Magín's managing committee included eighteen members, and not long after the group adopted its first development program.

From a practical perspective, the first plan of action was to acquire juridical status in accordance with the laws of the Cuban civil society. This process is rather lengthy and in no way just a formality—that is, all organizations that apply for NGO status are not granted it, as was the case with Magín. According to a 1985 Cuban law, Associations and their Regulation, to gain NGO status organizations must

- Provide the names of thirty members, together with the names, addresses, telephone numbers and ages of the top leadership.
- Prove that the organization is self-financing.
- Submit a written statement of goals, together with an explanation of the institution's internal structure.
- Obtain a "negative certificate" from the Ministry of Justice stating that there is no other registered NGO with a similar purpose. If there is a duplicate organization, the new applicant must associate with the one already registered.
- Obtain sponsorship of a "state reference institution" which affirms that the establishment of the NGO is in its interest. The reference institution subsequently has the right to attend the NGO's board meetings and inspect its accounts to confirm it is carrying out its stated purpose (Gunn 1995, 4).

While waiting on an answer regarding their NGO status, Magín developed a program with several goals including sensitizing society to understand sexist stereotypes of women; providing male and female communicators (journalists, teachers, etc.) the categories of analysis to understand the construction of gender; contributing to the strengthening of women's self-esteem; and familiarizing male and female communicators with information from international debates about gender, specifically the Platform of Action that came from the Fourth World Conference of Women in Beijing in 1995 (Magín 1996, 7–8).

Throughout 1995 and with the support of UNICEF, Magín organized countless workshops and international exchanges with feminists from all around the world, including Argentina, Belgium, Brazil, Canada, Chile, Colombia, Costa Rica, the Dominican Republic, Ecuador, England, Germany, Holland, Paraguay, Spain, Switzerland, and the United States. Included in their list of visitors were Angela Davis, Pratiba Parmer, and Alice Walker (Magín 1996, 7). They developed over fifty workshops that spanned a series of topics, all related to the priorities identified in their development program. The workshops were typically attended by about fifty participants and generated a variety of tools (literature, videos, and audiotapes, for example) to be distributed and shared by communicators to help sensitize them to issues related to the portrayal of women in the media. Through their ongoing discussions, Magín generated a list of ten recommendations for ways to tackle the problem of derogatory images of women in media. Perhaps the most eloquent synthesis of their work is recommendation number 10: "Promote equitable publication of the image of women in the programs, remembering that we are half of the population worldwide and also that we are mothers of the other half" (Magín 1996, 10, 17, 21).

Because Magín initially distanced itself from the word *feminism*, the FMC offered its support. As noted above, the fourth point in the Associations and their Regulation law mandates that it is illegal to duplicate efforts of existing organizations. Magín had an agenda distinct from the FMC and thus did not see themselves in violation of the government's policies. Magín's members were well-respected women, some of whom were quite well-known as cinematographers, radio personalities, artists, designers, soap-opera scriptwriters, television directors, journalists, and academics. These women joined Magín to create a space in which they could share their experiences (López Vigil 1998, 42). The members of Magín sought to maintain a positive relationship with the FMC and the Communist Party. Indeed, many of the members of Magín were also members of the Communist Party. A member of Magín who chose to remain anonymous in López Vigil's article explained, "We informed the Party of everything Magín did. In the beginning, the Cuban Women's Federation was on our side. We were well respected, we were part of them, and there were no problems. . . . We always said: 'If we have been able to get to the point of creating Magín, it's because of all we learned in the Women's Federation. If we've grown exceptionally fast, it's due to everything we previously did with the Revolution'" (quoted in López Vigil 1998, 42). Yet some remained uncomfortable with the tactics and even existence of Magín. In 1999 I spoke with Lizette Villa, the president of the Association of Artists of Film, Radio, and Television within the Cuban Union of Writers and Artists, about Magín. Lizette has a respected position within the government in the realm of cultural production. She spoke to me at length about women's images in the media and shared some TV documentaries that she had produced, the purpose of which was to offer positive images of women. Lizette, who considered herself a feminist, told me that she was aware of Magín, and that some of her friends were former leaders of the group. Still, as a feminist in the arts who is deeply concerned with the promotion of a positive image of women, she shied away from Magín. She explained that

> Magín was important in a conceptual way for communicators. . . . But it seems to me, and I say this because I met some of the leaders, they are my friends, and because I told them this, that I do not think they were transparent enough in terms of the . . . majority.
>
> I am telling you in a general way [what] I spoke to them about. From the beginning I told them, "I am not going to be in Magín because those

are not my principles or my ideas on how best to bring women together. I believe that we women need to work with those that we disagree with, with our different ideas, but with similar goals"—in this case, the communicators.

I do not like the selfish and opportunist attitudes; I cannot stand them and I am not ready to be around those attitudes. I tolerate them—if you want to be selfish it's your problem and I respect your selfishness and I respect your opportunism even though I do not like it personally; I respect it. My respect for another person is the most important thing, please understand that, but I do not like sharing time with them when I see that the main point of view focuses on those inequalities, not think-ing that everyone is the same. . . . I want diversity of thought, but with similar ideas, with similar purposes, with similar projects in favor of women, not with individual projects. . . .

I let them in the National Award of Film, Radio and Television that I organize; I let them give out their award as Magín, but I am not interested. It is clear though that many of them talk . . . about many interesting things . . . in feminist terms. They discussed some interesting things that we could not have discussed in any other space.

Lizette's feelings toward Magín are anything but straightforward; she suggested that Magín was not what she called "transparent enough." In other words, she was suggesting that the members of Magín were secretive in their organizing styles. This would seem counterintuitive, as the main goal of Magín was to dis-seminate information and tools to enable various members of society to chal-lenge the sexist stereotypes of women that predominate in the media. In reality, Magín's program centered upon outreach, which is anything but secre-tive. Due to the sensitive nature of some of the topics discussed in their work-shops, specifically violence against women, it is likely that Magín had methods to protect the anonymity of the women who shared such personal testimonies as their experiences with rape. However, creating a safe space and being orga-nizationally deceptive are quite different things. Villa seems particularly dis-turbed by what she perceived to be Magín's individualistic (antisocialist) approach to a collective (socialist) problem. Thus, in Villa's assessment, the Magíneras (as they called themselves) put their own individual needs ahead of the greater good of Cuba.

Magín's application for official NGO status suggests that they had no intention of organizing in opposition to the state. Initiating the application process meant that transparency was Magín's organizational goal. As Sonnia Moro pointed out in our interview, however, in response to Magín's formal petition the Ministry of Justice declared that Magín was duplicating the func-tions of other organizations—namely, the FMC and the Association of

Advertising Executives. So in September of 1996, at which point Magín's membership comprised about four hundred women, they were forced to stop organizing:

> In March of 1996, the Party's Politburo came out with a very tough, very restrictive and disturbing ideological document. All of a sudden, women from the Federation who had come to our workshops and participated in all our activities drew away from us. It was a sign of things to come. They had gotten the message to cut themselves off. In September, the Party's Central Committee called a meeting of its executive committee and Magín's steering committee. The purpose was to disband Magín. While it was a friendly and respectful meeting, as opposed to a trial, it was nevertheless clear from the beginning that if we resisted we would be subject to party disciplinary measures (anonymous quote in López Vigil 1998, 42).

The actual exchange with the Communist Party and process of deactivation is something that I heard very little about. Sonnia explained that Magín disagreed with the Communist Party's interpretation of the situation, but nevertheless respected its wishes. "When the Party decided to dissolve Magín, as comrades we women accepted it, because we were revolutionaries and among other things we did not want to be separated from the revolution," she noted. "But there were countless reasons why we did not agree and we expressed that to the Party." Belkis Vega also did not agree with the logic that Magín was duplicating the efforts of the FMC. Members of Magín had no desire to conflict with the Communist Party, as they supported the revolution and many were members of the party. She explained,

> We are not guilty—we had to stop existing because it was not legal; we are not going to have an illegal organization, that was not our intention. . . . In addition to that, we, or at least most of us, envision Magín as integral to the Communist Party. That is, it is not a different proposal for the social issue; we are working for the same social project. What we wanted was to include a different view of the same social project and for that reason we were not interested in being a clandestine organization, but an organization within this social project.

In short, the collective was told that their objectives were justifiable, but that justifiable did not always mean appropriate. Sonnia commented, "I cannot say exactly what the Party thinks of feminism. I have no doubt that at the highest levels there is a desire to achieve gender equality. However, I do think that *deactivating* Magín—and that is the word used by the civil servant who did it—was an act of paternalism and a misunderstanding of the very revolutionary role that Magín played (personal interview, 1999). It was suggested that the members could continue their work within the already existing channels—in this case, the FMC—but the women of Magín declined (López Vigil 1998, 43). The dissolution of the organization did not cause its founders to disappear; as Sonnia put it, "I like to say that Magín doesn't exist, but the Magíneras do." The different members of Magín are still active in individual ways—working on documentaries or writing articles about women who remain hidden from history. But according to the Communist Party's mandate they can no longer approach these issues collectively.

FEMINISM AND FEMINIST CONSCIOUSNESS

From some of the above testimonies we can see that feminism is often perceived to be either in direct contrast to Cuban socialism, a divisive ideology imported from the bourgeois north, and/or an unnecessary distraction since a classless society theoretically creates equality for all. As I discussed in the introduction of this book, I used a snowball sample to meet women that were active in what might be considered women-focused projects. As a result, the majority of the women with whom I was able to speak took the bold and unusual stance of identifying themselves as feminists. Though not all of the women called themselves this publicly, their willingness to embrace the term with a researcher from the United States is quite significant. Most of the women felt that the feminist consciousness that exists in Cuba is what they called an "unconscious" one; that is, women were aware of their rights to equality with men but didn't necessarily identify that vision as feminism. In this section I will share some of the women's definitions of feminism and understandings of feminist consciousness in Cuba.

When I interviewed her in 1999 Belkys Vega considered herself a feminist, but noted that if one was to ask her in a couple of years she might change her mind. It was through her work with Magín that she started calling herself a feminist.[11] She commented,

> In Cuba the term *feminism* has . . . been seen as somewhat negative. It has been seen as negative and this of course has not allowed some people that have . . . defended the feminist principle to call themselves feminist. There are a lot of women in Cuba who have fought for women's equality, for equal opportunities, for the right to [access] to all job positions, for being recognized as professionals in equal terms as men, [but] you can notice there have been a lot of problems with feminism. . . .
>
> [V]ery few of us know about the development of the movement. I believe that in Cuba there has been a feminist movement with other names. I think that an organization like Magín . . . raised more consciousness and it is more openly recognized as feminism. But I think that the way in which the term has been used has damaged the acceptance of feminist positions.

The "problems" to which Belkys refers stem from the pejorative meaning the Communist Party has superimposed upon the idea of feminism, and thus feminists. That is, Cubans have repeatedly heard that feminism is a divisive, Western, bourgeoisie, imperialist concept that encourages man-hating. Most women with whom I spoke in 1999 conveyed a similar message to that of Belkys—that feminism is largely misunderstood and misconstrued. One woman who chose to remain anonymous explained it this way:

> Consciously or unconsciously, I believe that the [Communist] Party has prejudices against feminism because of the idea that has been spread in Cuba that portrays feminism as extreme. . . . [Feminism is conveyed] as a position that subordinates the [socialist] struggle . . . and replaces it with feminist demands. That is the image of feminism, and I do not know why, I couldn't tell you what texts, what literature, or who disseminated this image of feminism in the country, but it has been a well-publicized image.

Through my discussions with women about the term *feminism*, it was conveyed to me both implicitly and explicitly that national unity is the Communist Party's priority, and from the Party's perspective feminism promotes difference, which is antithetical to unity. Because Cuba has been put on the defensive in the global-political realm, anything that is perceived to make the country any more vulnerable than it already is—in this case a wavering sense of nationalism—is understood to be disruptive to the larger revolutionary struggle. In other words, feminism is seen by the party as incompatible with nationalism. But from what I witnessed in my conversations with feminists in Cuba, their commitment to feminist ideals in no way undermined their commitment to the socialist project. Indeed, it is because of socialism that Cuban women feel entitled to their equality, so attacking socialism would be highly counterproductive to a feminist agenda.

Mayra Espina has considered herself a feminist since the mid-1980s, at which point she came into contact with other scholars and activists in the region who identified as feminists. Mayra tends not to use the term, but if she is asked if she is a feminist she answers honestly. Like most of the other women with whom I spoke she also explained that Cuban society, for the most part, does not understand feminism and presumes women who embrace the term to be man-haters. She described feminism as a revolutionary project that understands and celebrates difference and sheds light on relations of power:

> I believe that feminism is an everyday attitude about life that attempts to review the differences and the right to have those gender differences within a structure of equality. . . . What I have found in feminism is tolerance, in the enjoyment of the differences that I had not found in other social and life ideologies. That contact with feminism allowed me to

understand what difference means. . . . I think that feminism opens other doors . . . of understanding about the cultural, historical, and all kinds of differences. I believe that feminism has understood these differences better than other forms of social thought. I believe it is a way of understanding life and our differences and rejoice from them. And of course a fundamental aspect of feminist theory, as political life, as revolutionary, and as an everyday practice, is a radical position against any kind of power or domination and not just the kind that has to do with gender differences.

We can see here that Mayra uses feminism as a point of departure for understanding all sorts of imbalances in power. She is not suggesting that sexism is the most fundamental oppressive institution of inequality, but that feminist theory sheds light on much more than just gender inequities. From this perspective feminism is anything but individualistic.

I was also curious to know if the women I spoke with thought there is a feminist consciousness in Cuba. Marta Nuñez is a professor of sociology, economics, and women's studies and a member of the Communist Party who considers herself a feminist and has since 1994. As she explained in our 1999 interview, "I would not say there is a feminist consciousness [here]. And if it does exist it exists very unconsciously; an unconscious consciousness. If you ask anyone in Cuba, "Are you a feminist?" they would say, "No, feminist movements promote only women and women against men." But when you have personalized feminism . . . I do; I think that many . . . women are quite feminist unconsciously." That is, if a woman is presented with a specific scenario that resonates in her own life then she will be more likely to see feminism as something relevant to her. For example, if a single mother is asked if she supports more day-care centers for working mothers she would likely say yes, unaware that this is a top priority for many of the feminists with whom I spoke. When I asked Rita Perrera of the FMC if she thought there was a feminist consciousness in Cuba she echoed Nuñez's sentiment: "I think there is, but people are not aware of it." In other words, these women are suggesting that women in general have certain expectations as to their rights to equal treatment and opportunities in society, but this is more the result of living in a socialist atmosphere rather than one with high consciousness around women's issues. This mentality, I will argue below, is in part responsible for a backlash against feminism and a stagnant women's movement.

The different women I spoke with also had distinct interpretations about whether a women's movement exists in Cuba, and if so, how might it be characterized. Graciela González Olmedo, a professor of women's studies at the University of Havana, noted that the women's movement

is a strong movement. It is not [as] sufficiently strong and integrated as we would want it to be, but it has gained strength because we have [worked so] at least there is a consciousness and that consciousness has been transferred to each of the elements that can improvise or implement this change at [a] societal level. . . .

There are more strengths than weaknesses. . . . But I still feel that there is an exclusion of housewives. [We would like] to organize the women who are . . . from the . . . labor processes. That is, to strengthen the feminine movement at the grassroots level, the Federation of Cuban Women at the root (Personal interview, 1999).

In other words, Olmedo sees the women's movement as deeply connected to the FMC. Sonnia Moro, who says she has always been a feminist because she has always known that women have been at a disadvantage, described the women's movement as formal and restrictive and suggested that women need to find their voice. "The way I see it," she commented, "in Cuba the women's movement is a formal one, though it is still potentially quite strong. It suffers from inertia. Women act out as citizens, as professionals, artists, *campesinas* [peasants], and so on, but not as women per se. That weakens their potential to act from a gendered stance." The fact that different women I interviewed had varying ideas about a women's movement in Cuba is not in and of itself problematic. What it does suggest, however, is that a women's and/or feminist movement, if it does indeed exist, is only effective in some circles. The women who tended to feel more positive about a feminist movement were those who were professors at the university, particularly in women's studies, and/or engaged in their own intellectual research. This may be because they have more access to international dialogues, including those hosted by Cubans, where issues of gender predominate conversations. But some women felt there to be no women's movement in Cuba. For example, one 1999 interviewee who wished to remain anonymous suggested,

At a societal level I do not think it [feminism] is even a movement. I do not think there is even a feminist consciousness at a societal level. You may find it in small groups of women who are friends and who have spoken about these issues; you could find it in groups of men who are aware of women's issues and acknowledge them; you will find them in the young people who are not very clear about what feminism is, but who know that their problems and concerns pertain more to women than to any other group in society, but at a very disconnected and scattered level. It is not a movement, it is not a cohesive thing yet; it is not something that can bring together a major section of the population, not the majority, but certain sectors of the populations. . . . It is very slowly beginning to gain some ground, very slowly because it is very difficult in a country where everything is designed to come from men.

This suggests that the needs that she (and the circle of friends to whom she referred) felt should be prioritized were being left out of what might loosely be considered an agenda. For these women, research is not enough. The ebbs and flows of effectiveness of the women's movement within Cuban society are quite pronounced, indicating that the women's movement is only, at best, effective in some circles and ill-equipped to inspire meaningful change. From all of this we can see that there is not a revolutionary feminist movement in Cuba.

Revolutionary Feminism: The Case of Cuba

As I have discussed throughout this book, a revolutionary feminist movement is one that challenges sexism and larger political structures not explicitly perceived to be patriarchal. We also have seen that a revolutionary feminist movement is one where the leaders developed their political consciousness and organizational skills through their participation in a revolutionary movement that proceeded the emergence of feminism. I have suggested that to determine the strength and presence of a revolutionary feminist movement two things need be considered: whether autonomy exists within the movement, and whether it is a social or political phenomenon equipped to effect change. In Cuba we have what some may very loosely call a women's movement that is highly centralized, severely lacking autonomy, and at best, effective only in some circles, thus ill-equipped to inspire real change. There are many reasons that revolutionary feminism never blossomed in Cuba, not the least of which is the Cuban government's political and ideological hegemony. However, like everything in Cuba's political landscape, the answer is more complex than that.[12]

For a revolutionary feminist movement to present itself all five conditions—(1) gender-bending and (2) training as activists during the revolutionary movement; (3) a political opportunity structure; (4) a series of unmet needs; and (5) a collective feminist consciousness in the aftermath—need be present. I will look at each of these in turn. If we recall the insurrection against Fulgencio Batista and women's roles within that struggle, gender-bending was evident in at least a limited sense despite the fact that the percentage of women insurgents was presumably low. Many of the women postponed marriage, as it conflicted with their revolutionary commitments, certainly a subversive act with respect to gender prescriptions of the 1950s. Additionally, many of the tasks that women performed necessitated a public presence, which served to further undermine the practice of remaining in the home. Women also transported weapons, a decidedly masculine task regardless of the skirts and other feminine markers that enabled them to do so. However, the impact of such events was limited as the number of women active in the struggle was low, they had virtually no presence in positions of leadership, and the types of tasks women performed were largely bound by a traditional gendered division of labor.

The second necessary condition is the existence of a political opportunity structure, something that remains highly unavailable in postinsurrection Cuba. Initially the opportunity was lacking because the period immediately following the revolutionary triumph was one that necessitated a nation focused on one goal—consolidating the power of the revolution. Despite the fact that gender norms are typically challenged quite significantly through revolutionary processes, Nikki Craske argues that the periods when power is being consolidated tend to be those when more traditional gender roles emerge, often promoted and institutionalized by the revolutionary regime (1999, 143). Often in the consolidation period the easiest place to turn in an effort to establish some semblance of normality is to women—they are called upon again to be dutiful mothers and caretakers for a nation on the mend. But as we know, the power has long since been consolidated in Cuba. In simple terms, the Cuban state is the antithesis of a political opportunity. The government is hostile to social movements that step beyond the boundaries of the state, as the case of Magín helped to demonstrate. As we have seen, Magín was a group of professional women attempting to challenge the image of women in the media but because the government/Communist Party maintained that they were duplicating the efforts of the FMC they were forced to stop organizing. What this says is that the women's movement in Cuba must function within the ideological and institutional priorities set by the government. To imply that the work of Magín was duplicating the efforts of the FMC is to suggest that the FMC is indeed effectively challenging the images of women in the media. This, however, is not a goal on the FMC's agenda. The point here is that the only outlet for women's mobilization, the FMC, is so tightly bound to the Communist Party and government that true autonomy cannot exist. It is tempting to suggest that the closed nature of the Cuban state is the only reason that there is currently no revolutionary feminist movement in Cuba. Such an assessment would be shortsighted, because as we have seen with Chile under Augusto Pinochet—a political structure significantly more brutal and restrictive than that of Cuba under Castro—feminism was at its peak.

There are also logistical concerns for the development of revolutionary feminism that are lacking in Cuba. As I discussed in the introduction, one by-product of revolutionary movements is the fact that women acquire political and organizational training through their experiences in revolutionary movements. We saw that this happened in both El Salvador and Chile, and women then applied their training to the feminist movements in the postrevolutionary periods. The case of Cuba is slightly different, however. Though some women were exposed to political organizing, the number of women who actually received such training was fairly inconsequential. Additionally, the armed component of the revolutionary struggle was, from its inception, decidedly finite, suggesting that the roles that women held were specific to the context of war and not transferable to the civilian society, which followed the insurrection. That is, a woman delivering weapons beneath her skirt had very little political exposure that would be relevant in civilian society. As we have seen, in El Salvador the struggle was armed and temporary as well. But there are several differences between El Salvador and Cuba. On the one hand, Salvadoran women played significant roles in the urban popular movement which meant they were familiar with noncombat focused organizing, more so than the women in Cuba. And in El Salvador, in addition to some women holding high-level leadership positions, they were also well represented at the middle level. This meant that even in the context of armed struggle women became familiar with the actual organizing process of political actions. As well, the war was almost twice as long in El Salvador as in Cuba, which meant that women in El Salvador were politically active for a much longer time than were women in Cuba.

The fourth factor is the sense that for women, their revolution remains incomplete. In El Salvador and Chile the women experienced this in part because they were left with their practical gender needs unmet. This is in contrast to what we saw in Cuba, where the government was both quick and thorough in legally addressing women's basic needs, which meant that most women felt no need to mobilize as feminists. As we have seen, women's health, educational, and labor status, though not perfect, dramatically improved after the revolution. Women also have a sense of empowerment through their access to paid labor. They exercise far more control over their bodies in the sexual realm than in any other Latin American country because of their access to birth control and safe and free abortions. They are legally entitled to demand assistance with domestic chores, file for divorce, or claim paid maternity leave. We have seen that these gains are all terribly precarious due to the special period, the U.S. embargo, and difficulty in enforcing the laws, but the sense of empowerment they fostered in women has nonetheless had long-term effects. The establishment of women-focused social services almost immediately following the revolutionary triumph preemptively thwarted the want for a feminist social movement while allowing the government to claim that equality had been achieved.

As a result, the final factor—a collective feminist consciousness—is also absent in Cuba. This is in part due to the fact that women's needs were met, and that Castro worked hard and successfully to endear women to his revolutionary government. As the women we have met in these two chapters have explained, the feminist consciousness that they perceived to exist in Cuba is an unconscious one, not sufficient for energizing a revolutionary feminist movement. Also, external factors that in part were responsible for the creation of feminist consciousness in the rest of the region were absent in Cuba. As I have discussed throughout the book, the UN Decade for Women was important to the development of feminism in the region, for various reasons. First, in preparation for the international meetings national and regional conferences were organized. Organizational infrastructures and networks were both strengthened and created in El Salvador and Chile. Additionally, the conferences resulted in various plans of action to which some governments agreed to abide. What this suggests is that women's demands were becoming familiar enough around the world that national governments felt compelled to at least acknowledge some of the issues. As we saw, it was the UN Decade for Women that encouraged the establishment of the Family Code. But in Cuba the government treated the code's existence as proof that the woman question was answered, so there was no longer any need to discuss the issues that arose during the decade. Additionally, those who had access to international media became more familiar with the debates that were absent in Cuba and were offered visions of and models for women's organizing in all parts of the world. In some cases, high-level women of the FMC did have access but were short on sharing their experiences with the general public. One anonymous interviewee explained that "they [FMC] are the ones that almost always have representatives at these meetings. They get some sort of official notice [invitation] and get money to go to these. But the ideas [discussed] are not widely publicized [upon their return]." In other parts of the region awareness of these events tended to provide incentive for women activists who might otherwise feel isolated and as a result the regional encuentros began to flourish. In other words, all of these events were organizational manifestations of second-wave feminism to which Cuban women were not exposed. We did see in the mid-1990s that, in the case of Magín, this began to change a bit. Indeed, their organization was born at a regional conference for women journalists. But as we also saw, the Magíneras efforts to organize were prematurely ended by the Communist Party. Within the last several years, the women's studies program at the University of Havana has taken the important step of hosting several international conferences for scholars to discuss issues surrounding gender. There is no sign that these exchanges will stop but rather they are happening with more frequency. But by the time that more Cuban women (and men) were exposed to international dialogues about feminism, second-wave feminism had evolved into a third wave. This meant that most Cuban women missed an extremely vibrant period of feminist history, a period in which, as we saw in chapters 2 and 4, Salvadoran and Chilean women activists were leaders. What all of this suggests is that both internal and external factors have proven to stifle rather than facilitate revolutionary feminism in Cuba.

Conclusions: Some Thoughts on Feminism in Castro's Cuba

Clotilde Proveyer describes the Cuban Revolution as essentially feminist: "[F]eminism is to try to achieve the qualitative growth of women. If feminism is that we as women can be better from the human point of view, then I believe that the revolution, the social project, is essentially feminist." From Proveyer's perspective the woman question has indeed been answered. Above we have seen examples of Castro's desire to keep women sympathetic to the revolutionary project. To a large extent he has been successful, and as is the traditional pattern in socialist realities this has been at the expense of an organized feminist movement.[13] We also saw that women have the FMC to serve their needs, but if they move beyond its program and goals then their work is considered redundant and thus illegal. Women feel entitled to equality in their nation and in a sense take feminism for granted, both because many of their needs have been met and because of a fear of the word *feminism* itself; the suspicion toward the word is inseparable from international politics. Because the United States has been relentless in its attempt to bring the Cuban government to its knees, anything perceived to be American is considered just another part of this strategy. The U.S. embargo, in part, attempts to deprive Cubans of basic resources so they will lessen their support for the Cuban government; in other words, it is an attempt to use economic measures to divide a people. And just as U.S. policies are understood to be aggressively divisive, then so too are what are perceived to be U.S. ideologies—in this case, feminism. The irony here—and I will take this up in more detail in the book's conclusion—is that what we have seen in El Salvador and Chile is, despite the Left's assertion that feminism is a Western bourgeoisie concept, revolutionary feminists in Latin America have many more commonalities with the revolutionaries in their home countries than the feminists in the West. Given the chance I suspect that this may be even more the case in Cuba. Women are not oblivious to the fact that their basic needs are met (given available resources) as a result of policies and laws enacted by the socialist state. They are also quite aware that the unconscious feminist consciousness that they see as existing in Cuba is a result of their sense of entitlement to that which socialism intends to provide everyone, regardless of gender. Because of this, and echoing what Clotilde Proveyer said above, the Cuban Revolution could be considered inherently feminist. Using this logic, then why should we expect that Cuban feminism would be anything other than essentially revolutionary?

Conclusion

UNITY-INSPIRED DIVISIONS

It is not enough just to be a revolutionary and to be on the left; you have to be on the left, revolutionary, and feminist in order to place women in the position where they truly belong and that they should have held historically in this country.

—Irma Amaya, 1999

THE SALVADORAN, CHILEAN, and Cuban women revolutionaries we have met in this book are bearers of the conflicting identities of empowered revolutionary subjects and subservient gendered beings. In some cases (Cuba) these contradictions lay comfortably dormant and in others (El Salvador and Chile) they blossomed into articulate feminist movements. This book demonstrates that women, as a result of their gender and the attendant expectations of femininity, participate in revolutionary movements in ways that are not only strategically significant but distinct from men. I have also shown that despite the importance of women to revolutionary struggles, their work is often unacknowledged and unrewarded. Additionally, the participation of women in revolutionary struggles is directly related to the emergence of feminism in the aftermath of such movements.

As history has repeatedly shown, the answers to the "woman question" are anything but encouraging. What we have seen is a virtual failure of revolutions of the twentieth century to address women's issues in any substantial and effective way. Margaret Randall explains this in detail in her aptly titled book *Gathering Rage* (1992). On the other hand, the answers to the "revolution question" are more affirmative. What do women do for revolutions? A lot. What do revolutions give to feminism? A lot. By way of concluding this book I will revisit my answers to the revolution question in more detail by posing two new questions: What accounts for the general patterns that I have suggested exist? What are the implications for these patterns? I will argue that, for the most part, the significance of women's participation in revolutionary movements was seriously underacknowledged, which resulted in weaker revolutionary movements and stronger feminist movements. I will also argue that the untapped potential of women in revolutionary movements is indicative of a larger pattern of prematurely closing the door on women's ability to mediate and manage crises in general.

THE *WHY* QUESTION

The short answers to the revolution questions are that women offer a tremendous amount to revolutions, and revolutions equally substantial amounts to feminism. But despite the fact that women were so important to revolutionary movements, male leftists prevented them from enhancing these movements to their fullest potential, which meant that strategic alliances remained unexploited. There are several reasons why this happened: restrictive notions of femininity; limited conceptions of what constitutes a "rebel"; an insistence on creating a false polemic between women's and national struggles, the "logic" being that women's interests are considered divisive; and the resistance of male leftists to the political empowerment of women. I will take these up in turn.

The value of women's participation in revolutionary movements was simultaneously enhanced and limited by traditional notions of femininity. It was femininity that allowed women to transfer weapons in their fabricated pregnant bellies. It was femininity that enabled women to travel relatively safely through militarized airports with 100,000 U.S. dollars earmarked for the purchase of weapons. It was femininity that allowed women guerrillas to interact with unincorporated civilians in relatively unthreatening ways. It was femininity that allowed women to protest as mothers, confront the military face to face, and in some cases continue marching unharmed. It was in part femininity that facilitated the relocation of sixteen thousand displaced people to zones with strong guerrilla presence. It was femininity that allowed for the establishment of government programs organized entirely around socialist notions of paid and unpaid labor.

As we have seen throughout this book and as I have attempted to articulate through my notion of gendered revolutionary bridges, women participate in and contribute to revolutionary movements in very specific ways. The roles that women played and tasks that they performed were largely enabled by their femininity and had the effect of allowing them to literally and figuratively travel with more ease through civilian populations. As a result, women revolutionaries created bridges and alliances in ways that men would not have been able to. In some cases such positioning of women was intentional. For example, we might recall that during the war in El Salvador male leftists saw and exploited the potential of women revolutionaries. Toward the end of the war, as many of the current leaders of the feminist movement explained in chapter two, the leadership of the Farabundo Martí Front for National Liberation (Frente Farabundo Martí para la Liberación Nacional, or FMLN) directed women to start organizing women's groups. From the perspective of the FMLN's leadership, the goal of these organizations was not to foster feminism. Rather, their intentions were to develop support among potentially sympathetic women, and to encourage international solidarity organizations to financially support the FMLN vis-à-vis women's groups. In other words, women were recognized for their potential to create bridges that led to political and financial support for the revolutionary movement.

This strategic placement of women was not always intentional nor even noticed. In Chile women found themselves in mothers' centers designed to develop marketable skills to enable their insertion into the paid labor force. The mothers' centers were pillars in the prototypical socialist model for the emancipation of women that argues that women's access to paid employment puts them on equal footing with men. But these women who often, unbeknownst to their husbands, snuck out of their homes to drink tea and knit with other women were in no way motivated by a commitment to socialism, nor were they likely even aware of the fact that the mothers' centers under Salvador Allende had anything to do with a socialist platform. Regardless, an estimated one million women participated in the mothers' centers, implicitly conveying a prosocialist message to apolitical housewives.

Just as traditional notions of femininity allowed women's participation to be more powerful than was originally assumed or ever acknowledged, it was those same sexist expectations surrounding femininity that placed women in these roles in the first place—roles that were incorrectly seen as secondary. For the most part, women ended up in the so-called support positions by default. As we have seen, the Left is very much structured around a patriarchal division of labor. This means that the division of labor placed women in roles that remained invisible and unacknowledged. This positioning was no different than the placement of women in the unappreciated yet fundamental roles of their domestic lives. For example, as we have seen in chapter 6, during the special period in Cuba, a woman is expected to sustain her home by making her family's limited resources extend beyond their presumed limits. Certainly making food last longer than anticipated is invaluable to the survival of the family unit, but such activities remain invisible and unacknowledged, and are at best seen as secondary to a society's well-being. The same exact social structure that renders a woman's domestic work unimportant also minimizes her revolutionary contributions. For example, the job of transporting or purchasing of weapons was fairly low in the guerrilla hierarchy and therefore reserved for women. Those tasks that were considered most important to guerrilla warfare were the political and military strategizing performed by the leadership. In Allende's unarmed movement the true revolutionary tasks were those performed by union leaders and government functionaries designed to establish a worker-directed nation and economy, whereas guaranteeing that Chilean children had access to milk

on a daily basis was considered women's work and thus fell to the less important "caring ministries." Clearly, weapons were necessary to guerrilla war, and
the milk program was actually one in which Allende held tremendous pride.
Despite this, neither were understood to be as important to their respective
revolutionary movements as in reality they were. What the cases of El Salvador,
Chile, and Cuba further help to demonstrate is that regardless of the revolutionary structure—that is, armed or democratic—women's contributions were
both significant and underacknowledged.

In addition to the restrictive notions of femininity, the myopic vision of
what constitutes a "rebel" or "politico" also proved disempowering to women.
As we saw, the Salvadoran and Cuban guerrilla movements were organized
entirely around the vanguard structure. That is, a small group of self-appointed
leaders were empowered to make decisions for and act as the representatives
of an entire revolutionary movement. In this capacity they served as the
"brain" and public representations of their movements. In Cuba, for example,
all revolutionaries knew of Fidel Castro and Che Guevara. But as the women
we met in chapter 5 explained, their work was so invisible they did not always
know who their own immediate subordinates or leaders were. In Chile the
"true" politicos were the formal politicians and union leaders, two realms in
which women were significantly underrepresented. Guaranteeing the rights of
workers was considered the "real" political work, whereas organizing collective shopping and laundry facilities was women's work—despite the fact that
both were integral to the Popular Unity coalition's socialist vision. Such
restrictive notions of "revolutionary" superimposed upon a patriarchal division of labor rendered invisible and unimportant the strategic contributions of
women. Ironically, it was these same limited definitions that contributed to the
actual importance of women's contributions. Because women revolutionaries
were characterized as "collaborators" rather than leaders, their strategic value
was further downplayed and ignored. And perhaps more important, this secondary positioning meant that the potential of women to foster important
alliances remained untapped.

A third element that caused women's revolutionary potential to be short-
sightedly stifled is the all-too-common pattern of considering what are perceived to be "national" struggles as those most deserving of attention. The
Salvadoran, Chilean, and Cuban revolutionary movements were all national in
focus. That is, they sought to structurally transform the nation-state as it had
been previously constituted—most specifically, from capitalist to socialist. (In
the cases of El Salvador and Cuba, the revolutionaries also sought to purge
their countries of militaristic leaders). The ideological emphasis upon the state
meant that opposition existed to the recognition of gendered, ethnic, religious, or regional needs or interests. The argument was that when capitalism

was abolished, all other forms of oppression would automatically be eliminated. It is important to note that for the most part women were not insisting that "their" struggles should be prioritized. Indeed, women revolutionaries typically did not identify their gendered practical demands as such until the postrevolutionary periods, when new social movements emerged that were organized explicitly around identity. Despite the fact that interest-group movements did not seek to transform the actual state structure in reality their agendas did have national implications. Gender inequality, of course, is something that saturates an entire nation. What I am suggesting is that it was the logic of falsely identifying what is most urgent and what is a truly national movement that led the male leadership to remain unaware of the ability of women to effectively participate in the mediation of revolutionary crises. For example, during the war in El Salvador, the victory of the FMLN was certainly the priority of both men and women. And after the war, from the FMLN's perspective, the reconstruction and strengthening of political parties was of main concern. The logic that followed was that including women's practical demands would be divisive to the larger, national, movement. In reality, the opposite proved true. If we look at the example of the Association of Mothers Seeking Child Support (Asociación de Madres Demandantes) we might recall that the women who comprised this organization were able to build cross-party alliances between left- and right-wing women. Despite the fact that the right-wing women did not mobilize as a result of a motivation to bring about radical political change, the leaders of the Madres did expand support networks for what were rather progressive issues. In other words, women were able to transcend sectarianism, whereas the FMLN's leadership inspired divisiveness. If the FMLN had not insisted on separating "women's" from "national" demands, the feminists like those who started Women for Dignity and Life "Breaking the Silence" (Mujeres por la Dignidad y la Vida "Rompamos el Silencio," or DIGNAS) would not have been compelled to virtually leave the Left, and thus reduce its potential strength.

In revolutionary Chile the priority was the socialist project. Women Allendistas were not agitating for their own specific needs as the priority was clearly the establishment of a socialist state. The UP coalition's implicit ranking of struggles that presumed the goal of socialism was the only one with national implications provided women a glimpse of what would eventually reemerge in post-Pinochet Chile. As we saw, it was only during the dictatorship that women's feminist demands—namely, a democracy in which they were included—were able to take front stage. And this was only because women ended up in the vanguard of the anti-Pinochet movement for the reasons that I outlined in chapter 4. But as soon as Pinochet was out of power and the transition to democracy initiated, women's invaluable contributions to ushering in democracy were nearly forgotten and the new urgency became the democratic reconstruction of Chile. That is, just like during the tenure of the UP coalition, the Left's leadership declared that the national movement should take priority over identity-specific movements. What we have seen is that the results of the women's efforts were indeed national in scope regardless of the ideological structure of the movements. In other words, the political actions of women were entirely antithetical to divisiveness. Rather, women organized across very diverse political lines precisely to accomplish common goals. It was the political closed-mindedness of leftist men, those in the self-appointed vanguard, that caused them to remain oblivious to this alliance-building potential, thus undermining the power of the revolutionaries writ large.

The early years of post-1959 Cuba help to further demonstrate this point. Castro was much more savvy than the FMLN and the UP coalition. Almost immediately he established the Federation of Cuban Women (La Federación de Mujeres Cubanas, or FMC) in order to endear women to the Cuban revolutionary project. As we saw in chapter 6, the early creation of the FMC and eventual passage of laws said to promote egalitarianism between men and women thwarted the need or want for feminist movements. The FMC and the initial advances for women as a result of Castro's revolutionary agenda served to inspire women's commitment to the "national" project as it was explicitly attentive to their needs.

The final reason why women's abilities to develop political bridges was undermined was the result of male leftists being hostile to the idea of women's political empowerment. For example, in the FMLN most of the women we met spoke of their inability to receive political training and the sense that they had to prove themselves at least twice as much as did men. In Cuba, Gladys Marel García-Pérez spoke of the resistance of some men to taking orders from her. Also in Cuba, Nimia Menocal explained how, despite her training in chemistry, she would have been prevented from being involved in the building of bombs were it not for the insistence of Raúl Castro that she be allowed to participate in these activities. In Chile, women's political empowerment was inhibited by relegating them to the caring ministries. This same hostility and closed-mindedness of the male leaders became most apparent in the postrevolutionary periods. The argument in all three cases, and indeed for leftist movements around the world, is that feminism is simply a Western-imposed, bourgeois movement. The irony, of course, is that revolutionary feminism as organized and articulated by the women we have met in this book has far more in common with their own revolutionary roots—indeed, their typically anti-Western politics—than with the bourgeois feminism that male leftists claim is the antithesis of real revolution.

IMPLICATIONS

The implications of the male vanguard's hostility and/or obliviousness toward women's revolutionary potential are manifold. The first, and perhaps most significant to this project, is the simultaneous weakening of revolutionary and strengthening of feminist movements. The vanguard of their revolutions belittled women revolutionaries and their contributions while maintaining hostility toward feminism. Rather than feeling politically paralyzed, current and potential women revolutionaries abandoned the Left and created their own social movements. In other words, instead of waiting for revolutionaries to take up feminism and acknowledge their efforts, women opted to bring the revolution to their feminism. In the process the Left lost many disenchanted women to feminism, thus weakening the capacity to bring about revolutionary change.

Perhaps the most concrete manifestation of the Left's shortsightedness in maintaining an uncompromising ideological commitment to a purely class struggle combined with the resultant fear of feminism is its attempt to absorb feminism into state structures once given that opportunity. At the very least this has caused rifts between feminists and the Left as feminists have felt further betrayed by their former comrades. In other words, state-dominated feminism, in the name of unity, has further proved divisive to the left as in many cases feminists have all but separated from it. This is particularly true in post-transition Chile, where the first democratic government to follow Pinochet established the National Women's Service (Servicio Nacional de la Mujer, or SERNAM). As I explained in chapter 4, the feminists who led the anti-Pinochet movement demanded compensation and acknowledgment for their actions. One concrete way they suggested this could happen would be through the establishment of a ministry of women, with necessary resources from and influence upon the government. However, the government only superficially met the women's demands: it established a women's entity within the state, SERNAM, but it is lacking in real resources and power. Equally problematic for the feminists who ousted Pinochet is the fact that SERNAM is largely staffed by party functionaries rather than the grassroots feminists who were central to ushering in the transition to democracy.

In El Salvador the outcome was slightly different than in Chile. This is in part due to the fact that the FMLN did not gain the executive power and thus were not given the opportunity to use the state to absorb feminism. In El Salvador feminists have taken a two-pronged approach that combines reliance on formal state structures with grassroots movements. In the case of the women who comprise the Mélida Anaya Montes Women's Movement (Movimiento de Mujeres Mélida Anaya Montes, also known as the Mélidas), they have highly prioritized political representation as necessary for feminists, and women in general. However, as we saw in chapter 2, they have only been able to do this effectively as a result of the grassroots component of the feminist movement as represented by the DIGNAS and the Madres Demandantes. Similarly, the DIGNAS and the Madres would not have been able to advance their agendas without the support of feminists (namely, the Mélidas) working inside of formal state structures. As we might recall, the DIGNAS and the Madres are definitively autonomous from the Left, particularly when compared to the Mélidas. What this has meant for the Salvadoran Left is that yet again the discourse of unity has proved divisive and alienating to its former politicas. That is, many Salvadoran women became feminist casualties of the Left, virtually abandoning the parties for which just several years prior they had literally been willing to die.

The issue of the Cuban state and feminism, of course, presents entirely different issues. As we saw in chapter 6, the FMC and the Family Code preemptively thwarted the need for feminism. We also saw that once women decided a feminist organization was necessary they were prevented from organizing it—again, in the name of national unity. The founders and core members of the Colectivo Magín accepted this decision out of what they called respect for the Communist Party. As has been the pattern, the move toward state-imposed unity backfired. The Communist Party encouraged the women of Magín to work through the FMC. This, however, did not happen; rather, it inspired new tensions between the state-centered approach of the FMC and the members of Magín. What these three cases suggests is that antifeminist proclamations in the name of unity have been perhaps the most divisive ideologies ever introduced into revolutionary movements.

In addition to causing often irreparable fractures in the Left, the resistance of revolutionary leaders to acknowledge the full potential of women also meant that the Left prematurely closed the door to women's similar abilities to lessen those crises that fall beyond the boundaries of revolutionary movements. As I discussed above, women very much demonstrated their abilities to transcend sectarianism in the name of common goals. We saw, particularly in the cases of El Salvador and Chile, how women actually do politics differently than men. In postrevolutionary El Salvador we saw left-wing women forging alliances with right-wing housewives—who had literally been their armed enemies during the war—in order to advance a common agenda of child support. In chapter 4 we saw that the armed militants of the Movement for the Revolutionary Left (Movimiento de Izquierda Revolucionario, or MIR) and anti-Allende Christian Democrats were able to join forces toward one common goal: ousting Pinochet. In Cuba, we saw the women of Magín inviting the FMC, with all of its state-centric strategies, to join their efforts. If Magín's goal was to actually challenge the Cuban state, the group would have never attempted to incorporate the FMC into their efforts. In short, the agendas of the Salvadoran, Chilean, and Cuban feminists herein were certainly not anti-revolutionary. Rather, all of them demonstrated a foresight and commitment to larger goals that took priority over debilitating sectarianism.

If women can transcend sectarianism given common revolutionary goals, who is to say they could not also inspire collaborative efforts to mediate other crises? For example, in Cuba women may have been able to lessen some of the intense economic and social damage brought on by the U.S. embargo. Or in Chile and El Salvador, leftist parties could have been better positioned to weather the difficulties of reconstructing democratic structures in the wake of violent antidemocracy if they had larger political bases. This could have been accomplished rather easily simply by adding more women to the ballots and women focused issues to the agenda. Such suggestions are entirely simplistic and certainly not original, but sadly they need to continue to be reiterated, as male leftists persist in closing their eyes to the revolutionary potential of women.

SOME FINAL THOUGHTS

A feminist analysis of revolution helps us understand that women consistently have an untapped potential to offer revolutionary movements, and by extension to mend nonrevolutionary crises. This book suggests that arguments about the divisiveness of women's issues overlook the reality of women's revolutionary and feminist contributions. My research concludes that women demonstrate the potential to be precisely the opposite of divisive, despite the myopic visions of male leftists who fragment movements by pushing women and their potential supporters away from the Left. The politicoeconomic structure of the world today is entirely different than when these revolutionary movements began. The Cold War ended, and the United States "won." Additionally, the nation-state progressively loses its historic relevance as globalization becomes increasingly irreversible. On one hand, these global processes are largely the result of a U.S.-directed neoliberal economic model, which has eliminated virtually all social service organizations in the third world. Unquestionably, the predominance of neoliberalism most negatively affects women who struggle to secure food, housing, health care, education, and other basic services. However, on the other hand, the globalization of information makes the isolation of the most separated societies (namely Cuba) nearly impossible, thereby providing the vehicle for the proliferation of feminism around the world. This contradiction makes the future of revolutions entirely uncertain (see Foran 2003).

We are certain, however, that political and economic crises and injustices continue to exist and provide the impetus for future revolutionary struggles. Indeed, the need for opposition movements becomes arguably more urgent in the face of globalization. In response to these globally generated crises, new forms of resistance will emerge to challenge extreme forms of political, social and economic injustice. As we have seen, women possess the revolutionary capabilities to mobilize in creative and strategic ways that historically have proved fundamental to social movements. In fact, women have clearly demonstrated their ability and experience to lead emerging revolutionary movements. The final question remains: Will the male vanguard finally share the spotlight and provide women an opportunity to use their revolutionary savvy to construct the political bridges necessary for a successful movement?

APPENDIX: TIME LINES

EL SALVADOR

1876	Rafael Zaldívar y Lazo is the first president of independent El Salvador.
1912	Government establishes the National Guard to protect landowners.
1914	United States takes control of the Panama Canal.
1927	Farabundo Martí expelled from El Salvador.
1929	Great Depression and stock market crash cause drop in coffee prices in El Salvador.
1930	Salvadoran Communist Party (Partido Comunista Salvadoreña) is formed.
1930	Farabundo Martí returns to El Salvador and continues organizing peasants in the countryside.
1932	Farabundo Martí leads an unsuccessful uprising in San Salvador and western regions of the country. Approximately thirty thousand peasants, mostly indigenous people, are killed. Martí is publicly executed, and the Salvadoran Communist Party is outlawed. Women's committees support the uprising.
1938	Women's right to vote is recognized by the constitution, but not allowed by law.
1944	The Association of Democratic Women (Asociación de Mujeres Democráticas) and the Women's Democratic Front (Frente Democrático Femenino) are formed.
1945	The Salvadoran Women's League (Liga Femenina Salvadoreña) is formed.
1950	A law is passed that legalizes women's suffrage, which was constitutionally stipulated in 1938.
1957	The Sisterhood of Salvadoran Women (Fraternidad de Mujeres Salvadoreñas) is founded by the Communist Party.
1959	Success of the Cuban Revolution leads to changes in U.S.

foreign policy toward El Salvador. The United States creates the Alliance for Progress program.

1961   The Christian Democratic Party (Partido Democrático Cristiano) is formed.

1965   National Association of Salvadoran Educators (Asociación Nacional de Educadores Salvadoreños, or ANDES) is founded by Mélida Anaya Montes.

1969   The Sisterhood of Salvadoran Women is disbanded due to political pressure.

1972   José Napoleón Duarte, a Christian Democrat, mounts a reformist challenge to the military power in El Salvador and wins the general elections. The military ignores this victory and maintains power of the state. (The United States supports civilian-military juntas throughout the 1970s.)

1975   The Salvadoran Communist Party establishes the Association of Progressive Women of El Salvador (Asociación de Mujeres Progresivas de El Salvador).

1977   The Committee of Mothers and Relatives of Political Prisoners, Disappeared, and Assassinated of El Salvador (Comité de Madres y Familiares de Presos, Desaparecidos y Asesinados de El Salvador) is formed under the direct auspices of the Catholic Archdiocese.

1978   The Popular Forces of Liberation (Fuerzas Populares de Liberación) establish the Association of Women of El Salvador (Asociación de Mujeres El Salvador, or AMES).

1980   Archbishop Oscar Arnulfo Romero protests death-squad killings and is then assassinated while celebrating mass. Four church women from the United States are raped and killed. The United States terminates military aid to the Salvadoran government. A coalition of five guerrilla organizations join together to form the Farabundo Martí Front for National Liberation (Frente Farabundo Martí para la Liberación Nacional, or FMLN) in order to coordinate a guerrilla movement.

1981   Ronald Reagan begins his first term as president of the United States and reinstates military aid to El Salvador. The National Republican Alliance (Alianza Republicana Nacional, or ARENA) is formed by right-wing extremist Roberto D'Abuisson. The FMLN launches a premature "final offensive."

1983   Mélida Anaya Montes, founder of ANDES, is assassinated.

1984   With the support of the Reagan administration, José Napoleón Duarte defeats the ARENA party's D'Abuisson in the presidential race. The Christian Committee for the Displaced People of

El Salvador (Comité Cristiano Pro-Desplazados de El Salvador, or CRIPDES) is formed to relocate displaced citizens, provide food, health care, and literacy training, as well as to advocate for human rights.

1986   Several women's groups are formed, including the National Coordinating Committee of Salvadoran Women (Coordinadora Nacional de las Mujeres Salvadoreñas, or CONAMUS) to combat domestic violence; the Women's Institute for Research, Training, and Development (Instituto para la Investigación, Capacitación, y Desarrollo de la Mujer) to support grassroots women's groups in communication, law, and education; and the Association of Salvadoran Indigenous Women (Asociación de Mujeres Indigenas).

1987   The AMES joins the Salvadoran Women's Union (Unión de Mujeres Salvadoreñas), a coalition of five revolutionary women's associations connected to the FMLN.

1989   In honor of International Women's Day (8 March), CONAMUS opens the first battered women's shelter in El Salvador. The ARENA party's right-wing candidate, Alfredo Cristiani, wins the presidential election. The FMLN launches its final offensive. The government retaliates with a bombing campaign. The army assassinates six Jesuit priests.

1991   The Women for Dignity and Life "Breaking the Silence" (Mujeres por la Dignidad y la Vida "Rompamos el Silencio," or DIGNAS) is formed.

1992   On 16 January, the FMLN and government sign peace accords. The FMLN disarms its forces. On 25 July, the Mélida Anaya Montes Women's Movement (Movimiento de Mujeres Mélida Anaya Montes) is formed.

1995   The DIGNAS establish the Association of Mothers Seeking Child Support (Asociación de Madres Demandantes).

1997   The Non-Arrears Bill is passed by the Legislative Assembly and mandates that all political candidates obtain a clearance certification regarding their payment of child support.

CHILE

1918   Chile is granted independence from Spain.
1851–1861   A conservative government is in power.
1873–1875   Chilean industry is industrialized and urbanized.
1907   Miners organize a strike, are met by government troops; two thousand workers are killed.

1912   The Socialist Workers Party (Partido Obrero Socialista) is
                formed.
1919   The Chilean Women's Party (Partido de Mujeres Chilenas) is
                formed.
1920–1924   Arturo Alessandri is in office. While president he passes a pro-
                gressive constitution. His term ends prematurely due to the
                military exhibiting too much political power.
1927–1931   Military dictatorship of Carlos Ibáñez del Campo.
1931   Women are granted the right to vote in municipal elections.
1932   Constitutional order returns to Chile. Alessandri returns to
                power through democratic elections.
1933   The Socialist Party (Partido Socialista) is founded.
1936   Three different women's groups emerge: Feminine Action
                (Acción Feminina), the Movement of Chilean Women
                (Movimiento de la Mujer Chilena), and the Movement for the
                Emancipation of Women (Movimiento Pro-Emancipación de la
                Mujer).
1938   A coalition of members of the Communist, Radical, and
                Socialist Parties unites as the Popular Front (Frente Popular).
                Their presidential candidate is Pedro Aguirre Cerda.
1946–1952   Radical Party member Gabriel González Videla holds the presi-
                dential seat.
1949   Women gain full suffrage.
1952   Former dictator and self-proclaimed populist Carlos Ibáñez del
                Campo is reelected.
1959   Cuban Revolution triumphs. United States keeps closer watch
                on the region.
1960s   The guerrilla organization Movement for the Revolutionary
                Left (Movimiento de Izquierda Revolucionario) is formed.
1964   Christian Democrat Eduardo Frei narrowly wins the presiden-
                tial elections against Socialist Salvador Allende. (While president
                he will support the creation of the mothers' centers).
1970   Salvador Allende, representing the Popular Unity (Unidad
                Popular, or UP) coalition, becomes the first Marxist ever demo-
                cratically elected as president.
1971   Right-wing women organize the March of the Empty Pots and
                Pans against the UP government.
1972   A coalition of centrist and right-wing women organize against
                the UP coalition. Included in the march are Feminine Power
                (El Poder Femenino), and Solidarity, Order, and Liberty (Soli-
                daridad, Orden, y Libertad).

1973	On 11 September, with the support of the United Staes, army general Augusto Pinochet leads a coup against Allende.
1974	The Association of the Relatives of the Detained and Disappeared (Agrupación de Familiares de Detenido y Desaparecido) is established.
1982	The Movement of Shantytown Women (Movimiento de Mujeres Pobladores) is formed to coordinate the activities of the nearly five hundred grassroots organizations in place to combat poverty.
1983	The Movement for the Emancipation of Women '83 (Movimiento Pro-Emancipación de la Mujer '83) is formed. In the same year, ten thousand women come together in the Caupolicán Theater in Santiago to form the organization Mujeres por la Vida (Women for Life).
1986	The Right-wing National Renovation Party (Partido Renovación Nacional) is formed.
1988	On 5 October a plebiscite is held and the majority of Chileans favor the termination of Pinochet's power.
1989	Free elections are held and Christian Democrat Patricio Aylwin is elected president. Pinochet remains commander-in-chief of the army.
1991	In response to the demands of the women's movement, Patricio Aylwin creates the National Women's Service (Servicio Nacional de la Mujer).
1993	Christian Democrat Eduardo Frei Jr. is elected president.
1998	Pinochet is arrested in London on charges of crimes against humanity brought about by the Spanish government. Charges are eventually dropped and he is returned to Chile. He steps down as the head of the military and assumes the position of senator for life, a position written into the constitution he designed during his dictatorship.
2000	Former UP politico Ricardo Lagos, candidate of a centrist and leftist coalition, is elected president.

CUBA

1868–1878	Ten Years War for independence from Spain fails.
1890–1895	Economic downturn on the island; U.S. investments grow.
1892	While in exile, José Martí founds the Cuban Revolutionary Party (Partido Revolucionario Cubano), an organization that fights for independence from Spain.

1895   Martí lands on Cuban shore with a small group of insurgents; one month after his arival he is killed.

1898   Rebels come close to defeating Spain. United States intervenes after battleship *Maine* blows up in Havana harbor. United States eventually defeats Spain and claims control of Cuba, Puerto Rico, Guam, and the Philippines.

1899–1902   United States occupies Cuba and gains control of the naval base at Guantanamo Bay.

1902–1924   United States controls Cuban politics through the Liberal and Conservative Parties. Losing party often declares fraud and threatens to revolt. United States troops land in 1908, 1912, and 1917–1923.

1925–1933   Gerardo Machado is pro– United States strong-arm ruler.

1933   General strike topples Machado. The military, including sergeant Fulgencio Batista, seizes power, then hands it over to Ramón Grau San Martín. Grau's radical advisor, Antonio Guiteras, advocates reforms. United States encourages Batista to exile Grau and assassinate Guiteras in January 1934.

1940   Fulgencio Batista elected president and remains president until 1944. He drafts a constitution that grants broad protections for women and labor. Batista subsequently allows the Communist Party and labor unions political representation.

1944–1948   Grau returns to power, but his rule is corrupt.

1948   Carlos Prío Socorrás steals elections from Eduardo ("Eddie") Chibás.

1951   In protest, Chibas commits suicide during a radio broadcast.

1952   Fulgencio Batista seizes power in a coup. Within twenty-four hours students lead a protest with a mock burial of the 1940 constitution.

1953   On 26 July, Fidel Castro leads attack on Moncada Barracks in Santiago. The rebels are ruthlessly pursued by Batista's army and police, many are assassinated on the spot, many are tortured and others, including Fidel and Raúl Castro, are put on trial and then imprisoned on the Isle of Pines.

1955   Castro is released from prison and exiled to Mexico.

1956   Fidel Castro, Che Guevara, Raúl Castro, and seventy-nine other rebels, sailed from Mexico to Cuba on the *Granma* to launch their uprising in Oriente province. Shot up on the beach, only twelve survive to flee into the Sierra Maestre mountains where they organize the Revolutionary Movement of 26 July (Movimeiento Revolucionario 26 de Julio).

1957	Rebels gain strength; Batista loses some U.S. support when he uses U.S.-supplied weapons to suppress a revolt in the navy.
1958	Castro forms the Mariana Grajales Women's Platoon and women are officially allowed to become combatants.
1959	On 1 January Batista flees the island and surrenders Cuba to Castro and the rebel movement.
1960	The United States declares an economic embargo against Cuba and prohibits all economic trade and travel to the island. Castro establishes the Federation of Cuban Women (Federación de Mujeres Cubanas) in order to incorporate women into the construction of socialism.
1961	Cuban exile army, with U.S. support, attempts to overthrow Castro and is defeated at the Bay of Pigs. Castro then declares Cuba a socialist state. Later in the year Castro declares Cuba a literate nation.
1962	The United States and the USSR come close to nuclear war over Soviet missiles in Cuba. Soviets remove missiles in exchange for U.S. pledge not to invade Cuba.
1975	The Family Code is passed.
1990	As a result of the collapse of the Soviet Union, the Cuban government declares a special period of economic crisis, allowing some private enterprise and foreign investment.
1992	Cuban constitution is modified to include strong language mandating equality between men and women.
1993	Cuban women journalists come together at a conference and form the Colectivo Magín.
1995	The United Nations Development Program releases a Human Development Report that recognizes Cuba as the leader in gender equality within the developing world.
1996	The Communist Party declares the Colectivo Magín illegal.

NOTES

1. In nearly every case I use the real names of the women interviewed, per their requests. Most of the women with whom I spoke were already publicly known, thus making pseudonyms largely ineffective. Furthermore, the interviewees were committed to an accurate historical record, thus making their identities important.

    Throughout the book, the ages of the interviewees and their positions in coalitions and government, when given, were applicable at the time of the interviews.

2. Julieta Kirkwood is seen as a leading Chilean socialist-feminist of the 1980s for her poignant analyses of the positions of women, the Left, and feminism. (See 1982, 1983, 1986, and 1989.)

3. In Karen Kampwirth's book *Women and Guerrilla Movements* (2002) she notes that one of the Salvadoran women she interviewed also came to a feminist consciousness while a political prisoner. Though the reasons were different, the irony of prison-facilitated feminism is noteworthy.

4. These include Haydée Santamaría, Celia Sánchez Manduley, Melba Hernández, and Vilma Espín, all of whom will be discussed in chapter 5.

5. Molyneux has since responded to such critiques and expanded her original arguments (see Molyneux 1998).

6. Institutional feminists are those who work within state structures and NGOs to advance feminist agendas. Largely as a result of feminist mobilization during the dictatorships that have since been transformed to democracies, there has been a proliferation of such NGOs and women's ministries. For a case-study analysis of this debate see Donna Murdock, "When Women Have Wings: Feminist NGO Strategies and Social Class in Medellin, Columbia," Ph.D. diss., Emory University, 2003.

7. Related to this, the United Nations–sponsored conferences on the status of women have also been influential to Latin American feminists. The UN declared 1975–1985 the International Decade for Women. During that time meetings happened in Mexico (1975), Copenhagen (1980), and Nairobi (1985). Since the Decade for Women ended, the Fourth World Conference on Women took place in Beijing in 1995, with a follow-up conference, Beijing plus Five, in 2000.

8. See Jaquette 1973 for one of the earliest overviews of women in Latin American guerrilla movements.

9. Gender-bending is a process also applicable to men, though this study focuses only on women.

10. I thank Lois Hect Oppenheim for sharing this term with me.

11. They were called the "elections of the century" for four reasons: (1) they were the first elections to follow the signing of the peace accords; (2) they were arguably the first democratic elections ever held in El Salvador; (3) they were the first elections in which all members of the political spectrum were represented, and (4) the voting

cycle in El Salvador is such that the executive, legislative, and local branches are rarely up for re-election at the same time, which was the case during these elections (Saint-Germain 1997, 90).

12. I conducted these interviews with Salvadoran feminists who were in the United States on speaking tours or had relocated during the war as U.S. representatives of the FMLN.

13. Due to the fact that at the last moment my visa was changed to a one-month tourist visa I was unable to spend as much time in Cuba as I would have liked.

14. I traveled to Cuba with Arizona State University's Latin American studies scholars program.

CHAPTER 1   GENDER AND THE REVOLUTIONARY STRUGGLE
IN EL SALVADOR, 1979–1992

1. "On March 15, 1993, the U.N.-sponsored Truth Commission released its long-awaited report. The report was based on the testimony of two thousand persons who had come forward, under promises of confidentiality, to testify as witnesses about the fate of seven thousand victims and on secondary information about the fate of more than eighteen thousand victims. The report found that 85 percent of the nine thousand human rights abuses investigated, and 95 percent of the killings, were committed by government-supported death squads and the military" (Keen and Haynes 2000, 498).

2. This is term that resulted from the United Nations negotiations and has been adopted by the FMLN.

3. I use the terms *revolutionary movement, revolutionary struggle,* and *resistance movement* interchangeably to refer to both the armed and unarmed movements that sought to overthrow the Salvadoran government and military.

4. In addition to the testimonies of women I interviewed, the information for this section is drawn from the following sources: (Bethell 1991; Cohen and Wali 1990; Keen and Hayes 2000; Montgomery 1995; Pérez-Brignoli 1989; Skidmore and Smith 1997, and Stephen 1994).

5. For a general overview of U.S. policy toward the region see Peter Smith, *Talons of the Eagle: Dynamics of U.S.-Latin American Relations* (New York: Oxford University Press, 1996) and Lars Schoultz, *Beneath the United States: A History of U.S. Policy Towards Latin America* (Cambridge, Mass: Harvard University Press, 1998).

6. See Arthur F. McGovern, *Liberation Theology and Its Critics: Toward an Assessment* (New York: Orbis, 1989) and by Daniel H. Levine, *Popular Voices in Latin American Catholicism* (Princeton, N.J.: Princeton University Press, 1992).

7. In this case I am referring to organizations that do not see themselves as either feminine or feminist but are, nonetheless, made up of women.

8. "Mélida Anaya Montes was murdered . . . because she would not back off [of] a principled position that directly challenged Cayetano Carpio, the commander-in-chief of the FPL. The principle over which they struggled was whether *guerra prolongada* (prolonged war), Carpio's tactic, or Anaya Montes's position, which sought a political solution to the war, would [prevail]. Following Anaya Montes's assassination Cayetano Carpio, considered the father of the revolution, committed suicide" (Golden 1991, 167). And, as we know, the war ended with a negotiated settlement.

9. The 1995 interview was conducted by a colleague of mine working from questions that I wrote. In September of 1998 I was able to interview Esperanza Ramos myself. She is currently a member with a twenty-year history in ANDES and its Women's Secretariat the Cooperativa Asociación Nacional de Educadores Salvadoreñas (or CO-ANDES). At the time of the 1998 interview the current president of CO-ANDES, also at the interview, was Kenya Isabel Santos Martinez.

10. The *capucha* is a "form of torture in which the prisoner's head is covered with a hood (usually the inside of the hood is coated with toxic chemicals). As the prisoner breathes, the hood sticks to his or her face, resulting in suffocation" (Stephen 1994, 237).

11. Regarding Argentina, see Arditti 1999, and Fisher 1993; regarding Chile, see Chuchryk 1989b, 1994; regarding Guatemala, see Schirmer 1993; and regarding Latin America in general, see Craske, 1999; Miller, 1991, and Muños and Portillo 1986.

12. From the perspective of Evelyn Stevens, as articulated in her highly problematic essay "Marianismo: The Other Face of Machismo," such positioning is the result of the fact that Latin American society is organized around what she calls "marianismo, " or "the cult of feminine spiritual superiority, which teaches that women are semi-divine, morally superior to and spiritually stronger than men" (1973a, 91). Here I must clarify that my intention is not to suggest that Salvadoran, and indeed Latin American, society writ large is structured as Stevens suggests, but to highlight the revered role of the mother in Catholic discourse and ideology. For an excellent essay that critiques Stevens's work and articulates the need to move beyond her paradigm, see Marysa Navarro, "Against *Marianismo*," pp. 257–72 in *Genders Place: Feminist Anthropologies of Latin America*, ed., Rosario Montoya, Leslie Jo Frazier, and Janise Hurtig (New York: Palgrave, 2002).

13. Ernesto "Che" Guevara is the most revered and respected of all guerrilla leaders, strategists, and fighters. Born in Argentina, Che considered himself an internationalist who fought against imperialism in all parts of the world. He played a leading role in the Cuban Revolution and was later killed in Bolivia in 1967.

14. Luciak explains that the numbers most likely underestimate at least 10 to 15 percent of the FMLN's membership who were not processed. Additionally he notes an inconsistency between ONUSAL's figure that 29.1 percent of the FMLN were women in contrast the FMLN's wartime claim of 40 percent (2001, 4, 7, and 244–45 n. 10).

15. She has since left the FMLN.

16. After seven months in jail, Mária Marta Valladares was eventually released in a prisoner exchange with Inés Duarte, who was the president's daughter, an official for the Christian Democratic Party, and the manager of Liberty Radio, a station owned by the Duarte family and financed with U.S. aid. The kidnap, organized to force the release of Maria Marta Valladares (as well as other political prisoners) "was one of the most successful operations of the urban front in recent times" (Díaz 1992, 174). This was an extremely risky operation given that it occurred in the capital city of San Salvador, which had about twenty-five-thousand soldiers readied for its protection and defense.

CHAPTER 2   FEMINISM IN POSTWAR EL SALVADOR, 1992–1999

1. The organization takes its name from Mélida Anaya Montes (also known as Comandante Ana María), second in command of the Popular Forces of Liberation (Fuerzas Populares de Liberación) and founder of the teacher's union (ANDES) discussed in chapter 1.

2. See also Stephen 1997, 102–4.

3. The year 1979 is identified by Mary Thomson (1986, 94) and Lynn Stephen (1994, 206), whereas Patricia Hipsher (2001, 138) suggests 1978 was the year that AMES was formed.

4. As I explained in the introduction to this book, they were called "the elections of the century" for four reasons: (1) they were the first elections to follow the signing of the peace accords, (2) the first democratic elections ever held in El Salvador; (3) they were also the first elections in which all members of the political spectrum

were represented, and (4) the voting cycle in El Salvador is such that the executive, legislative, and local branches are rarely up for reelection at the same time, which was the case during these elections (Saint-Germain 1997, 90).

5. The Mujeres '94 platform included the following points: "An end to incest, rape, and sexual harassment; land, credit, and technical assistance for women; adequate housing with ownership for women; worker training, more places in the workforce, and equal salaries to men; [a] stop [to] the rising costs of basic wage goods; equal opportunity for girls in schools; coordinated medical attention for women in more and better hospitals; consistent sexual education and the expression of women's sexuality without prejudices; free and voluntary motherhood; responsible fatherhood and an increase in food rations; respect for the environment and a better quality of life for women; development policies that take care of women's needs; laws that don't discriminate against women . . . women should hold 50 percent of the positions of power" (Stephen 1994, 218).

6. I am grateful to Victoria Polanco for sharing this term with me.

7. The booklet to which she is referring is called: *Hacer Política Desde Las Mujeres: Una propuesta feminista para la participación política de las mujeres salvadoreñas* by Sonia Baires, Gloria Castañeda, and Clara Murguialday. San Salvador: Las DIGNAS. (1993).

8. The training of which López speaks was the initial feminist consciousness-raising workshops in which the DIGNAS participated.

9. For parallel discussions of this phenomenon see Lind 1992 and Chinchilla 1992.

10. This is an organization set up through the Peace Accords.

11. Leonel Gonzalez's real name is Salvador Sánchez. During the war he was the commander-in-chief of the FPL.

12. See also Hipsher 2001, 146, for a similar observation regarding sectarianism and the Salvadoran women's movement.

13. For similar testimonies, see Hipsher 2001; Kampwirth 2002; Luciak 2001; Stephen 1997; and Vasquez 1995.

14. Though I doubt Ilja Luciak (2001) would disagree with this point he does provide impressive data regarding the formal commitment of the FMLN to incorporating women into the party vis-à-vis affirmative action programs.

CHAPTER 3   THE TENURE OF SALVADOR ALLENDE THROUGH
A FEMINIST LENS, 1970–1973

Another version of the Allende quote that makes up this chapter's epigraph, most likely due to editing and translation, reads, "This is surely the last time I will address you. My words are not spoken in bitterness, but in disappointment. There will be a moral judgment against those who betrayed the oath they took as soldiers of Chile, legitimately designated as commanders in chief. . . . Long live Chile! Long live the people! Long live the workers! These are my last words. And I am convinced my sacrifice will not be in vain. I am certain that this sacrifice will be a moral lesson that will punish cowardice, treachery, and treason" (quoted in Spooner 1994, 17).

1. I credit Lois Hect Oppenheim for sharing this term and these observations with me.

2. Allende only garnered thirty thousand more votes than the second place candidate: Allende had 36.2, Alesssandri 34.9, and Tomic 27.8 percent of the votes (Oppenheim 1999, 38).

3. For the most recent and thorough overview of the mobilization of right-wing women in Allende's Chile see Margaret Power, *Right-Wing Women in Chile: Feminine Power and the Struggle Against Allende 1964–1973* (University Park: Pennsylvania State University Press, 2002).

4. In addition to the testimonies of women I interviewed, the information for this section is drawn from the following sources: Agosín 1996; Baldez 2002; Franceschet 2001; Keen and Hayes 2000; Oppenheim 1999, and Spooner 1994.

5. For more detailed accounts of women's mobilization in early twentieth century Chile see, Franceschet 2001; Gaviola, Largo, and Palestro 1994; Miller 1991, and Valdés and Weinstein 1993.

6. For an overview of MEMCH see "MEMCH: Antología para una historia del movimiento femenino en Chile." (N/D). This booklet was assembled by contemporary feminist activists who have also organized using the name MEMCH.

7. Relying upon the women's self-identification of social class status is a bit problematic. Many of the women I interviewed appeared to be members of the upper class of Chilean society despite their self-identification as middle class. A report put out by the *Grupo Iniciativa Mujeres,* a coalition of eleven nongovernmental women's organizations, defines one's socioeconomic class status in Chile as based on the neighborhood she lives in, her type of housing, her level of education and professional status, activities performed by the head of household, monthly salary, and the type of car she drives (1999, 4–7). In one case, I sat in the luxurious home of a woman who described herself as middle class despite the fact that in every one of the aforementioned categories she met the criteria for upper class. (I don't know her monthly income, but based on the fact that her home was one of three on her property, the other two inhabited by her daughter and the domestic who worked for her, I have to assume that her and/or her husband's salary was at the level specified in the report as upper class.)

8. Though I was unable to, Carmen encouraged me to go to the part of the country where the mining happened so that I could see that, as she said, "the mountains are gone" as a result of the mining.

9. Gladys Marín, long-time member of the Communist Party, was the first woman to run for president in Chile (see Marín 1998).

10. Price and supply associations (*juntos de abastecimiento y precio*, or JAPs) were formed in order to ensure that people had access to basic goods. They were organizations that were often supported through the voluntary labor of women.

11. Though Soledad did not share her brother's name with me, a colleague called my attention to his identity: "On March 28, 1985, three professionals, who were secret Communist Party members, were taken away by the police and killed. Two, José Manuel Parada and Manuel Guerrero, were dragged from their place of work, the *Colegio Latinoamericano* (Latin American School), in broad daylight. The three dead men, their throats slashed, were found two days later" (Oppenheim 1999, 177).

12. As we will see in the case of Cuba, predating the UN Decade for Women did not mean that a government would be unable to adequately address the needs of women. In 1960 Fidel Castro formed the Federation of Cuban Women (Federación de Mujeres Cubanas), which worked from an exhaustive platform that addressed women's practical gender needs.

13. Despite the fact that the mothers' centers were government sponsored, they were not the sort of projects to which she is referring.

14. In our discussion about Allende's policies of socializing housework I mentioned to Soledad that his programs sounded quite similar to what Angela Davis has described in her essay "The Approaching Obsolescence of Housework: A Working-Class Perspective." Davis argues, "socialized housework implies large government subsidies in order to guarantee accessibility to the working-class families whose need for such services is most obvious" (1983, 223). Soledad was familiar with Davis's essay (and has met her), and concurred regarding the similarities with the Allende government.

15. See Baldez 2002 for a detailed discussion of the parallels between anti-Allende and anti-Pinochet women.

16. After a "dress rehearsal" for the coup on the twenty-ninth of June 1973 Salvador Allende reaffirmed his commitment to democracy, even in the face of an imminent military uprising:"Comrades . . . the people know what I have repeatedly told them. The Chilean revolutionary process has to follow its own path in accordance with our history, our institutions, our characteristics. Therefore, the people must understand that I have to be faithful to what I say. We will make the revolutionary changes within democratic pluralism, democracy and freedom. This does not mean—hear me well—this does not mean that we will tolerate antidemocrats, the subversives, and least of all the fascists, comrades" (Cockroft 2000, 237).

CHAPTER 4   DICTATORSHIP, DEMOCRACY, AND FEMINISM
             IN POST-ALLENDE CHILE, 1973–1999

1. The use of the term *democracy* for Chile's current political status is a bit problematic. Certainly Chile is experiencing more democracy than during the dictatorship of Augusto Pinochet, but there is still a climate of fear that impacts the freedom of expression in the country, and this became very obvious as my stay in Chile progressed. The current Chilean constitution was drafted by Pinochet, and is thus anything but a democratic document; and the current government, albeit socialist in name, is tightly restricted by the binomial electoral system, unable to gain a leftist or even center-left majority in the house and thus implement structural and political changes. It is important, then, to understand democracy in Chile not only in contrast to a dictatorship but also in comparison to the open pluralistic system that allowed for the election of a Marxist president. For further discussion of these debates, see Matear 1997, 99 n. 1; McSherry, 1998; Oppenheim, 1999; and Oxhorn and Ducatenzeller, 1998.

2. Basso refers to "we" because I interviewed her together with Soledad Parada.

3. For a more detailed discussion, see Spooner 1994, 66–67.

4. As was reported in both the Spanish and English press in the United States during the week of 10–17 March 1998, Pinochet finally stepped down as the head of the armed forces and assumed the position of senator for life. This transition and refusal to relinquish power was met with protest. One senator proclaimed his opposition, stating that Pinochet has never been elected to any position in Chile and certainly did not deserve to be a senator for life, while street protesters echoed this same sentiment and were met with riot police.

5. See for example, Agosín 1996; Baldez 2002; Boyle 1993; Chuchryk 1984, 1989a, 1989b, 1994; Fisher 1993; Franceschet 2001; Frohmann and Valdés 1995; Gaviola, Largo and Palestro 1994; Maloof 1999; Molina 1986; Muñoz Dálbora 1987; Noonan 1997; Palestro 1991; Safa 1995; Sepúlveda 1996; Valdés and Weinstein 1993; and Valenzuela 1995.

6. Chuchryk 1994 is generally regarded as the most exhaustive survey of this period; for a more recent account see Baldez 2002.

7. When I was in the office of the AFDD it was not uncommon to see women with three or four pictures of loved ones safety-pinned to their breast, every photo representing a disappeared relative.

8. Viviana Díaz explained that in the first year of the AFDD's work, of the 1,198 detained and disappeared, 74 were women (personal interview, 1999).

9. At the time of the interview she was the vice president. Then president Sola Sierra passed away while I was in Chile.

10. The Chilean police, *carabineros*, continue to use these same water-canon-equipped tanks in response to public protests.

11. When I asked Chilean women about feminism in contemporary Chile, nearly all remarked that International Women's Day is still celebrated, so therefore some sort of feminist movement remains present.

12. Mujeres por la Vida does not officially still exist, though Teresa Valdés and Graciela Borquez both described to me the tight networks that resulted from the coalition and remain intact.

13. Ricardo Lagos was elected president of Chile in January 2000. See Winn 2000, 6–10, for a discussion of this narrow victory.

14. The documentary *In Women's Hands* (Field and Mandelbaum 1993) includes footage of these types of demonstrations and other campaign tactics employed by the women.

15. For recent discussions of this period see Baldez 2002 and Franceschet 2001 and 2003.

16. Courtney Rivard complicates this a bit and suggests that the type of transition to democracy, either punctuated (as in the case of Chile) or chronic (as in the case of El Salvador) have differing effects on the status of women's movements in post-transition states. She elaborates her theory through the case of Honduras in Rivard 2003.

17. The critique of Bajo Suspecha, that the *historicas* have not adjusted their framework, analysis, and strategies to run parallel with the contemporary era of globalization, is one that has been taken up at the regional level. Alvarez et al 2003, explain how one of the newer points of contention within the feminist *encuentros* has been this very struggle, indeed, in part initiated by the young women of Bajo Suspecha.

18. This analysis is parallel to John Foran's (1992) theory of the necessity of a personalistic dictator, among other things, for a successful revolution in order to keep the opposition focused, united, and triumphant.

19. For the purposes of this study I do not consider the movement against Pinochet to be a revolutionary struggle but rather a radical social movement to reinstate democracy.

CHAPTER 5   THE CUBAN INSURRECTION THROUGH A FEMINIST LENS, 1952–1959

1. In the language of the revolutionary movement these skirts were called "the deceivers" (Waters 2003, 30).

2. In addition to the testimonies of women I interviewed, the information for this section is drawn from Foran 1994; Franqui 1968; García-Pérez 1998; Keen and Haynes 2000; Maloof 1999; Pérez-Stable 1999; Smith and Padula 1996, and documents that I found in the archives maintained by the Federation of Cuban Women. For a detailed overview of Cuban history, Pérez-Stable 1999 is an excellent source. For a detailed case study of the structure of the Cuban revolutionary movement, see García-Pérez 1998.

3. This number comes from an interview a colleague did with María Antonia Figueroa. Figueroa was at the trial of Fidel Castro where he was found guilty and sentenced to jail. Keen and Haynes (2000, 440) however, report that Castro was in jail for nineteen months.

4. It is important to note that Macaulay's article is focused upon the difficulty in actually quantifying numbers in the rebel army.

5. In the nineteenth century, Mariana Grajales was the most revered mother of the resistance. She was known as the "the lioness," mother of "the bronze Titan" (General Antonio Maceo). Seven of her thirteen children died in combat, and she is one of the few women to be honored with a monument in Cuba (Smith and Padula 1996, 11).

6. This quote comes from a document that is not clearly marked. It appears to be transcripts from a speech one of the members of the brigade made at some sort of anniversary celebration of the founding of the brigade. I found this and other

similar documents in some makeshift archives—literally, boxes in drawers—at one of the offices of the Federation of Cuban Women in Havana in August 1999.

CHAPTER 6   THE WOMEN'S MOVEMENT IN
POSTINSURRECTION CUBA, 1959–1999

1. The use of these mansions formerly owned by sugar barons is evident all over Havana. They serve to house everything from the Federation of Cuban Women to cultural centers to embassies.
2. It is important to note, however, that many women complained to me that despite the institutional availability and protection of health care most hospitals are severely understocked in everything from simple bandages to antibiotics. This situation has been exacerbated by the combination of the "special period" (to be discussed later) and the U.S. Embargo against Cuba (personal interviews, 1999).
3. This has not always been the case in Cuba, even in the Castro era. Under the 1938 criminal code, which remained on the books until 1979, abortion was allowed in only three circumstances: to save the life of the mother, in the case of rape, or to avoid birth defects from hereditary diseases. What is not often mentioned is that the Castro government actively opposed abortion for several years. Another obstacle to women obtaining abortions was that after 1959 many doctors left Cuba as their lucrative professions became nationalized and subsequently their incomes dropped. Thus, there was a period when the maternal death rate increased dramatically from self-adminsitered abortions. By 1980 the Ministry of Health was alarmed by figures of deaths from illegal abortions and attempted a program to both discourage abortions and make them safer and more accessible. It was in the 1980s that abortion became available without charge through the tenth week of pregnancy (Smith and Padula 1996, 73–76).
4. Molyneux's (2001b) article is a detailed analysis of the evolution of the FMC.
5. My initial introduction to Ms. Perrera was less than cordial. My colleagues and I had come to Cuba to do research on various aspects of women's experiences throughout the twentieth century. As I explained in the introduction of this book one must receive official permission from the Ministry of Culture to conduct research in Cuba—permission that my colleagues and I were denied. Ms. Perrera was annoyed that we did not contact the FMC about our research agendas. According to Ms. Perrera we should have known that everything related to women must be channeled through and thus unofficially monitored by the FMC.
6. For an interesting overview of NGOs in Cuba, including a discussion specifically of the FMC, see Gillian Gunn, "Cubas NGOs: Government Puppets or Seeds of Civil Society," Washington, D.C.: Center for Latin American Studies at Georgetown University, 1995.
7. CDRs are Committees to Defend the Revolution, established by the government and organized by neighborhood. They were originally established to prepare the Cuban people for an invasion from the United States. They remain intact and now serve as the eyes and ears of the revolutionary regime. I, however, met some CDR "volunteers" who had no commitment to their task other than to keep their record clean by performing it.
8. Cubans are most likely to gain access to the U.S. dollar through their contact with foreigners—for example, taxi drivers, hotel wait staff, prostitutes, black-market vendors, and the like. If one works as a professor or medical doctor, for example, she will be paid with Cuban pesos.
9. The "political spectrum" in Cuba is difficult to characterize. One can, however, think of it in terms of degree of criticism leveled against the government combined with membership or not in the Communist Party. It is important to note, though, that not

all members of the Communist Party were uncritical of the government—most of the women I interviewed were members and some had quite severe criticisms.

10. The classic Cuban film *Portrait of Teresa* (Vega 1979) was made by the government in 1979 in an attempt to sensitize the Cuban population to this reality. While in Cuba many of the women I interviewed suggested this film to me both to demonstrate the government's awareness regarding the Cuban woman's reality and to provide me with a daily picture of the scenarios they often described in a somewhat abstract manner.

11. Something very telling in my interviews across countries is that when I asked women that did identify as feminists when they started using that term, the vast majority could trace that personal transformation to almost the exact event. I find this striking, as it implies that the identity is far more than a mere label but rather a political commitment that at a certain point begins to shape one's life and worldview. This indicates that feminism, when embraced, is taken quite seriously.

12. For an excellent collection of essays that speak to the complexity of Cuba, see María López Vigil, *Neither Heaven Nor Hell* (Washington, D.C.: Ecumenical Program on Central America and the Caribbean, 1999).

13. For a detailed overview of the failure of socialist projects to welcome feminism, see Randall 1992.

References

Print and Visual Sources

Acosta, Mariclaire. (1993). "The Comadres of El Salvador: A Case Study." Pp. 126–39 in *Surviving Beyond Fear: Women, Children, and Human Rights In Latin America*, edited by Marjorie Agosín. New York: White Pine Press.

Agosín, Marjorie. (1987). *Scraps of Life: Chilean Arpilleras*. Toronto: Williams-Wallace.

———, ed. (1993). Surviving Beyond Fear: Women, Children, and Human Rights in Latin America. New York: White Pine Press.

———. (1996). *Ashes of Revolt: Essays on Human Rights*. New York: White Pine Press.

Alegría, Claribel, and Darwin J. Flakoll, eds. (1989). *On the Front Line: Guerrilla Poems of El Salvador*. Willimantic, Conn.: Curbstone Press.

Alvarez, Julia. (1994). *In the Time of the Butterflies*. New York: Plume.

Alvarez, Sonia. (1990). *Engendering Democracy in Brazil: Women's Movements in Transition Politics*. Princeton, N.J.: Princeton University Press.

———. (1994). "The (Trans)formation of Feminism(s) and Gender Politics in Democratizing Brazil." Pp. 13–63 in *The Women's Movement in Latin America: Participation and Democracy*, 2d ed., edited by Jane Jaquette. Boulder, Colo.: Westview Press.

Alvarez, Sonia E., Elisabeth Jay Friedman, Erika Beckman, Maylei Blackwell, Norma Stoltz Chinchilla, Nathalie Lebon, Marysa Navarro, and Marcela Ríos Tobar. (2003). "Encountering Latin America and Caribbean Feminisms." *Signs: Journal of Women in Culture and Society* 28 (2): 537–79.

Aman, Kenneth, and Christian Parker, eds. (1989). *Popular Cultures in Chile: Resistance and Survival*. Boulder, Colo.: Westview Press.

Andreas, Carol. 1977. "The Chilean Woman: Reform, Reaction, and Resistance." *Latin American Perspectives* 4 (4): 121–25.

Arditti, Rita. (1999). *Searching for Life: The Grandmothers of the Plaza de Mayo and the Disappeared Children of Argentina*. Berkeley and Los Angeles: University of California Press.

Arguelles, Lourdes. (1993). "Crazy Wisdom: Memories of a Cuban Queen." Pp. 194–204 in *Sisters, Sexperts, Queers: Beyond the Lesbian Nation*, edited by Arlene Stein. New York: Plume.

Arguelles, Lourdes, and Ruby Rich. (1984). "Homosexuality, Homophobia, and Revolution: Notes toward an Understanding of the Cuban Lesbian and Gay Male Experience, Part I." *Signs: Journal of Women in Culture and Society* 9 (4):120–36.

———. (1985). "Homosexuality, Homophobia, and Revolution: Notes toward and Understanding of the Cuban Lesbian and Gay Male Experience, Part II." *Signs: Journal of Women in Culture and Society* 11 (1): 120–36.

Armstrong, Robert, and Janet Shenk. (1982). *El Salvador: The Race of Revolution*. Boston: South End Press.

Asociación de Mujeres Comunicadoras (Magín). (1996). "¡Dí, mama! ¿Tú sabes qué cosa es género?" New York: United Nations Development Fund for Women.

Azicri, Max. (1981). "Women's Development through Revolutionary Mobilization: A Study of the Federation of Cuban Women." Pp. 276–308 in *Cuban Communism*, edited by Irving Louis Horowitz. New Brunswick, N.J.: Transaction.

———. (1988). *Cuba: Politics, Economics, and Society*. London: Pinter.

Baires, Sonia, Gloria Castañeda, and Clara Murguialday. (1993). *Hacer Política Desde Las Mujeres: Una propuesta feminista para la participación política de las mujeres salvadoreñas*. San Salvador: Las DIGNAS.

Baires, Sonia, Dilcia Marroquín, Clara Murguialday, Ruth Dolanco, and Norma Vásquez. (1996). *Mami, mami, demanda la cuotala necesitamos: Un análisis feminista sobre la demanda de cuota alimenticia a lo Procuraduría*. San Salvador: Las DIGNAS.

Baldez, Lisa. (2002). *Why Women Protest: Women's Movements in Chile*. Cambridge: Cambridge University Press.

Balari, Eugenio R., Violeta Chang Banos, and Ana González Mora. (1980). "La mujer cubana: el camino hacia su emancipación." Havana: Instituto Cubano de Investigaciones y Orientación de la Demanda Interna.

Belli, Giocanda. (1994). *The Inhabited Woman*. Willimantic, Conn.: Curbstone Press.

———. (2002). *The Country Under My Skin: A Memoir of Love and War*. New York: Knopf.

Bengelsdorf, Carollee. (1988). "On the Problem of Studying Women in Cuba." Pp. 119–36 in *Cuban Political Economy: Controversies in Cubanology*, edited by Andrew Zimbalist. Boulder, Colo.: Westview Press.

———. (1994). *The Problem of Democracy in Cuba: Between Vision and Reality*. New York: Oxford University Press.

Benjamin, Medea, Joseph Collins, and Michael Schott. (1984). *No Free Lunch: Food and Revolution in Cuba Today*. San Francisco: Institute for Food and Development.

Berger Gluck, Sherna, and Daphne Patai, eds. (1991). *Women's Words: The Feminist Practice of Oral History*. New York: Routledge.

Bethell, Leslie, ed. (1991). *Central America Since Independence*. New York: Cambridge University Press.

———, ed. (1993a). *Chile since Independence*. Cambridge: Cambridge University Press.

———, ed. (1993b). *Cuba: A Short History*. Cambridge: Cambridge University Press.

Boyle, Catherine M. (1993). "Touching The Air: The Cultural Forces of Women in Chile." Pp. 156–72 in *'Viva': Women and Popular Protest in Latin America*, edited by Sarah A. Radcliffe and Sallie Westwood. London: Routledge.

Brenner, Phillip. (1999). "Washington Loosens the Knot (Just a Little)." *NACLA: Report on the Americas* 32 (5): 41–45.

Bunck, Julie Marie. (1989). "The Cuban Revolution and Women's Rights." Pp. 443–64 in *Cuban Communism*, edited by Irving Louis Horowitz. New Brunswick, N.J.: Transaction.

Bunster, Ximena. (1993). "Surviving beyond Fear: Women and Torture in Latin America." in *Surviving Beyond Fear: Women, Children and Human Rights In Latin America*, edited by Marjorie Agosín. New York: White Pine Press.

Byrne, Hugh. (1996). *El Salvador's Civil War: A Study of Revolution*. Boulder, Colo.: Lynne Rienner.

Cagan, Elizabeth. (1999). "Women and Grassroots Democracy in El Salvador: The Case of Comunidad Segundo Montes." Pp. 173–95 in *Democratization and Women's Grassroots Movements*, edited by Jill M. Bystydzienski and Joti Sekhon. Bloomington: Indiana University Press.

Casal, Lourdes. (1980). "Revolution and *Conciencia*: Women in Cuba." Pp. 183–206 in

Women, War, and Revolution, edited by Carol R. Berkin and Clara M. Lovett. New York: Holmes and Meier.

Chaney, Elsa M. (1974). "The Mobilization of Women in Allende's Chile." Pp. 267–80 in *Women in Politics*, edited by Jane Jaquette. New York: John Wiley and Sons.

———. (1979). *Supermadre: Women in Politics in Latin America.* Austin: University of Texas Press.

Chinchilla, Norma. (1992). "Marxism, Feminism, and the Struggle for Democracy in Latin America." Pp. 38–49 in *The Making of Social Movements in Latin America*, edited by Arturo Escobar and Sonia Alvarez. Boulder, Colo.: Westview Press.

———. (1993). "Gender and National Politics: Issues and Trends in Women's Participation in Latin American Movements." Pp. 37–54 in *Researching Women in Latin America and the Caribbean*, edited by Edna Acosta-Belén and Christine E. Bose. Boulder, Colo.: Westview Press.

Chuchryk, Patricia. (1984). "Protest, Politics and Personal Life: The Emergence of Feminism in a Military Dictatorship, Chile 1973–1983." Ph.D. diss., York University, Toronto.

———. (1989a). "Feminist Anti-Authoritarian Politics: The Role of Women's Organizations in the Chilean Transition to Democracy." Pp. 149–84 in *The Women's Movement in Latin America: Feminism and the Transition to Democracy*, edited by Jane Jaquette. Boston: Unwin Hyman.

———. (1989b). "Subversive Mothers: The Women's Opposition to the Military Regime in Chile." Pp. 86–97 in *Surviving Beyond Fear: Women, Children and Human Rights in Latin America*, edited by Marjorie Agosín. New York: White Pine Press.

———. (1994). "From Dictatorship to Democracy: The Women's Movement in Chile." Pp. 65–107 in *The Women's Movement In Latin America: Participation and Democracy*, edited by Jane Jaquette. Boulder, Colo.: Westview Press.

Cockroft, James D, ed. (2000). *The Salvador Allende Reader: Chile's Voice of Democracy.* Melbourne: Ocean Press.

Comité de Defensa de los Derechos de la Mujer. (1985a). "Editorial: Estamos Dando a Luz La Unidad." *Vamos Mujer*, no. 2: 3.

———. (1985b). "Fidel en la clausura del IV Congreso de la F.M.C." *Vamos Mujer*, no. 2: 7.

———. (1985c). "Julieta Kirkwood." *Vamos Mujer*, no. 2: 9.

———. (1985e). "Situación Nacional." *Vamos Mujer*, no. 5: 4–5.

———. (1986a). "Compañera Combatiente!" *Vamos Mujer*, no. 1: 12–13.

———. (1986b). "Día Internacional de la Mujer." *Vamos Mujer*, no. 1: 9.

———. (1986c). "Situación Nacional." *Vamos Mujer*, no. 1: 4–5.

Cohen, Pamela, and Monona Wali, dirs. (1990). *María's Story.* Produced by Pamela Cohen and Catherine M. Ryan. Los Angeles: Camino Film Projects.

Colburn, Forrest D. (1999). "Post–Cold War Feminism in El Salvador." *Dissent*, Winter, 43–46.

Cole, Johnetta B. (1980). "Women in Cuba: The Revolution within the Revolution." Pp. 162–78 in *Comparative Perspectives of Third World Women: The Impact of Race, Sex, and Class*, edited by Beverly Lindsay. New York: Praeger.

Collier, Simon, and William F. Sater. (1996). *A History of Chile, 1808–1994.* Cambridge: Cambridge University Press.

Collier, Simon, Thomas E. Skidmore, and Harold Blakemore, eds. (1992). *The Cambridge Encyclopedia of Latin America and the Caribbean.* Cambridge: Cambridge University Press.

Constable, Pamela, and Arturo Valenzuela. (1993). *A Nation of Enemies: Chile under Pinochet.* New York: W. W. Norton.

Craske, Nikki. (1999). *Women and Politics in Latin America*. New Brunswick, N.J.: Rutgers University Press.

Crummet de los Angeles, María. (1977). "El Poder Femenino: The Mobilization of Women against Socialism in Chile." *Latin American Perspectives*, no. 4: 103–13.

Dandavati, Annie G. (1996). *The Women's Movement and the Transition to Democracy in Chile.* New York: Peter Lang.

Davis, Angela. (1983). *Women Race and Class*. New York: Vintage.

De Shazer, Mary K. (1994). *A Poetics of Resistance: Women Writing in El Salvador, South Africa, and the United States.* Ann Arbor: University of Michigan Press.

Debray, Régis. (1971). *The Chilean Revolution: Conversations with Allende.* New York: Pantheon.

Díaz Caro, Viviana, Sola Sierra Henríquez, and Gustavo Adolfo Becerra. (1997). *20 años: Un camino de imágenes.* Santiago: Agrupación De Familiares de Detenidos Desaparecidos.

Díaz, Nidia. (1992). *I Was Never Alone: A Prison Diary from El Salvador.* New York: Ocean Press.

Las DIGNAS, ed. (1996). *Montañas con Recuerdos de Mujer.* San Salvador: Las DIGNAS.

Dix, Robert H. (1984). "Why Revolutions Succeed and Fail." *Polity*, no. 41: 423–46.

Dolgoff, Sam. (1976). *The Cuban Revolution: A Critical Perspective.* Montreal: Black Rose.

Dore, Elizabeth, ed. (1997). *Gender Politics in Latin America: Debates in Theory and Practice.* New York: Monthly Review Press.

Dunkerley, James. (1982). *The Long War: Dictatorship and Revolution in El Salvador.* London: Verso.

———. (1988). *Power in the Isthmus: A Political History of Modern Central America.* London: Verso.

Eckstein, Susan. (1994). *Back from the Future: Cuba under Castro.* Princeton, N.J.: Princeton University Press.

Ehlers, Tracy. (1991). "Debunking Marianismo: Economic Vulnerability and Survival Strategies among Guatemalan Wives." *Ethnology* 30 (1): 1–16.

Eisenstein, Zillah R., ed. (1979). *Capitalist Patriarchy and the Case for Socialist Feminism.* New York: Monthly Review Press.

Espín, Vilma. (1991). *Cuban Women Confront the Future.* Melbourne: Ocean Press.

Esteva Fabregat, Claudio. (1995). *Mestizaje in Iberoamérica.* Tucson: University of Arizona Press.

Evenson, Debra. (1986). "Women's Equality in Cuba: What Difference Does a Revolution Make?" *Law and Inequality*, no. 4: 295–326.

Facultad Latinoamericana de Ciencias Sociales (FLACSO), ed. (1998). *Chile 97 Análisis y Opiniones.* Santiago: FLACSO.

Fantasia, Rick, and Eric L. Hirsch. (1995). "Culture in Rebellion: The Appropriation and Transformation of the Veil in the Algerian Revolution." Pp. 144–59 in *Social Movements and Cultures*, edited by Hank Johnston and Bert Klandermans. Minneapolis: University of Minnesota Press.

Fernández, Ferran Yamile. (1995). "Mujeres Cubanas Camino a Beijing '95." Mujer/Fempress, no. 163: 10.

Ferrada, Rosa. (1993). "La Violencia contra la Mujer Viola los Derechos Humanos." Santiago: Movimiento Pro-Emancipación de la Mujer Chilena.

Field, Rachel and Juan Mandelbaum. (1993). "*In 'Women's Hands: The Changing Roles of Women.*" Part of the *Americas* television series. South Burlington, Vt.: Annenberg/Corporation for Public Broadcasting.

Fisher, Jo. (1993). *Out of the Shadows: Women, Resistance, and Politics in South America*. London: Latin American Bureau.

Fitzsimmons, Tracy. (2000). "A Monstrous Regiment of Women? State, Regime, and Women's Political Organizing in Latin America." *Latin America Research Review* 35: 216–29.

Fleites-Lear, Marisela. (2000). "Women, Family and the Cuban Revolution: A Personal and Socio-political Analysis." Pp. 33–54 in *Cuban Transitions at the Millennium*, edited by Eloise Linger and John Cotman. Largo, Md.: International Development Options.

Federación de Mujeres Cubanas (FMC). (1973). "FMC Political Orientation Guide." Havana: FMC.

———. (1984). "La eliminación de todas las formas de discriminación contra la mujer en Cuba." Havana: FMC.

FMC archives. (N.d., no title). Transcriptions of exchange with the members of the Mariana Grajales Women's Platoon. Havana: FMC (obtained 1999).

Fonow, Mary Margaret, and Judith Cook, eds. (1991). *Beyond Methodology: Feminist Scholarship as Lived Research*. Bloomington: Indiana University Press.

Foran, John. (1992). "A Theory of Third World Social Revolutions: Iran, Nicaragua, and El Salvador Compared." *Critical Sociology* 19: 3-27.

———. (1994). "The Causes of Latin American Social Revolutions: Searching for Patterns in Mexico, Cuba, and Nicaragua." Pp. 209–44 in *Conflicts and New Departures in World Society*, edited by Volker Bornschier and Peter Lengyel. New Brunswick, N.J.: Transaction.

———, ed. (1997a). *Theorizing Revolutions*. New York: Routledge.

———. (1997b). "Discourses and Social Forces: The Role of Culture and Cultural Studies in Understanding Revolutions." Pp. 203–26 in *Theorizing Revolutions*, edited by John Foran. New York: Routledge.

———, ed. 2003. *The Future of Revolutions: Rethinking Radical Change in the Age of Globalization*. New York: Zed.

Franceschet, Susan. (2001). "Gender and Citizenship: Democratization and Women's Politics in Chile." Ph.D. Diss. Carleton University, Ottowa.

———. (2003). " 'State Feminism' and Women's Movements: The Impact of Chile's Servicio Nacional de la Mujer on Women's Activism." *Latin American Research Review* 38 (1): 9–40.

Franqui, Carlos. (1968). *The Twelve*. New York: Lyle Stuart.

Friedman, Elisabeth J. (1998). "Paradoxes of Gendered Political Opportunity in the Venezuelan Transition to Democracy." *Latin American Research Review* 33 (3): 87–135.

Frohmann, Alicia, and Teresa Valdés. (1995). "Democracy in the Country and in the Home: The Women's Movement in Chile." Pp. 276–301 in *The Challenges of Local Feminisms: Women's Movements in Global Perspective*, edited by Amrita Basu. Boulder, Colo.: Westview Press.

García-Pérez, Gladys Marel. (1998). *Insurrection and Revolution: Armed Struggle in Cuba, 1952–1959*. Boulder, Colo.: Lynne Rienner.

Garreton, Manuel Antonio. (1989). *The Chilean Political Process*. Boston: Unwin Hyman.

Gaviola, Edda, Eliana Largo, and Sandra Palestro. (1994). *Una Historia Necesaria: Mujeres En Chile: 1973–1990*. Santiago: ASDI, Suecia.

Geiger, Susan. (1992). "What's So Feminist about Doing Women's Oral History?" Pp. 305–18 in *Expanding the Boundaries of Women's History: Essays on Women in the Third World*, edited by Cheryl Johnson-Odim and Margaret Strobel. Bloomington: Indiana University Press.

Gil, Frederico G., Ricardo Lagos [Escobar], and Henry Landsberger, eds. (1979). *Chile at the Turning Point: Lessons of the Socialist Years, 1970–1973*. Philadelphia: Institute for the Study of Human Issues.

Golden, Renny. (1991). *The Hour of the Poor, the Hour of Women: Salvadoran Women Speak*. New York: Crossroad.

Goldstone, Jack A. (1980). "Theories of Revolution: The Third Generation." *World Politics*, no. 32: 425–53.

———. (1982). "The Comparative and Historical Study of Revolutions." *Annual Review of Sociology*, no. 8: 197–207.

Gonzalez, Juan. (2000). *Harvest of Empire: A History of Latinos in America*. New York: Viking-Penguin.

Goodwin, Jeff. (1988). "Revolutionary Movements in Central America: A Comparative Analysis." Cambridge, Mass.: Harvard University Center for Research on Politics and Social Organization.

———. (1997). "State-Centered Approaches to Social Revolutions: Strengths and Limitations of a Theoretical Tradition." Pp. 11–37 in *Theorizing Revolutions*, edited by John Foran. New York: Routledge.

Grau, Olga, Riet Delsing, Eugenia Brito, and Alejandra Farías, eds. (1997). *Discurso, Genero y Poder: Discursos públicos: Chile 1978–1993*. Santiago: ARCIS-LOM.

Grewal, Inderpal, and Caren Kaplan, eds. (1994). *Scattered Hegemonies: Postmodernity and Transnational Feminist Practices*. Minneapolis: University of Minnesota Press.

Grupo Iniciativa Mujeres. (1999). "Encuesta Nacional: Opinión y Actitudes de las Mujeres Chilenas Sobre la Condición de Género." Santiago: Grupo Iniciativa Mujeres.

Guevara, Che. (1962). *On Guerrilla Warfare*. New York: Frederick A. Praeger.

Gunn, Gillian. (1995). "Cuba's NGOs: Government Puppets or Seeds of Civil Society?" Washington D.C.: Center for Latin American Studies at Georgetown University.

Gutierrez, Tomas Alea, and Juan Carlos Tabio, dirs. (1994). *Strawberry and Chocolate*. Produced by Miguel Mendoza. Burbank, Calif.: Miramax Films/Buena Vista Home Video.

Halebsky, Sandor, and John Kirk with Carollee Bengelsdorf, eds. (1992). *Cuba in Transition: Crisis and Transformation*. Boulder, Colo.: Westview.

Harding, Sandra, ed. (1987). *Feminism and Methodology*. Bloomington: Indiana University Press.

Herrera, Morena. (1996). "Posguerra, Ex-Guerrilleras y Feminismo En El Salvador." Pp. 128–34 in *Montañas Con Recuerdos De Mujer*, edited by Las DIGNAS. San Salvador: Las DIGNAS.

Hipsher, Patricia. (2001). "Right- and Left-wing Women in Post-Revolutionary El Salvador: Feminist Autonomy and Cross-Political Alliance-Building for Gender Equality." Pp. 133–64 in *Radical Women in Latin America: Left and Right*, edited by Victoria González and Karen Kampwirth. University Park: Pennsylvania State University Press.

Horowitz, Irving Louis, ed. (1989). *Cuban Communism*. New Brunswick, N.J.: Transaction.

Jaquette, Jane S. (1973). "Women in Revolutionary Movements in Latin America." *Journal of Marriage and the Family* 35 (2): 344–54.

———, ed. (1994). *The Women's Movement in Latin America: Participation and Democracy*. Boulder, Colo.: Westview Press.

———. (1995). "Rewriting the Scripts: Gender in the Comparative Study of Latin

American Politics." Pp. 111–33 in *Politics in Latin America in Comparative Perspective*, edited by Peter Smith. Boulder, Colo.: Westview Press.

Jaquette, Jane S., and Sharon L. Wolchik, eds. (1998). *Women and Democracy: Latin America and Eastern and Central Europe*. Baltimore: Johns Hopkins University Press.

Kampwirth, Karen. (1997). "From Feminine Guerrillas to Feminist Revolutionaries: Nicaragua, El Salvador, Chiapas." Paper presented to the Latin American Studies Association, Guadalajara, Mexico, 17–19 April 1997.

———. (2002). *Women and Guerrilla Movements: Nicaragua, El Salvador, Chiapas, Cuba.* University Park: Pennsylvania State University Press.

———. (2004). *Feminism and the Legacy of Revolution: Nicaragua, El Salvador, Chiapas.* Athens, Ohio: Ohio University Press.

Kaplan, Temma. (1982). "Female Consciousness and Collective Action: The Case of Barcelona, 1910–1918." *Signs: Journal of Women in Culture and Society* 7 (3): 545–60.

Keen, Benjamin. (1996). *A History of Latin America*. Boston: Houghton Mifflin.

Keen, Benjamin, and Keith Haynes. (2000). *A History of Latin America*. Boston: Houghton Mifflin.

Kirkwood, Julieta. (1982). *Ser Política En Chile: Las Feministas y Los Partidos*. Santiago: Facultad Latinoamericana de Ciencias Sociales.

———. (1983). "Feminismo y Participación Política en Chile." Pp. 61–83 in *Temas Socialistas*, edited by Eduardo Ortíz. Santiago: Vector/Centro de Estudios Económicos y Sociales.

———. (1986). *Ser Política en Chile: Los Nudos de la Sabiduría Feminista*. Santiago: Facultad Latinoamericana de Ciencias Sociales.

———. (1989). "Del amor a la necesidad." Pp. 9–13 in *Caminado: Luchas y Estrategias de Las Mujeres Tercer Mundo*, edited by Colectivo Isis Internacional. Santiago: Colectivo Isis Internacional.

Kornbluh, Peter, ed. 2003. *The Pinochet File: A Declassified Dossier on Atrocity and Accountability*. New York: New Press.

Küppers, Gaby, ed. (1994). *Compañeras: Voices from the Latin American Women's Movement*. London: Latin American Bureau.

Lancaster, Roger. (1992). *Life is Hard: Machismo, Danger, and the Intimacy of Power in Nicaragua*. Berkeley and Los Angeles: University of California Press.

Landau, Saul. (2000). "Hope Comes to Chile." *Progressive* 64 (5): 24–27.

Larguía, Isabel, and John Dumoulin. (1986). "Women's Equality and the Cuban Revolution." Pp. 344–66 in *Women and Change in Latin America*, edited by June Nash and Helen Safa. South Hadley, Mass.: Bergin and Garvey.

Leiner, Marvin. (1993). *Sexual Politics in Cuba: Machismo, Homosexuality, and AIDS*. Boulder, Colo.: Westview Press

Levine, Daniel H. (1992). *Popular Voices in Latin American Catholicism*. Princeton, N.J.: Princeton University Press.

Lewis, Oscar, Ruth M. Lewis, and Susan M. Rigdon, eds. (1977). *Four Women: Living the Revolution: An Oral History of Contemporary Cuba*. Urbana: University of Illinois Press.

Lidid, Sandra, and Kira Maldonado, eds. (1997). *Movimiento Feminista Autónomo (1993–1997)*. Santiago: Ediciones Numero Critico.

Lind, Amy. (1992). "Power, Gender, and Development: Popular Women's Organizations and the Politics of Needs in Ecuador." Pp. 134–49 in *The Making of Social Movements in Latin America*, edited by Arturo Escobar and Sonia Alvarez. Boulder, Colo.: Westview Press.

Lobao, Linda. (1990). "Women in Revolutionary Movements: Changing Patterns of

Latin American Guerrilla Struggle." Pp. 180–204 in *Women And Social Protest*, edited by Guida West and Rhoda Lois Blumberg. Oxford: Oxford University Press.

López Vigil, María. (1998). "Cuban Women's History—Jottings and Voices." *Envío* 17 (208): 27–43.

———. (1999). Cuba: *Neither Heaven nor Hell*. Washington, D.C.: Ecumenical Program on Central America and the Caribbean.

Lorber, Judith. (1994). *Paradoxes of Gender*. New Haven, Conn.: Yale University Press.

Luciak, Ilja A. (1998). "La Igualdad de Género y la Izquierda Revolucionaria: El Caso de El Salvador." Pp. 137–73 in *Género y Cultura En América Latina*, vol. 1, edited by María Luisa Tarrés Barraza. Pedregal de Santa Teresa: El Colegio de México.

———. (2001). *After the Revolution: Gender and Democracy in El Salvador, Nicaragua, and Guatemala*. Baltimore: Johns Hopkins University Press.

Lungo Uclés, Mario. (1995). "Building an Alternative: The Formation of a Popular Project." Pp. 153–79 in *The New Politics of Survival: Grassroots Movements in Central America*, edited by Minor Sinclair. New York: Monthly Review Press.

Lutjens, Sheryl L. (1994). "Remaking the Public Sphere: Women and Revolution in Cuba." Pp. 366–93 in *Women and Revolution in Africa, Asia, and the New World*, edited by Mary Ann Tétrault. Columbia: University of South Carolina Press.

———. (1995). "Reading between the Lines: Women, the State, and Rectification in Cuba." *Latin American Perspectives*, no. 22: 100–124.

———. (1997). "The Politics of Revolution in Latin America: Feminist Perspectives in Theory and Practice." Paper presented to the Latin American Studies Association, Guadalajara, Mexico, 17–19 April.

Macauley, Neil. (1978). "The Cuban Rebel Army: A Numerical Survey." *Hispanic American Historical Review*, no. 58: 284–95.

Maloof, Judy, ed. (1999). *Voices of Resistance: Testimonies of Cuban and Chilean Women*. Lexington: University Press of Kentucky.

Marín, Gladys. (1998). "Allende: Un Revolucionario Para El Siglo XXI." *Alternativa* Edición Especial: Seminario Internacional "A 25 Años del golpe militar," año 2: 19–24.

Matear, Ann. (1997). " '*Desde La Protesta a La Propuesta*': The Institutionalization of the Women's Movement in Chile." Pp. 84–100 in *Gender Politics in Latin America: Debates in Theory and Practice*, edited by Elizabeth Dore. New York: Monthly Review Press.

Mattelart, Michelle. (1975). "Chile: The Feminine Side of the Coup, or When Bourgeois Women Take to the Streets." In *NACLA's Latin America and Empire Report*, no. 9: 14–25.

———. (1980). "Chile: The Feminine Version of the Coup d'Etat." Pp. 279–301 in *Sex and Class in Latin America: Women's Perspectives on Politics, Economics and the Family in the Third World*, edited by June Nash and Helen Safa. Brooklyn, N.Y.: Bergin.

McAuley, Christopher. (1997). "Race and the Process of the American Revolutions." Pp. 168–202 in *Theorizing Revolutions*, edited by John Foran. New York: Routledge.

McGarrity, Gayle, and Cárdenas Osvaldo. (1995). "Cuba." Pp. 77–107 in *No Longer Invisible: Afro-Latin Americans Today*, edited by the Minority Rights Group. London: Minority Rights Publications.

McGovern, Arthur. (1989). *Liberation Theology and Its Critics: Toward an Assessment*. New York: Orbis.

McSherry, J. Patrice. (1998). "The Emergence of 'Guardian Democracy'." *NACLA: Report on the Americas* 22 (3): 16–24.

Meyer, Julie. (1994). "Breaking Many Taboos: Women in Solidarity." *Crossroads* 40: 11–14.

Miller, Francesca. (1991). *Latin American Women and the Search for Social Justice*. Hanover, N.H.: University Press of New England.

Mitchell, Juliett. (1984). *Women, the Longest Revolution*. New York: Pantheon.

Moghadam, Valentine. (1994). "Islamic Populism, Class, and Gender in Postrevolutionary Iran." Pp. 189–222 in *A Century of Revolution: Social Movements in Iran*, edited by John Foran. Minneapolis: University of Minnesota Press.

———. (1997). "Gender and Revolutions." Pp. 137–67 in *Theorizing Revolutions*, edited by John Foran. New York: Routledge.

Mohanty, Chandra Talpade. (1991). "Under Western Eyes: Feminist Scholarship and Colonial Discourses." Pp. 51–80 in *Third World Women and The Politics of Feminism*, edited by Chandra Mohanty, Ann Russo, and Lourdes Torres. Bloomington: Indiana University Press.

———. (1992). "Feminist Encounters: Locating the Politics of Experience." Pp. 74–92 in *Destabilizing Theory: Contemporary Feminist Debates*, edited by Michele Barret and Anne Phillips. Stanford, Calif.: Stanford University Press.

Molina, Natacha G. (1986). *Lo Femenino y Lo Democrático En El Chile De Hoy*. Santiago: Vector Centro De Estudios Económicos y Sociales.

Molyneux, Maxine. (1985). "Mobilization without Emancipation? Women's Interests, the State, and Revolution in Nicaragua." *Feminist Studies*, no. 11: 227–54.

———. (1998). "Analysing Women's Movements." *Development and Change* 29 (2): 219–45.

———. (2001a). *Women's Movements in International Perspective and Beyond*. New York: Palgrave.

———. (2001b). "State, Gender and Institutional Change: The Federación de Mujeres Cubanas." Pp. 76–98 in *Women's Movements in International Perspective and Beyond*. New York: Palgrave.

Momsen, Janet. (1991). *Women and Development in the Third World*. London: Routledge.

Montgomery, Tommie Sue. (1995). *Revolution in El Salvador: From Civil Strife to Civil Peace*. San Francisco: Westview Press.

Moore, Carlos. (1988). *Castro, the Blacks, and Africa*. Berkeley and Los Angeles: University of California Press.

Moore, Henrietta L. (1988). *Feminism and Anthropology*. Minneapolis: University of Minnesota Press.

Morgan, Robin, ed. (1984). *Sisterhood is Global: The International Women's Movement Anthology*. Garden City, N.Y.: Anchor.

Movimiento Pro-Emancipación de la Mujer Chilena (MEMCH). (n/d). "MEMCH: Antología para una historia del movimiento femenino en Chile." Santiago: MEMCH.

Mujeres de Chile (MUDECHI). (1985). "Informe General de la Directiva Nacional de MUDECHI." Santiago: Comité de Defensa de los Derechos de la Mujer.

Muños, Susana and Lourdes Portillo. (1986). *Las Madres: The Mothers of the Plaza de Mayo*. Los Angeles: Direct Cinema.

Muñoz Dálbora, Adriana. (1987). *Fuerza feminista y democracia: Utopía a realizar*. Santiago: Ediciones Documentas.

Murdock, Donna. (2003). "When Women Have Wings: Feminist NGO Strategies and Social Class in Medellin, Colombia." Ph.D. diss., Emory University.

Murray, Nicola. (1979a). "Socialism and Feminism: Women and the Cuban Revolution, Part 1." *Feminist Review*, no. 2: 99–108.

———. (1979b). "Socialism and Feminism: Women and the Cuban Revolution, Part 2." *Feminist Review*, no. 3: 57–73.

Navarrete, María Ofelia. (2003). "Maria's Stories." Pp. 22–30 in *Feminist Futures: Reimagining Women, Culture and Development*, edited by Kum-Kum Bhavnani, Priya Kurian, and John Foran. New York: Zed.

Navarro, Marysa. (2002). "Against *Marianismo*." Pp. 257–72 in *Gender's Place: Feminist Anthropologies of Latin America*, edited by Rosario Montoya, Leslie Jo Frazier, and Janise Hurtig. New York: Palgrave.

Nazzari, Muriel. (1983). "The 'Woman Question' in Cuba: An Analysis of Material Constraints on Its Solution." *Signs: Journal of Women in Culture and Society* 9 (2): 246–63.

New Americas Press, ed. (1989). *A Dream Compels Us: Voices of Salvadoran Women*. Boston: South End Press.

Noonan, Rita K. (1997). "Women against the State: Political Opportunities and Collective Action Frames in Chile's Transition to Democracy." Pp. 252–67 in *Social Movements: Readings on Their Emergence, Mobilization, and Dynamics*, edited by Doug McAdam and David A. Snow. Los Angeles: Roxbury.

Oppenheim, Lois Hect. (1998). "Reconstructing Democracy and the Role of Women in Politics in Chile." Paper presented to the Latin American Studies Association, Chicago, 24–26 September 1998.

———. (1999). *Politics in Chile: Democracy, Authoritarianism, and the Search for Development*. Boulder, Colo.: Westview Press.

Orans, Sylvia. (1987). "Cuban Women Move Out from Sexism's Shadow." *Guardian*, 11 February.

Oxhorn, Philip D., and Graciela Ducatenzeller, eds. (1998). *What Kind of Democracy? What Kind of Market? Latin America in the Age of Neoliberalism*. University Park: Pennsylvania State University Press.

Pages, Raisa. (2000). "From Economically Dependent to Independent." *Granma International* (Havana), 8 March.

Palestro, Sandra. (1991). "Mujeres en Movimiento 1973–1989." Santiago: Facultad Latinoamericana de Ciencias Sociales.

Pearce, Jenny. (1986). *Promise Land: Peasant Rebellion in Chalatenango El Salvador*. London: Latin American Bureau.

Pérez, Louis A., Jr. (1998). "Foreword." Pp. ix–x in *Insurrection and Revolution: Armed Struggle in Cuba, 1952–1959* by Gladys Marel García-Pérez. Boulder, Colo.: Lynn Rienner.

Pérez-Brignoli, Hector. (1989). *A Brief History of Central America*. Berkeley and Los Angeles: University of California Press.

Pérez-Sarduy, Pedro, and Jean Stubbs, eds. (1993). *AfroCuba: An Anthology of Cuban Writing on Race, Politics, and Culture*. New York: Latin American Bureau.

Pérez-Stable, Marifeli. (1999). *The Cuban Revolution: Origins, Course, and Legacy*. Oxford: Oxford University Press.

Pisano, Margarita. (1990). "Reflexiones Feministas." Santiago: La Morada/Centro de Análisis y Difusión de la Condición de la Mujer.

Power, Margaret. (2002). *Right-Wing Women in Chile: Feminine Power and the Struggle Against Allende 1964–1973*. University Park: Pennsylvania State University Press.

Radcliffe, Sarah A. and Sallie Westwood, eds. (1993). *"Viva": Women and Popular Protest in Latin America*. London: Routledge.

Ramos, Ana. (1971). "La mujer y la revolución en Cuba." *Casa de las Américas*, March–June, 56–72.

Ramos Escandon, Carmen. (1997). "Reading Gender in History." Pp. 149–60 in *Gender Politics in Latin America: Debates in Theory and Practice*, edited by Elizabeth Dore. New York: Monthly Review Press.

Randall, Margaret. (1974). *Cuban Women Now*. Toronto: Women's Press.

———. (1981a). *Women In Cuba: Twenty Years Later*. Brooklyn, N.Y.: Smyrna Press.

————. (1981b). *Sandino's Daughters: Testimonies of Nicaraguan Women in Struggle.* Vancouver: Zed.

————. (1992). *Gathering Rage: The Failure of Twentieth Century Revolutions to Develop a Feminist Agenda.* New York: Monthly Review Press.

————. (1994). *Sandino's Daughters Revisited: Feminism in Nicaragua.* New Brunswick, N.J.: Rutgers University Press.

Ready, Kelley. (2001). "A Feminist Reconstruction of Parenthood within Neoliberal Constraints: La Asociacón de Madres Demandantes in El Salvador." Pp. 165–88 in *Radical Women in Latin America: Left and Right,* edited by Victoria González and Karen Kampwirth. University Park: Pennsylvania State University Press.

Reinharz, Shulamit. (1992). *Feminist Methods in Social Research.* Oxford: Oxford University Press.

Riquelme, Alfredo. (1999). "Voting for Nobody in Chile's New Democracy." *NACLA: Report on the Americas* 32 (6): 31–33.

Rivard, Courtney. (2003). "A Struggle for Democracy: Overcoming Corruption and Patriarchy. A Study of Women's Activism in Honduras." B.A. honor's thesis, Emory University.

Roberts, Kenneth M. (1998). *Deepening Democracy? The Modern Left and Social Movements in Chile and Peru.* Stanford, Calif.: Stanford University Press.

Rojas, Marta, and Mirta Rodríguez Calderón, eds. (1971). *Tania.* New York: Random House.

Saa, María Antonieta. (1985). "Por la vida y algo más . . . " *Mujer/Fempress,* no. 46: 9.

————. (1987). "Queremos Votar en las Próximas Elecciones." *Mujer/Fempress,* no. 66: 8.

Safa, Helen. (1995). "Women's Social Movements in Latin America." Pp. 227–41 in *Women in the Latin American Development Process,* edited by Christine E. Bose and Edna Acosta Belén. Philadelphia: Temple University Press.

Saint-Germain, Michelle. (1997). "Mujeres '94: Democratic Transition and the Women's Movement in El Salvador." *Women and Politics* 18 (2): 75–99.

Salinas Alvarez, Cecilia. (1994). *Las Chilenas de la Colonia: Virtud Sumisa, Amor Rebelde.* Santiago: Lom Ediciones.

Santamaría, Haydeé. (1980). *Moncada: Memories of the Attack That Launched the Cuban Revolution.* Secaucus, N.J.: Lyle Stuart.

Sargent, Lydia, ed. (1981). *Women and Revolution: A Discussion of the Unhappy Marriage of Marxism and Feminism.* Boston: South End Press.

Schirmer, Jennifer. (1993a). "The Seeking of Truth and the Gendering of Consciousness: The COMADRES of El Salvador and the CONAVIGUA Widows of Guatemala." Pp. 30–64 in *"Viva": Women and Popular Protest in Latin America,* edited by Sarah A. Radcliffe and Sallie Westwood. New York: Routledge.

————. (1993b). "Those Who Die for Life Cannot Be Called Dead: Women and Human Rights Protests in Latin America." Pp. 31–57 in *Surviving Beyond Fear: Women, Children and Human Rights in Latin America,* edited by Marjorie Agosín. Freedonia, Vt.: White Pine Press.

Schneider, Cathy. (1995a). "Chile: The Underside of the Miracle." Pp. 151–55 in *Free Trade and Economic Restructuring in Latin America,* edited by Fred Rosen and Deidre McFadyen. New York: Monthly Review Press.

————. (1995b). *Shantytown Protest in Pinochet's Chile.* Philadelphia: Temple University Press.

Schnookal, Deborah, ed. (1991). *Cuban Women Confront the Future.* Melbourne: Ocean Press.

Schoultz, Lars. (1998). *Beneath the United States: A History of U.S. Policy toward Latin America.* Cambridge, Mass.: Harvard University Press.

Selbin, Eric. (1997). "Revolution in the Real World: Bringing Agency Back In." Pp. 123–36 in *Theorizing Revolutions*, edited by John Foran. New York: Routledge.

———. (1999). *Modern Latin American Revolutions.* Boulder, Colo.: Westview Press.

Sen, Gita, and Caren Grown. (1987). *Development, Crises, and Alternative Visions: Third World Women's Perspectives.* New York: Monthly Review Press.

Sepúlveda, Emma, ed. (1996). *We, Chile: Personal Testimonies of the Chilean Arpilleristas.* Falls Church, Va.: Azul Editions.

Servicio Nacional de la Mujer (SERNAM). (1994). "Plan de Igualdad de Oportunidades para las Mujeres 1994–1999." Santiago: SERNAM.

Shayne, Julia Denise. (1995). "Salvadorean Women Revolutionaries and the Birth of Their Women's Movement." MA thesis, San Francisco State University.

———. 1999. "Gendered Revolutionary Bridges: Women in the Salvadoran Resistance Movement, 1979–1992." *Latin American Perspectives* 26:85–102.

———. 2000. " 'The Revolution Question': Feminisms in Cuba, Chile, and El Salvador Compared (1952–1999)." Ph.D. diss., University of California–Santa Barbara.

Sinclair, Minor, ed. (1995). *The New Politics of Survival: Grassroots Movements in Central America.* New York: Monthly Review Press.

Skidmore, Thomas E., and Peter H. Smith. (1997). *Modern Latin America*, 4th ed. New York, Oxford: Oxford University Press.

Skocpol, Theda. (1979). *States and Social Revolutions.* Cambridge: Cambridge University Press.

———. (1994). *Social Revolutions in the Modern World.* Cambridge: Cambridge University Press.

Smith, Lois M. (1989). "Progress, Science, and Myth: The Health Education of Cuban Women." *Cuban Studies*, no. 19:167–96.

Smith, Lois M. and Alfred Padula. (1988). "Twenty Questions on Sex and Gender in Revolutionary Cuba." *Cuban Studies*, no. 18: 149–58.

———. (1996). *Sex and Revolution: Women in Socialist Cuba.* Oxford: Oxford University Press.

Smith, Peter. (1996). *Talons of the Eagle: Dynamics of U.S.–Latin American Relations.* New York: Oxford University Press.

Spivak, Gayatri Chakravorty. (1987). *In Other Worlds: Essays in Cultural Politics.* New York: Methuen.

Spooner, Mary Helen. (1994). *Soldiers in a Narrow Land: The Pinochet Regime in Chile.* Berkeley and Los Angeles: University of California Press.

Stacey, Judith. (1991). "Can There Be a Feminist Ethnography?" Pp. 111–19 in *Women's Words: The Feminist Practice of Oral History*, edited by Sherna Berger Gluck and Daphne Patai. New York: Routledge.

Stephen, Lynn, ed. (1994). *Hear My Testimony: María Teresa Tula, Human Rights Activist of El Salvador.* Boston: South End Press.

———. (1997). *Women and Social Movements in Latin America: Power from Below.* Austin: University of Texas Press.

Sternbach, Nancy Saporta, Marysa Navarro-Aranguren, Patricia Chuchryk, and Sonia E. Alvarez. (1992). "Feminisms in Latin America: From Bogota to San Bernardo." Pp. 207–39 in *The Making of Social Movements in Latin America: Identity, Strategy, and Democracy*, edited by Arturo Escobar and Sonia E. Alvarez. Boulder, Colo.: Westview Press.

Stevens, Evelyn P. (1973a). "Marianismo: The Other Face of *Machismo* in Latin America."

Pp. 89–101 in *Female and Male in Latin America: Essays*, edited by Ann Pescatello. Pittsburgh: University of Pittsburgh Press.

————. (1973b). "The Prospect for a Women's Liberation Movement in Latin America." *Journal of Marriage and the Family* 35 (2): 313–21.

Stewart, Shane. (2003). "2003 Elections: Stopping Neoliberalism in the Streets and at the Polls." Retrieved online 30 October 2003 from http://www.cispes.org/english/Updates_and_Analysis/elections.html.

Stoner, Kathryn Lynn. (1988). "Ofeila Domínguez Navarro: The Making of a Cuban Socialist Feminist." Pp. 119–40 in *The Human Tradition in Latin America*, edited by Wiliam H. Beezley and Judith Ewell. Wilmington, Del.: Scholarly Resources.

————. (1991). *From the House to the Streets: The Cuban Women's Movement for Legal Reform 1898–1940*. Durham, N.C.: Duke University Press.

Tarrow, Sidney. (1994). *Power in Movement: Social Movements, Collective Action and Politics*. Cambridge: Cambridge University Press.

Tétreault, Mary Ann, ed. (1994). *Women and Revolution in Africa, Asia, and the New World*. Columbia: University of South Carolina Press.

Thomson, Marilyn. (1986). *Women of El Salvador: The Price of Freedom*. Philadelphia: Institute for the Study of Human Issues.

Thompson, Martha. (1995). "Repopulated Communities in El Salvador." Pp. 109–51 in *The New Politics of Survival: Grassroots Movements in Central America*, edited by Minor Sinclair. New York: Monthly Review Press.

Trinh, T. Minh-Ha. (1989). *Woman/Native/Other: Writing Postcoloniality and Feminism*. Bloomington: Indiana University Press.

Ueltzen, Stefan, ed. (1993). *Como Salvadoreña Que Soy: Entrevistas Con mujeres en la lucha*. San Salvador: Editorial Sombrero Azul.

United Nations Development Program. (1995). "Human Development Report 1995: Gender and Human Development." Oxford: Oxford University Press.

Valdés, Teresa. (1987a). "La Unidad: Una Construcción Delicada." *Mujer/Fempress*, no. 58: 10.

————. (1987b). "Las Mujeres y La Dictadura Militar En Chile." Report no. 94. Santiago: Facultad Latinoamericana de Ciencias Sociales.

————. (1987c). "Ser Mujer en Sectores Populares Urbanos." Pp. 205–58 in *Espacio y Poder: Los Pobladores*, edited by Facultad Latinoamericana de Ciencias Sociales (FLACSO). Santiago: FLACSO.

————. (1991). "Being Female and Poor: A Double Oppression." Pp. 97–112 in *Popular Culture in Chile: Resistance and Survival*, edited by Kenneth Aman and Christian Parker. Boulder, Colo.: Westview Press.

Valdés, Teresa, and Enrique Gomariz, eds. (1995). *Latin American Women: Compared Figures*. Santiago: Instituto de la Mujer, Ministerio de Asuntos Sociales de España/Facultad Latinoamericana de Ciencias Sociales.

Valdés, Teresa, and Marisa Weinstein. (1993). *Mujeres que sueñan: Las Organizaciones De Pobladoras En Chile: 1973–1989*. Santiago: Facultad Latinoamericana de Ciencias Sociales.

Valenzuela, Luisa. (2003). "The Woof and the Warp." Pp. 31–34 in *Feminist Futures: Reimagining Women, Culture and Development*, edited by Kum-Kum Bhavnani, Priya Kurian, and John Foran. New York: Zed.

Valenzuela, María Elena. (1987). *La Mujer en el Chile Militar*. Santiago: Ediciones Chile y América.

Vallina, Elvira Díaz, and Julio César González Pagés. (2000). "The Self Emancipation of Women." Pp. 15–31 in *Cuban Transitions at the Millennium*, edited by Eloise Linger and John Cotman. Largo, Md.: International Development Options.

Vásquez, Norma. (1996). "Las Mujeres y Las Relaciones Genericas en el Proyecto del FMLN." Pp. 20–30 in *Montañas Con Recuerdos de Mujer*, edited by Las DIGNAS. San Salvador:Las DIGNAS.

Vásquez, Norma and Clara Murguialday. (1996). *Unas + Otras × Todas = Asociación de Madres Demandantes: Una lucha colectiva por la cuota y la paternidad responsable*. San Salvador: Las DIGNAS.

Vega, Pastor, dir. (1979). *Portrait of Teresa*. Produced by Evelio Delgado. New York: New Yorker Video.

Waters, Mary-Alice, ed. (2003). *Marianas in Combat: Teté Puebla and the Mariana Grajales Women's Platoon in Cuba's Revolutionary War, 1956–58*. New York: Pathfinder Press.

Waylen, Georgina. (1994). "Women and Democratization: Conceptualizing Gender Relations in Transition Politics." *World Politics* 46 (3): 327–54.

———. (1996). "Democratization, Feminism and the State in Chile: The Establishment of SERNAM." Pp. 103–17 in *Women and the State: International Perspectives*, edited by Shirin M. Rai and Geraldine Lievesley. London: Taylor and Francis.

Wickham-Crowley, Timothy P. (1992). *Guerrillas and Revolution in Latin America. A Comparative Study of Insurgents and Regimes since 1956*. Princeton, N.J.: Princeton University Press.

———. (1997). "Structural Theories of Revolution." Pp. 38–72 in *Theorizing Revolutions*, edited by John Foran. New York: Routledge.

Winn, Peter. (2000). "Lagos Defeats the Right—By a Thread." In *NACLA: Report on the Americas* 33 (5): 5–10.

Wright, Thomas, and Rody Oñate. (1998). *Flight from Chile: Voices of Exile*. Albuquerque: University of New Mexico Press.

Interviews and Meetings

All interviews were conducted by the author unless otherwise noted.

Acuña, María Elena. (1999). Member of Bajo Sospecha. Santiago, Chile.

Aguayo, Carmen Gloria. (1999). Minister for Salvador Allende. Santiago, Chile.

Amaya, Irma. (1998). Coordinator of the Movimiento de Mujeres Mélida Anaya Monte and assistant deputy, Frente Farabundo Martí para la Liberación Nacional. San Salvador, El Salvador.

Andrade, Carmen. (1999). National Coordinator of Servicio Nacional de la Mujer's woman as head of household program. Santiago, Chile.

Anonymous. (1999). Retired political analyst. Havana, Cuba.

Astorga, Alicia de. (1995). Member of Asociación Nacional de Educadores Salvadoreños and Cooperativa Asociación Nacional de Educadores Salvadoreñas. San Vicente, El Salvador. Joint interview with Esperanza Ramos, conducted by Leslie Schuld.

Baltra, Mireya. (1999). Minister of labor under Salvador Allende. Santiago, Chile.

Basso, Alicia. (1999). Former leader of the Communist Party; member of Salvador Allende's presidential advisory group. Santiago, Chile. Joint interview with Soledad Parada.

Borquez, Graciela (Chela). (1999). Cofounder of Mujeres por la Vida; member of the Christian Democrats. Santiago, Chile.

Cañas, Mercedes. (1998). President of the Centro Para Estudias Feministas. San Salvador, El Salvador.

Díaz Caro, Viviana. (1999). President of Agrupación de Familiares de Detenido y Desaparecido. Santiago, Chile.

"Elsy." (1994). Ex-combatant with the Fuerzas Populares de Liberación. Cuscatlan, El Salvador.

Espina, Mayra. (1999). Sociologist; member of the Cuban Communist Party. Havana, Cuba.

Figueroa, María Antonia. (1999). Former treasurer for the Movimiento Revolucionario 26 de Julio. Havana, Cuba.

Flores, Luis. (1994). Member of the Fuerzas Populares de Liberación. San Francisco. Joint interview with José Landaverdes.

García-Pérez, Gladys Marel. (1999). Militant in the Movimiento Revolucionario 26 de Julio. Havana, Cuba.

González Plascencia, Yolanda. (1999). Researcher, historian. Havana, Cuba.

González, Ximena. (1999). Journalist in Salvador Allende's communication office. Santiago, Chile.

Guzmán, Gloria. (1994). Director of the women's program of the archbishop. San Salvador, El Salvador. Interview conducted by Victoria Polanco.

———. (1998). Member, Mujeres por la Dignidad y la Vida "Rompamos el Silencio." San Salvador, El Salvador.

Herrera, Morena. (1998). Ex-combatant with the Frente Farabundo Martí para la Liberación Nacional; member of Mujeres por la Dignidad y la Vida "Rompamos el Silencio." San Salvador, El Salvador.

Hola, Eugenia. (1999). Researcher with Centro de Estudios de la Mujer. Santiago, Chile.

Landaverde, José. (1994). Member of the Fuerzas Populares de Liberación. San Francisco. Joint interview with Luís Flores.

Lazo Carerra, Carmen. (1999). Socialist Party militant. Santiago, Chile.

López, Aracely. (1998). Former member of the Comité de Madres y Familiares de Presos, Desaparecidos y Asesinados de El Salvador; member of Madres Demandantes. San Salvador, El Salvador.

——— and Dilcia Maroquin. (1994). Members of Mujeres por la Dignidad y la Vida "Rompamos el Silencio." San Salvador, El Salvador. Small group meeting.

López Solorza, María Mirtala. (1998). Substitute congresswoman for the Frente Farabundo Martí para la Liberación Nacional and leader in the Comité Cristiano Pro-Desplazados de El Salvador. San Salvador, El Salvador.

Mendez, Lety. (1998). Member of the Frente Farabundo Martí para la Liberación Nacional's women's secretariat. San Salvador, El Salvador.

Menocal, Nimia. (1999). Former member of the Movimiento Revolucionario 26 de Julio. Havana, Cuba.

Morales, María. (1993). Member of the Movimiento de Mujeres Mélida Anaya Montes. San Francisco, CA, United States.

Navarrete de Dubon, Maria Ofelia (Maria Serrano). (1998). Ex-combatant with the Frente Farabundo Martí para la Liberación Nacional; deputy for the Frente Farabundo Martí para la Liberación Nacional. San Salvador, El Salvador.

Moro, Sonnia. (1999). Founding member of Colectivo Magín. Havana, Cuba.

Nuñez, Marta. (1999). Professor of women's studies, University of Havana. Havana, Cuba.

Orteaga Araya, Miriam. (1999). Former member of the Movimiento de Izquierda Revolucionario; coordinator of the Ana Clara Centro de Capacitación para Mujeres. Santiago, Chile.

Parada, Soleda. (1999). Director of the Women's Secretariat under Salvador Allende. Santiago, Chile. Joint interview Alicia Basso.

Peña Menodza, Lorena (Rebecca Palacios). (1998). President of the Movimiento de

Mujeres Mélida Anaya Montes, and deputy of the Frente Farabundo Martí para la Liberación Nacional. San Salvador, El Salvador.

Perrera, Rita. (1999). Staff member of the foreign affairs department of the Federación de Mujeres Cubanas. Havana, Cuba.

Pollarolo, Fanny. (1999). Psychiatrist; Socialist Party deputy; cofounder of Mujeres por la Vida. Santiago, Chile.

Proveyer, Clotilde. (1999). Professor of women's studies, University of Havana. Havana, Cuba.

Ramos, Esperanza. (1995). Member of Asociación Nacional de Educadores Salvadoreños and Cooperativa Asociación Nacional de Educadores Salvadoreñas. San Vicente, El Salvador. Joint interview with Alicia de Astorga, conducted by Leslie Schuld.

Ríos, Marina. (1998). Coordinator of the Movimiento de Mujeres Mélida Anaya Montes's work with the maquiladoras. San Salvador, El Salvador.

Rodar, Ana Matilde. (1994). Ex-combatant with the Fuerzas Populares de Liberación; administrator with the Movimiento de Mujeres Mélida Anaya Montes. San Salvador, El Salvador.

Silva, Clotilde (Cloti). (1999). Former leader of Movimiento de Mujeres Pobladores; currently coordinator of the Servicio Nacional de la Mujer's project against domestic violence. Santiago, Chile.

Valdés, Teresa. (1999). Cofounder of Mujeres por la Vida; head of gender studies at the Facultad Latinoamericana de Ciencias Sociales. Santiago, Chile.

Vallina, Angela Elvira Díaz. (1999). Former member of the Movimiento Revolucionario 26 de Julio. Havana, Cuba.

Vásquez, Isabel. (1994). Organizational director of the Coordinadora Nacional de las Mujeres Salvadoreñas. San Salvador, El Salvador. Small group meeting.

Vásquez, Vilma. (1998). President of Madres Demandantes. San Salvador, El Salvador.

Vega, Belkys. (1999). Cuban cinematographer and founding member of Colectivo Magín. Havana, Cuba.

Villa, Lizette. (1999). President of the Asociación de Artistas de Cine, Radio, y Televisión de la Unión de Escritures y Artistas (Cuba). Havana, Cuba.

Weber, Paulina. (1999). Cofounder of Movimiento Pro-Emancipación de la Mujer '83 and co-coordinator of its Casa de La Mujer. Santiago, Chile.

Index

abortion, 3; in Chile, 89, 112; in Cuba, 138, 156, 184n3; in El Salvador, 54

Acuña, María Elena, 105–106

AFDD. *See* Association of Relatives of the Detained and Disappeared

Agosín, Marjorie, 68, 73, 105

agrarian reform. *See* land reform

agro economy: in El Salvador, 20

Aguayo, Carmen Gloría, 75, 76, 80, 81, 82, 87, 109

Allende, First Lady Laura, 75, 92

Allende, Salvador, 2, 7, 11, 14, 67, 77, 108, 111, 172, 180; Allendista Women's Unit, 74, 83–84, 88; culture trains, 84; election of, 68, 70–71; health care, 81; Marxism, 67, 70, 71, 86, 114, 172; maternity leave, 83, 86; milk program, 82, 87, 161–162; revolutionary agenda of, 67, 71, 181n14; right wing women against, 68, 82, 84–85, 88, 172, 180n3; suicide of, 71; and the "woman question," 73, 78, 84, 87, 109; women's secretariat, 75, 81–82, 83, 86, 87, 109. *See also* Popular Unity; Socialist Party in Chile

Allesandri, Arturo, 69, 172

Amaya, Irma, 37, 39, 40, 50, 57, 58, 59, 159

ANDES. *See* National Association of Salvadoran Educators

Araujo, Arturo, 21

ARENA. *See* National Republican Alliance

Association of Mothers Seeking Child Support (*Asociación de Madres Demandantes*, AMD): El Salvador, 47, 50, 51, 54–57, 163, 166, 171

Association of Relatives of the Detained and Disappeared (*Agrupación de Familiares de Detenido y Desaparecido*, AFDD): Chile, 15, 91, 94, 95–96, 173, 182n7

Aylwin, Patricío, 94, 105, 107, 173

Bajo Sospecha (Under Suspicion): Chile, 105, 183n17

Baltra, Míreya, 74, 76, 78, 82, 83, 88

Basso, Alicia, 78, 89, 91, 93, 111

Batista, Fulgencio, 116–117, 120, 121, 135, 174, 175 (*see also* July 26 Revolutionary Movement); demonstrations against, 124, 130–131

BPR. *See* Farabundo Martí Front for National Liberation

bombing campaign in El Salvador, 23, 24, 32, 171

Borquez, Graciela (Chela), 90, 100–101, 103, 106, 113

campesino/as, 13, 51, 73, 80

carabineros [Chilean police], 92, 99, 104, 182n10

"caring ministries," 77, 109, 162, 164

Castro, Fidel, 120, 121, 122, 124, 128; "History Will Absolve Me," 119; incarceration and exile of, 119, 123, 125, 174, 183n3; role as leader, 10, 118, 135,

MR-26-7. *See* July 26 Revolutionary
Movement
Mujeres '94 (Women '94): El Salvador,
13, 50, 63, 180n5

National Association of Salvadoran Edu-
cators (*Asociación Nacional de Educadores
Salvadoreños*, ANDES), 24, 26–28, 33,
44, 65, 170, 178n9, 179n1
The National Coordinating Committee
of Salvadoran Women (*Coordinadora
Nacional de las Mujeres Salvadoreñas*,
CONAMUS), 48, 171
National Republican Alliance. *See* politi-
cal parties in El Salvador
National Women's Service (*Servicio
Nacional de la Mujer*, SERNAM):
Chile, 106, 107–108, 165, 173
Navarrete, Maria Ofelia, 39, 65
Non-Arrears Bill, 58, 171
non-governmental organizations in Cuba,
139, 146, 148, 184n5. *See also* Colectivo
Magín.

oligarchy: in Chile, 68, 69; in El Salvador,
19, 21, 23
ONUSAL. *See* United Nations Observer
Mission in El Salvador
Orthodox Party in Cuba, 123, 124

Palacios, Rebecca. *See* Lorena Peña
Mendoza
Parada, Soledad, 75, 81, 83, 86, 87, 109,
111, 181nn11, 14
patriarchy: division of labor, 12, 35, 44,
61, 73, 81, 109, 110, 114, 132, 142;
institutions, 78, 88, 103; at the micro
level, 8, 88, 103. *See also* Farabundo
Martí Front for National Liberation;
July 26 Revolutionary Movement;
Pinochet
peace accords in El Salvador. *See* Chapultepec Accords
peasants, 21, 128, 169. *See also*
campesino/as

Peña Mendoza, Lorena, 41, 49, 57, 58,
62, 65
Pinochet, Augusto, 2, 93, 108, 155; and the
Christian Democratic Party, 93; and his
constitution, 93, 94, 103, 108, 182n1;
and the coup d'état, 7, 11, 67, 73, 90,
173; detention of, 14–15, 173; and feminist opposition to, 90, 97–104, and the
"No" campaign, 103, 105; as patriarch,
90, 99, 105, 109; and the plebiscite, 11,
94, 102–104, 173, senator for life, 94,
173, 182n4, and the United States, 93.
(*See also* United States involvement in
Chile); women in support of, 22
poblaciónes/pobladoras [shantytowns/
shantytown dwellers], 75, 76, 91, 97
political parties in Chile: and Pinochet,
91, 112; Chilean Women's Party, 68, 69,
172; Christian Democratic Party, 70,
71, 72, 75, 79, 80, 81, 87, 94, 100, 101,
102, 173, Christian Left, 83, 101, Communist Party, 15, 70, 74, 75, 76, 78, 91,
94, 101, 172, 181n9, Conservative
Party, 68; Democratic Party, 68; Liberal
Party, 68; Movement for United Popular Action, 75, 82, 83, 100–101;
National Renovation Party, 173; Party
for Democracy, 77, 103; Popular
Action Front, 70; Popular Front, 70,
172; Radical Party, 68, 70, 83, 172;
Socialist Workers Party, 172. *See also*
Allende, Salvador; Popular Unity; and
Socialist Party in Chile
political parties in El Salvador: Christian
Democratic Party, 22, 170, 179n16;
Communist Party, 21, 47, 48, 169, 170;
Farabundo Martí Front for National
Liberation, 24, 163 (*see also* democracy
in El Salvador; elections in El Salvador;
Farabundo Martí Front for National
Liberation); National Republican
Alliance, 24, 170
political prisoners: in Chile, 2, 95; in
Cuba, 127; in El Salvador, 27, 177n3;
women in support of, 95, 128–129

Pollarolo, Fanny, 96, 100–101

popular movement in El Salvador, 25–26, 28, 34, 39, 43, 48, 62, 65, 156. *See also* Christian Committee for the Displaced People of El Salvador; Committee of Mothers and Relatives of Political Prisoners, Disappeared, and Assassinated of El Salvador; National Association of Salvadoran Educators

Popular Front. *See* Political Parties in Chile

Popular Unity (*Unidad Popular*, UP), 14, 67, 72, 75, 87, 91, 92, 103, 109, 114, 164; election of, 70, 72, 172; political tensions within, 71, 78, 87, 113; program of, 72–73, 162, 163; and the role of women, 68, 73, 110. *See also* Allende, Salvador; Socialist Party in Chile

Price and Supply Associations (*Juntos de Abastecimiento y Precio*, JAPs): Chile, 77, 79, 81, 181n10

prolonged war, 7, 8, 26, 178n8

Prío Socarrás, Carlos, 116, 174

PRTC. *See* Farabundo Martí Front for National Liberation

rape, 30, 33, 65, 148, 170, 184n3

refugees, 24, 31. *See also* Christian Committee for the Displaced People of El Salvador

revolution, 75; armed versus electoral, 2, 11, 85–86, 162; attempted, 19; the Cuban, 2, 22, 70, 158, 169, 172, 179n13; failed, 16, 62; negotiated, 11 (*see also* Chapultepec Accords; FMLN); partial, 11, 17, 67, 71, 90, 114; successful, 11, 67, 72. *See also* gendered-revolutionary bridges; revolutionary feminism; "revolution question"

revolutionary feminism: and Chile, 61, 108–114; contributing factors, 10, 61, 109, 154; and Cuba, 154–157; definition of, 9–10, 60, 108–109, 154, 164; and El Salvador, 60–66

Revolutionary Movement of the Left (*Movimiento de Izquierda Revolucionario*, MIR): Chile, 2, 70, 85, 100, 101, 102, 172

"revolution question," 3, 9, 159–160; and Chile, 73, 90; and Cuba, 115; and El Salvador, 24, 46, 60

Revuelta, Natalia, 119, 128

RN. *See* Farabundo Martí Front for National Liberation

Romero, Archbishop Oscar, 23, 29, 170. *See also* liberation theology

Sanchez, Celia, 122, 177n4

the Sandinistas, 113

Santamaría, Haydée, 118, 119, 121, 122, 123, 127, 129, 177n4

Seranno, María. *See* Navarrete, María Ofelia

SERNAM. *See* National Women's Service

sexism, 3, 4, 10, 44, 60, 64, 66, 78, 103, 142. *See also* sexist; machismo; machista

sexist, 8, 84, 146, 148. *See also* machismo; machista; sexism

Shantytowns. *See* Poblaciones

Socialist Party in Chile, 70, 74, 76, 82, 83, 92, 96, 101, 103, 107, 112; formation of, 69–70, 172. *See also* Allende, Salvador; Popular Unity

soup kitchens, 3, 4, 98

special period in Cuba, 142, 143–145, 156, 161, 175, 184n2

suffrage in Chile, 68, 70, 172

torture, 23, 27, 34, 65, 91, 179n10

union activists: in Chile, 6, 81, 91; in El Salvador, 28, 24, 33, 36. *See also* National Association of Educators of El Salvador

United Nations Convention of the Elimination of All Forms of Discrimination Against Women (CEDAW), 103

About the Author

Julie Shayne is an assistant professor in the Departments of Sociology and Women's Studies at Emory University.